In the Studio is a series from Hauser & Wirth Publishers that gives readers a behind-the-scenes view of artists at work. Generously illustrated and written by a leading scholar or critic, each book focuses on a major artist and offers an overview of their influences, materials, and techniques.

Explore the series:
Phyllida Barlow by Frances Morris
Lee Lozano by Lucrezia Calabrò Visconti
Takesada Matsutani by Mika Yoshitake
Jack Whitten by Yinka Elujoba

Justin Paton is an Aotearoa New Zealand–born writer and chief curator at the Art Gallery of New South Wales in Sydney, Australia, where in 2023 he curated the exhibition *Louise Bourgeois: Has the Day Invaded the Night or Has the Night Invaded the Day?* Paton's projects in Sydney have included *Adrián Villar Rojas: The End of Imagination* (2022) and *Mike Hewson: The Key's Under the Mat* (2025), both in the Nelson Packer Tank, and Francis Upritchard's monumental outdoor work *Here Comes Everybody* (2022). His books include *McCahon Country* (2019), a study of modernist painter Colin McCahon, and *Dreamhome: Stories of Art & Shelter* (2023).

In the Studio

Louise Bourgeois

Justin Paton

Hauser & Wirth Publishers

“What is important is not so much where my motivation came from as how it managed to survive.”

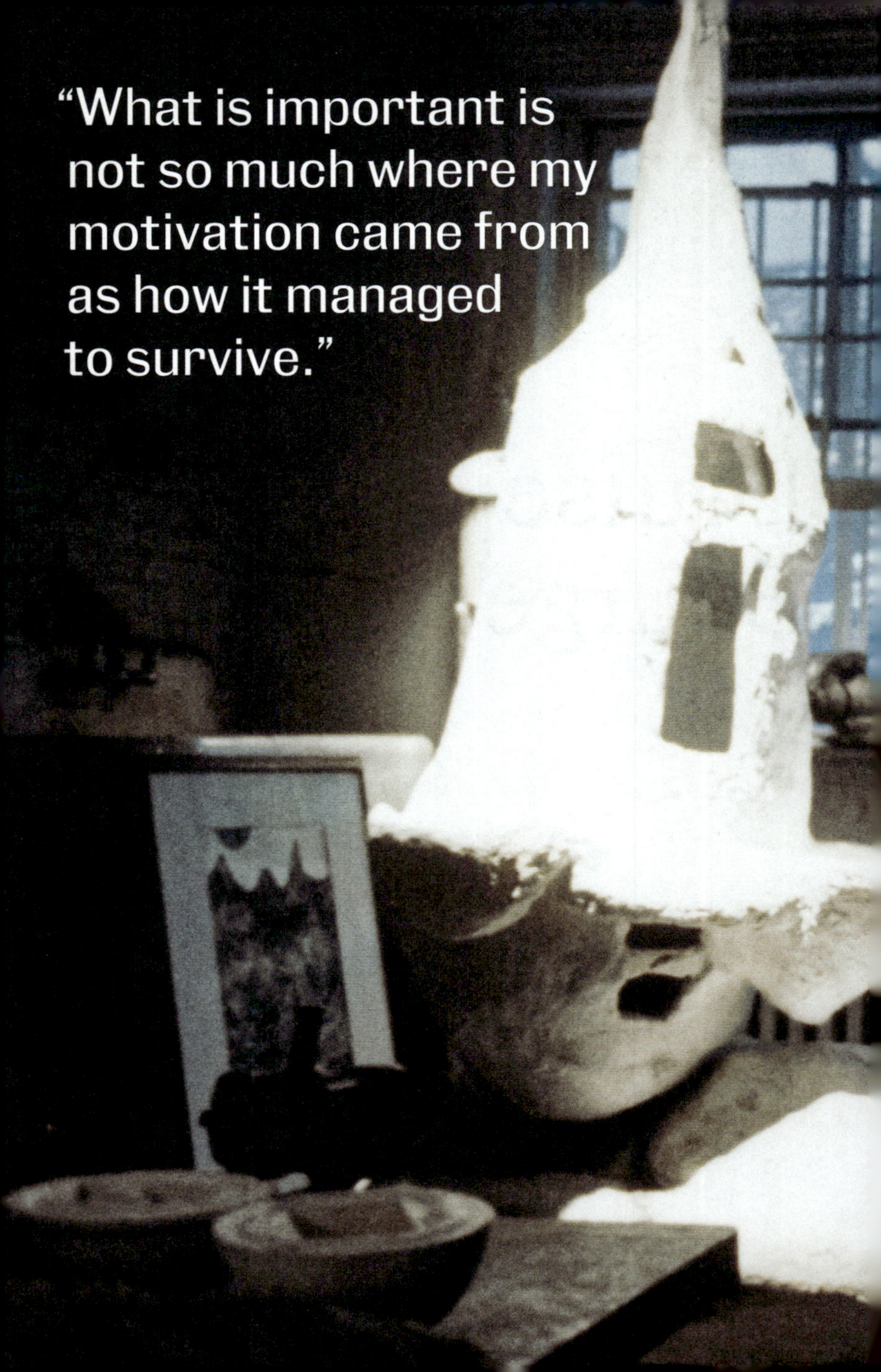

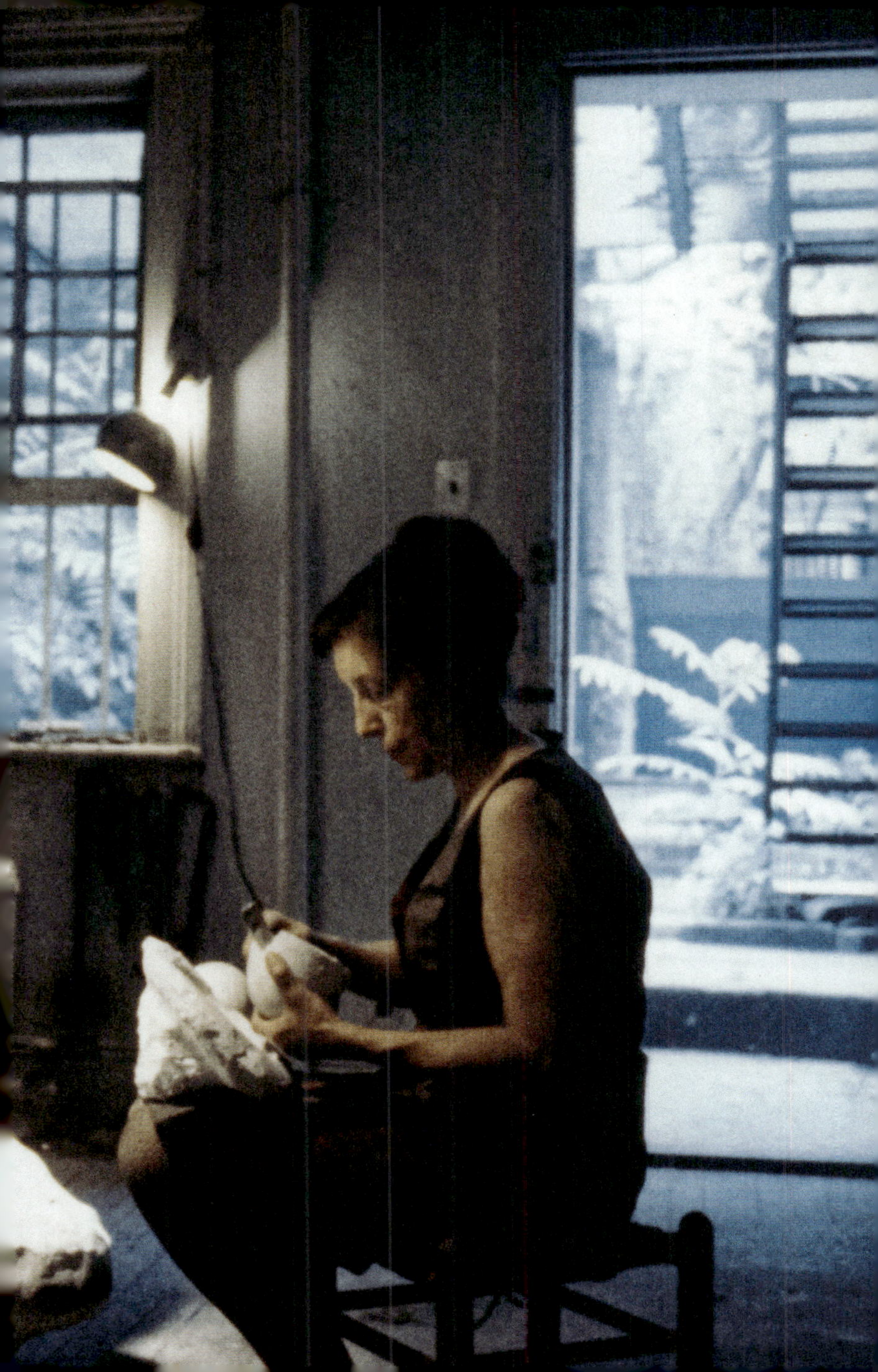

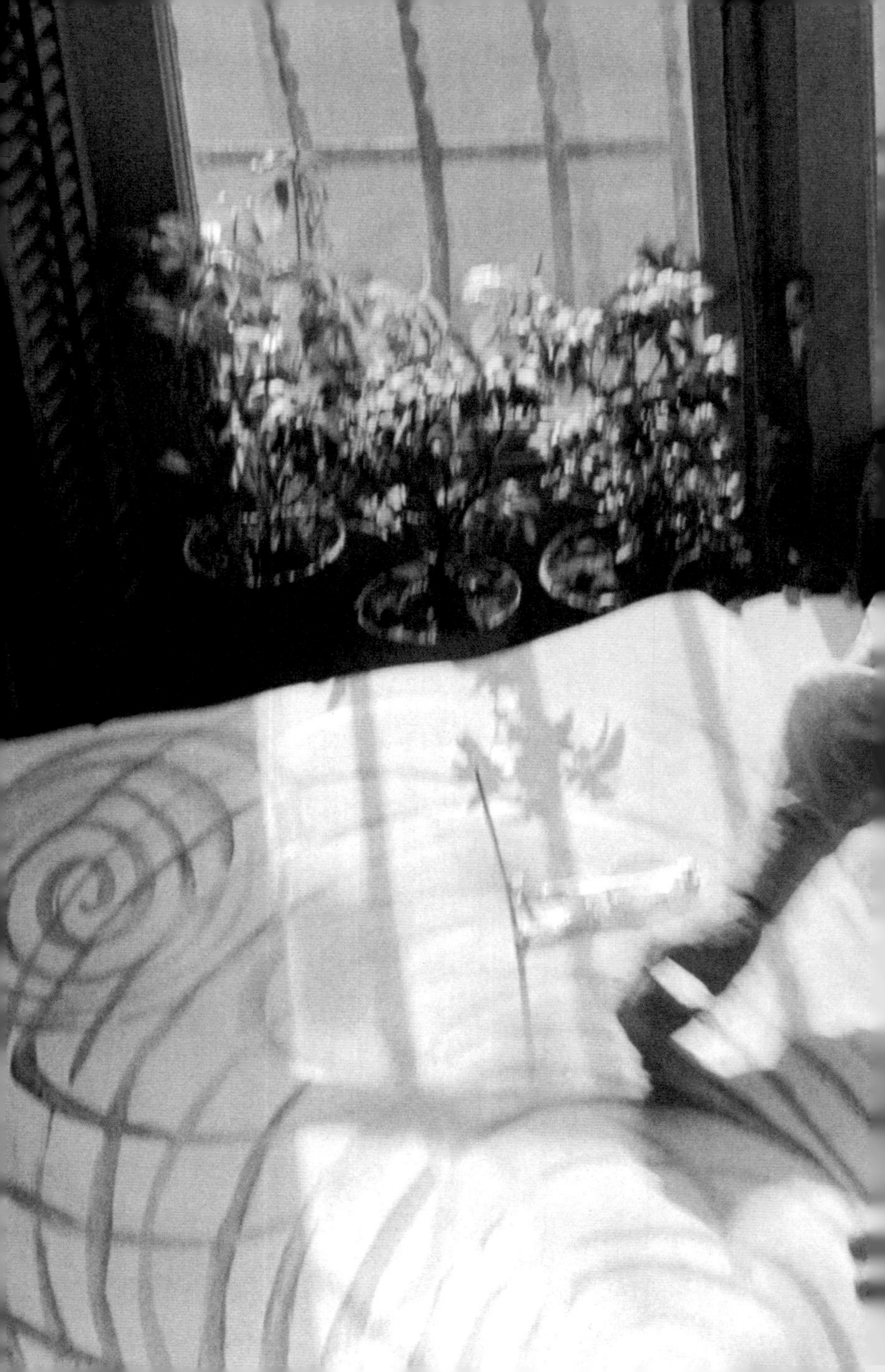

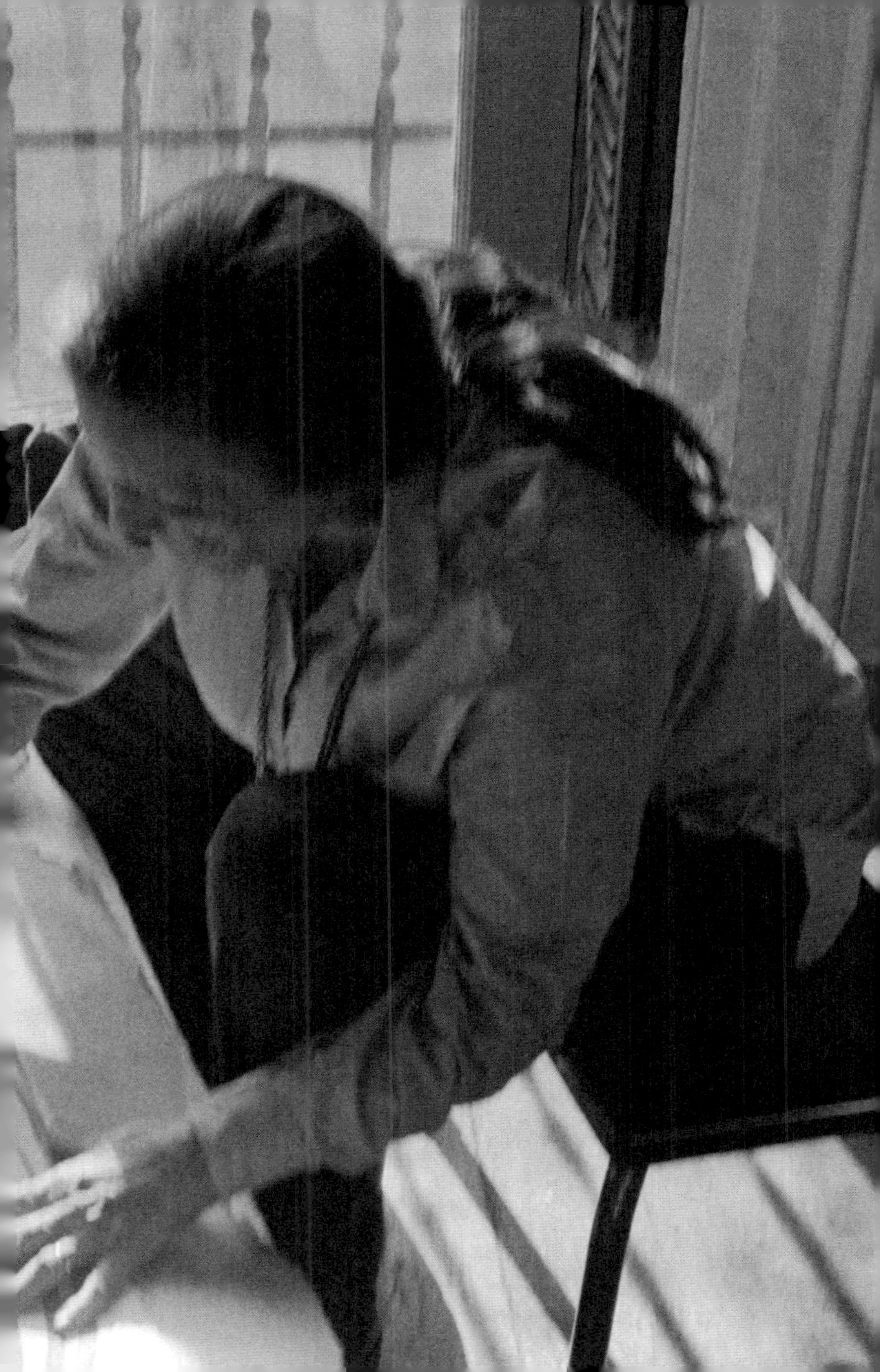

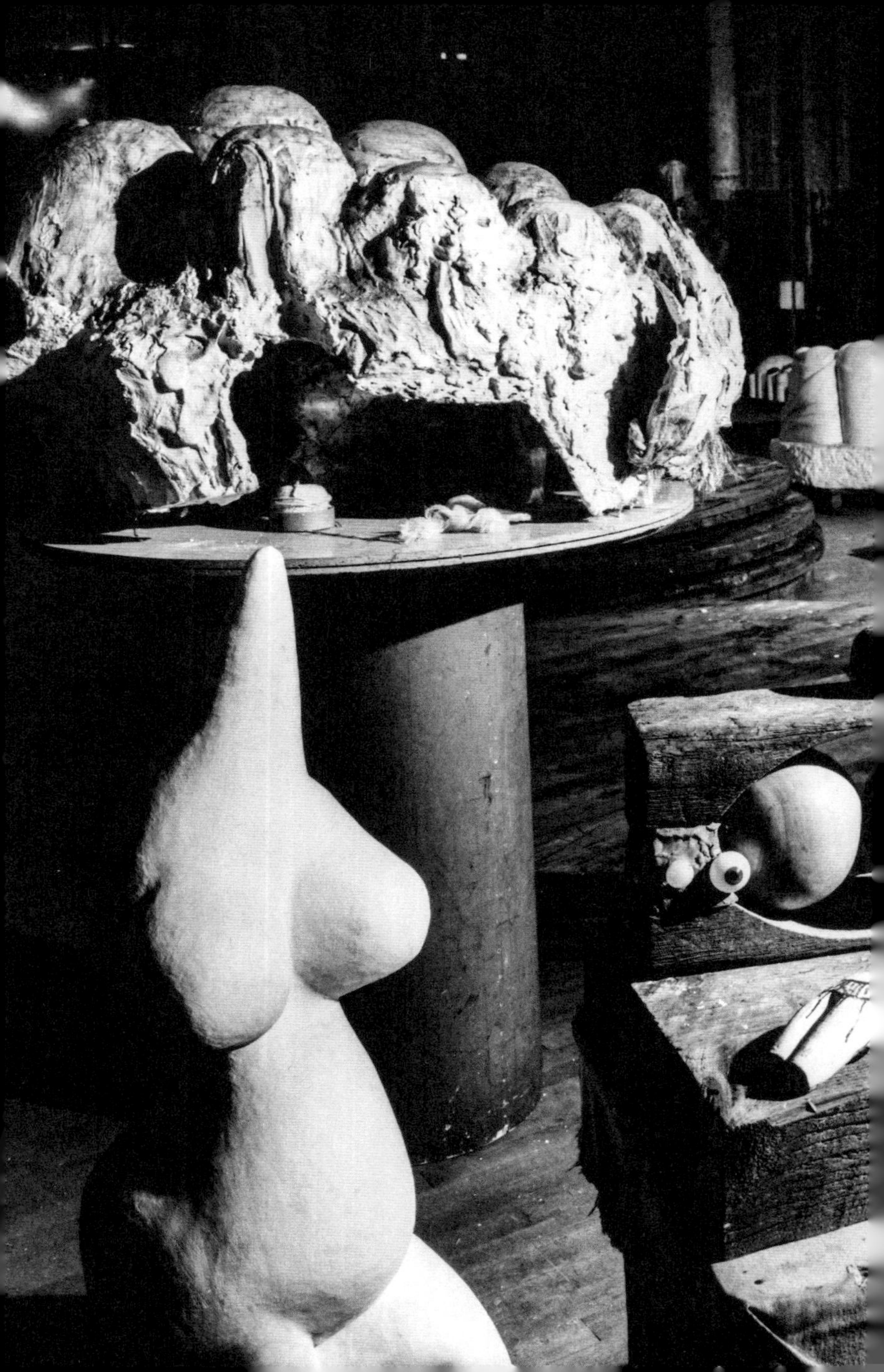

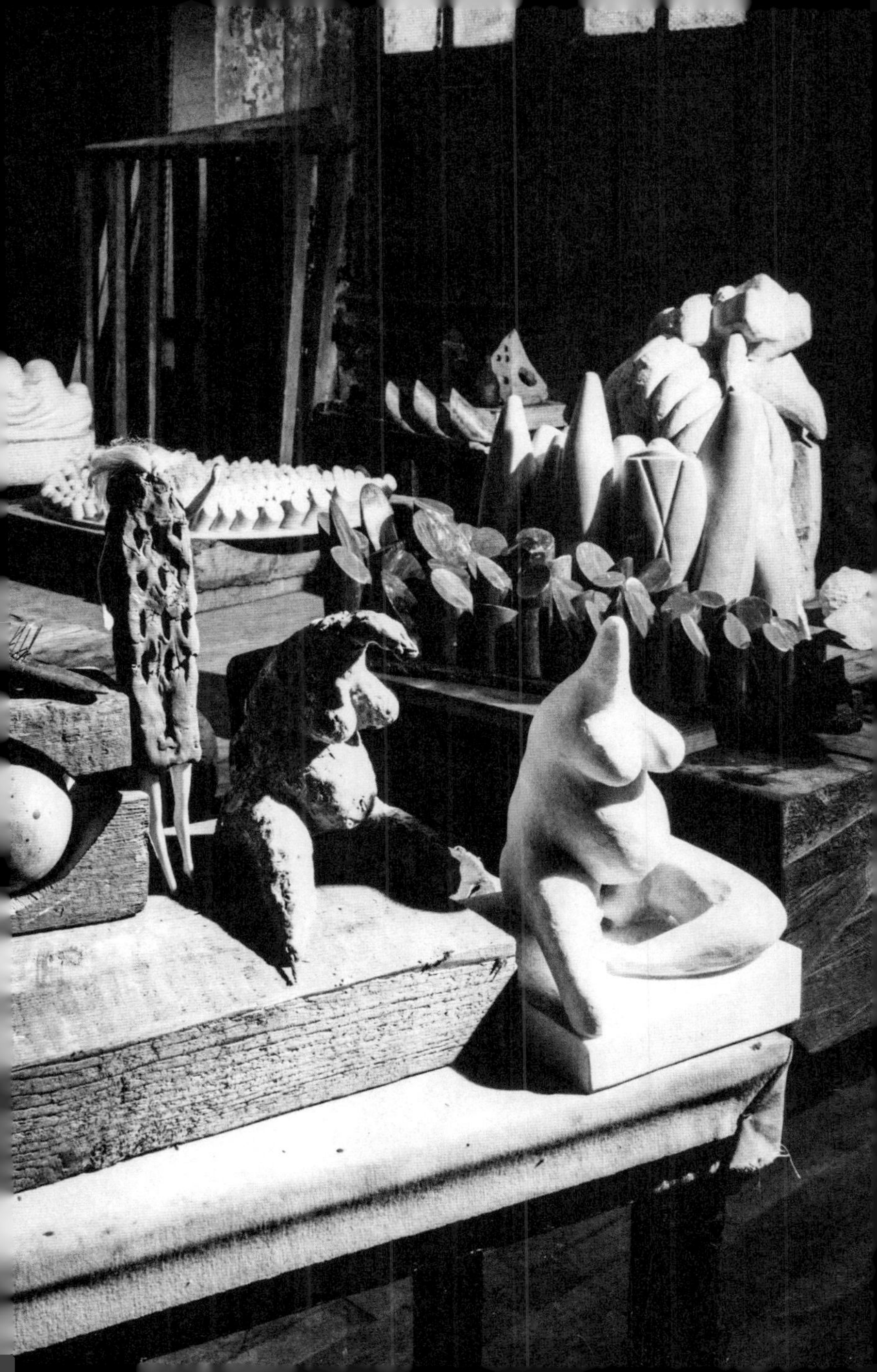

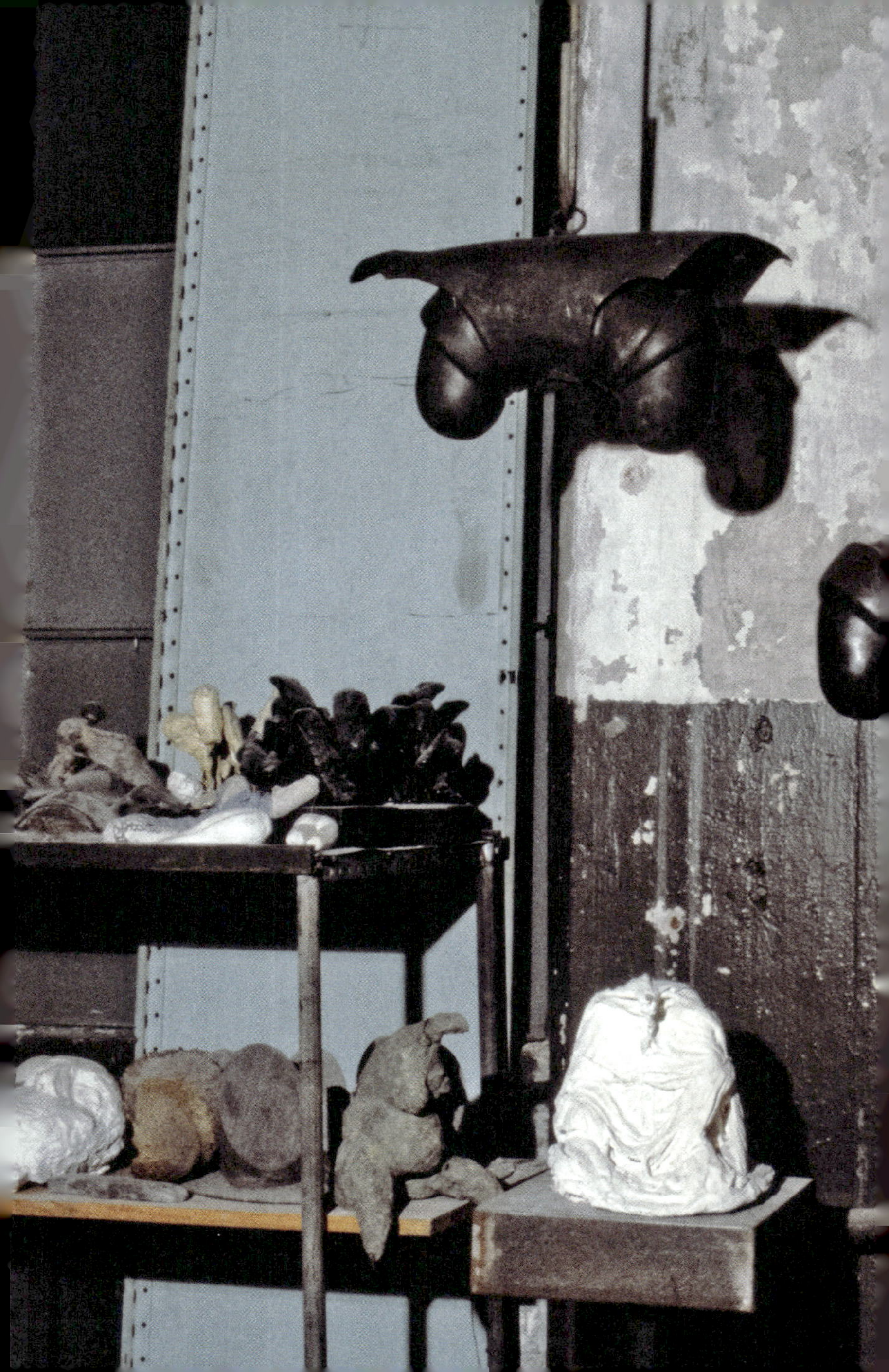

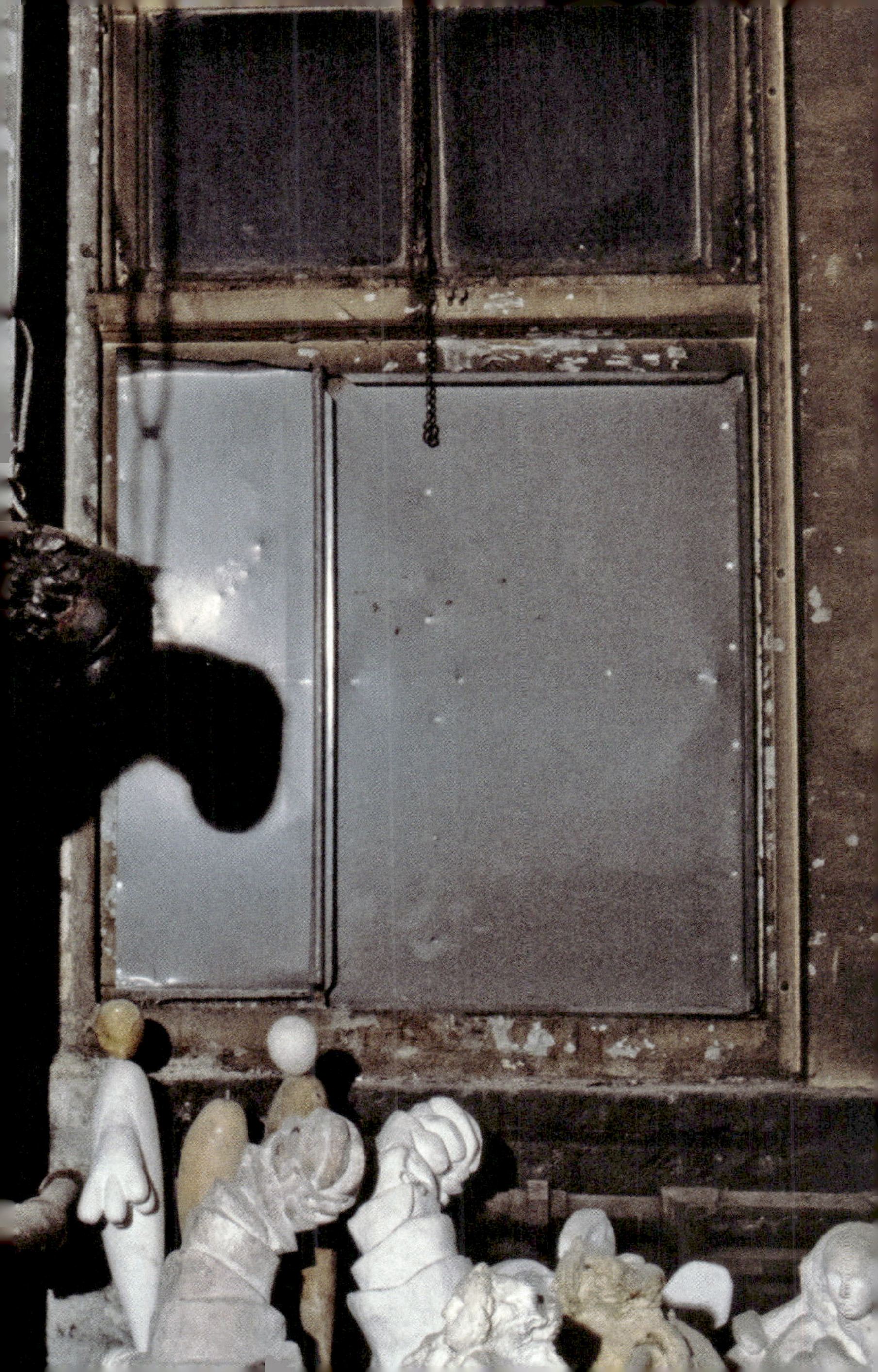

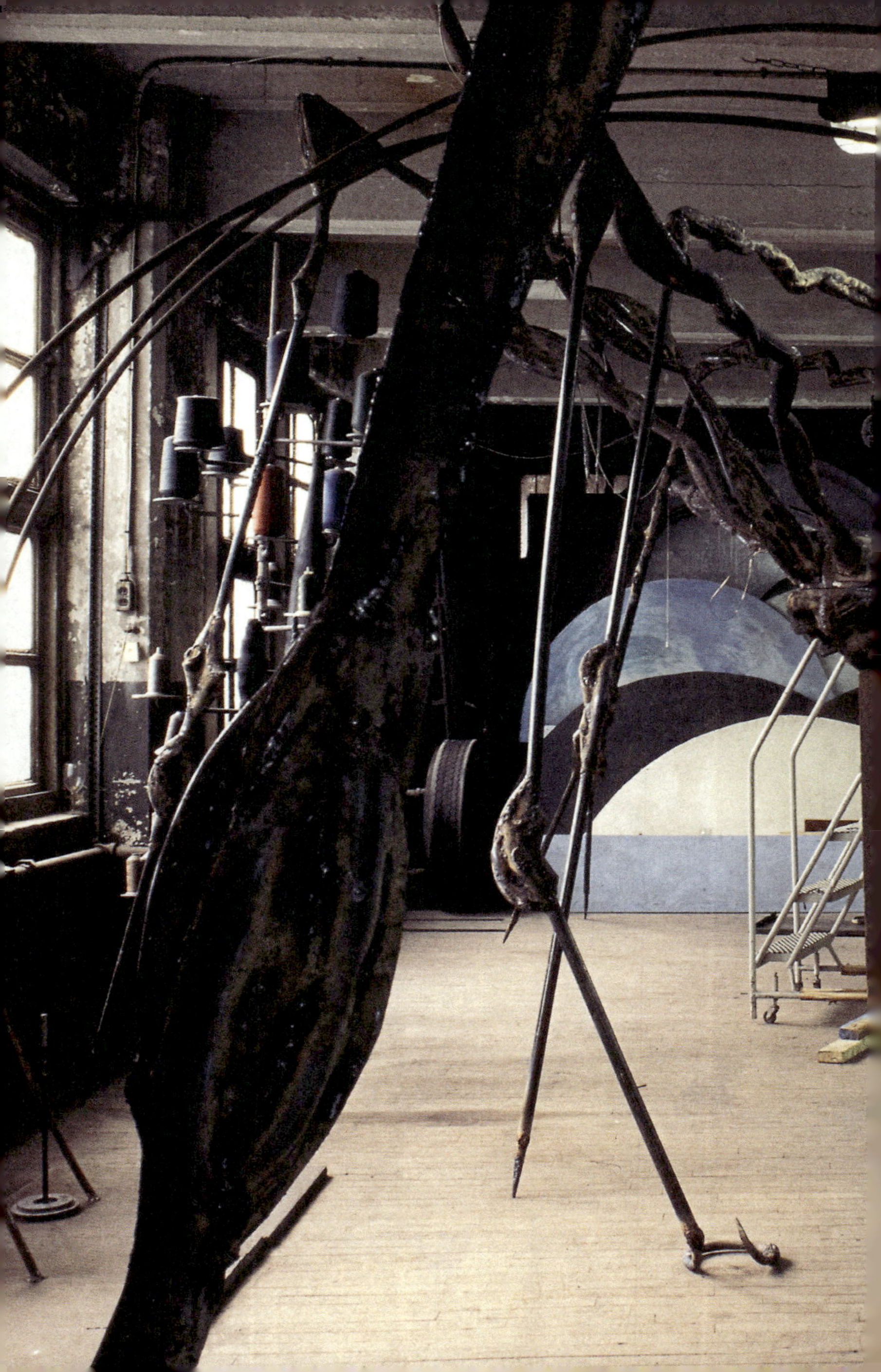

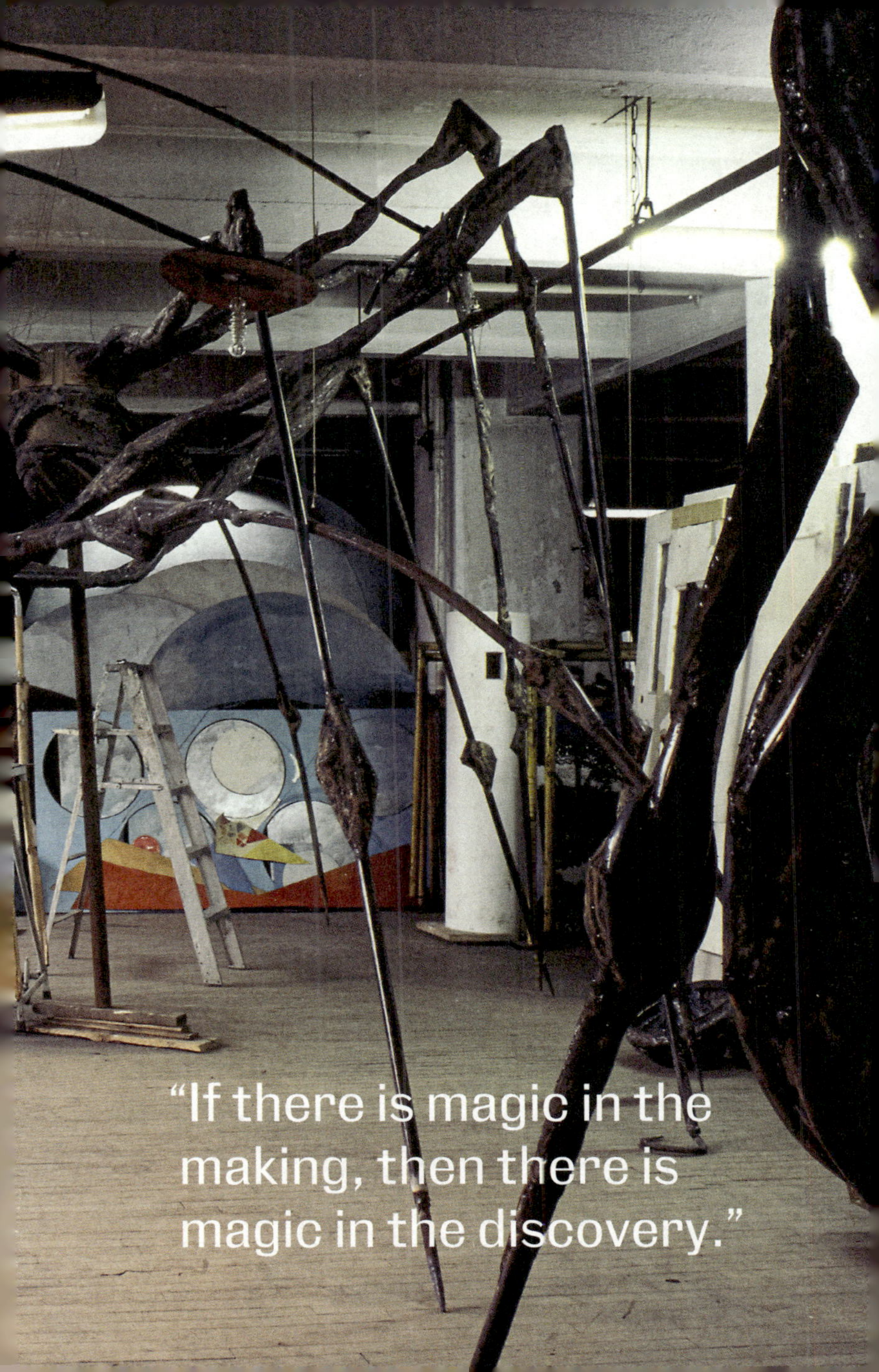
“If there is magic in the making, then there is magic in the discovery.”

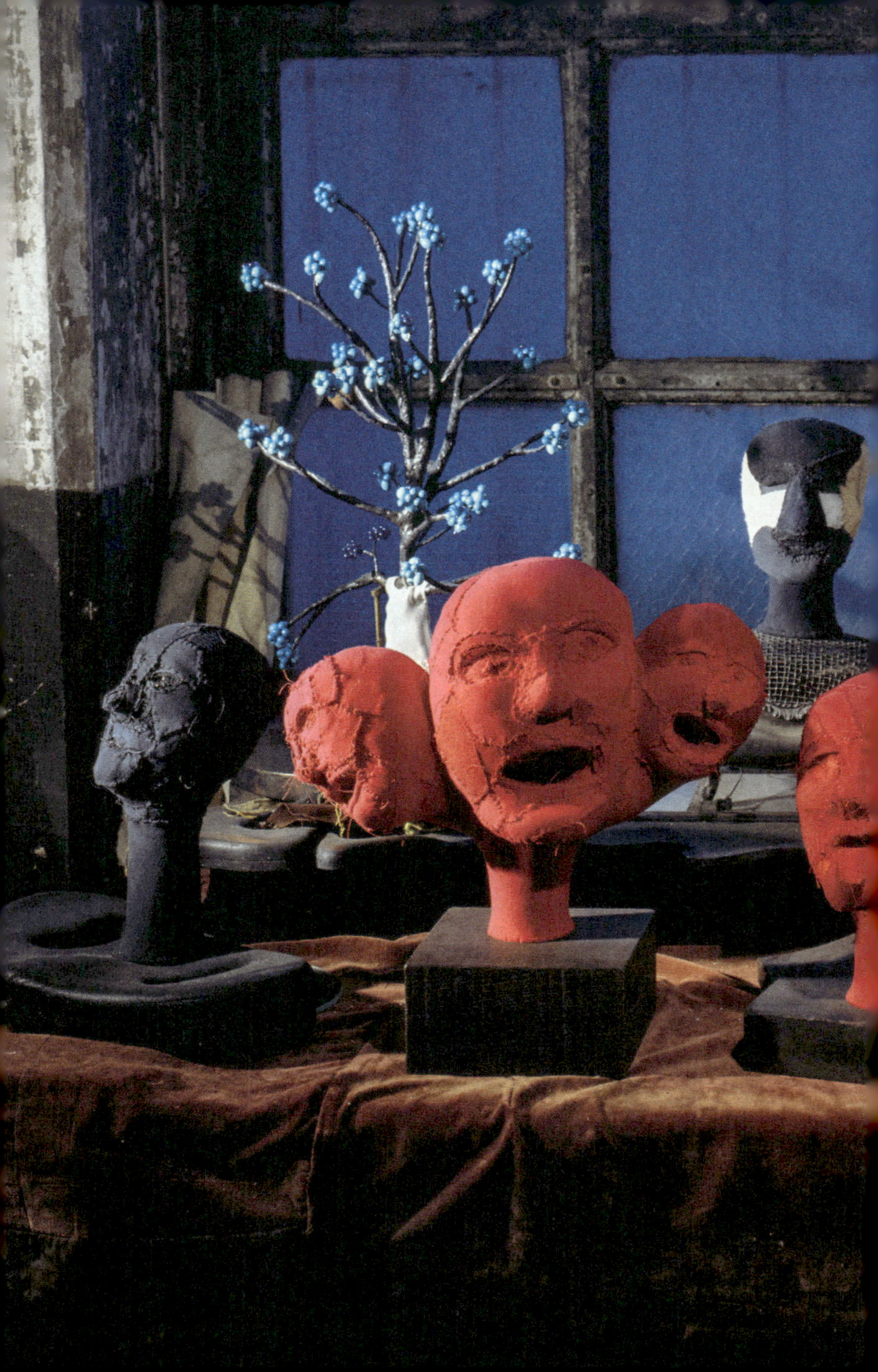

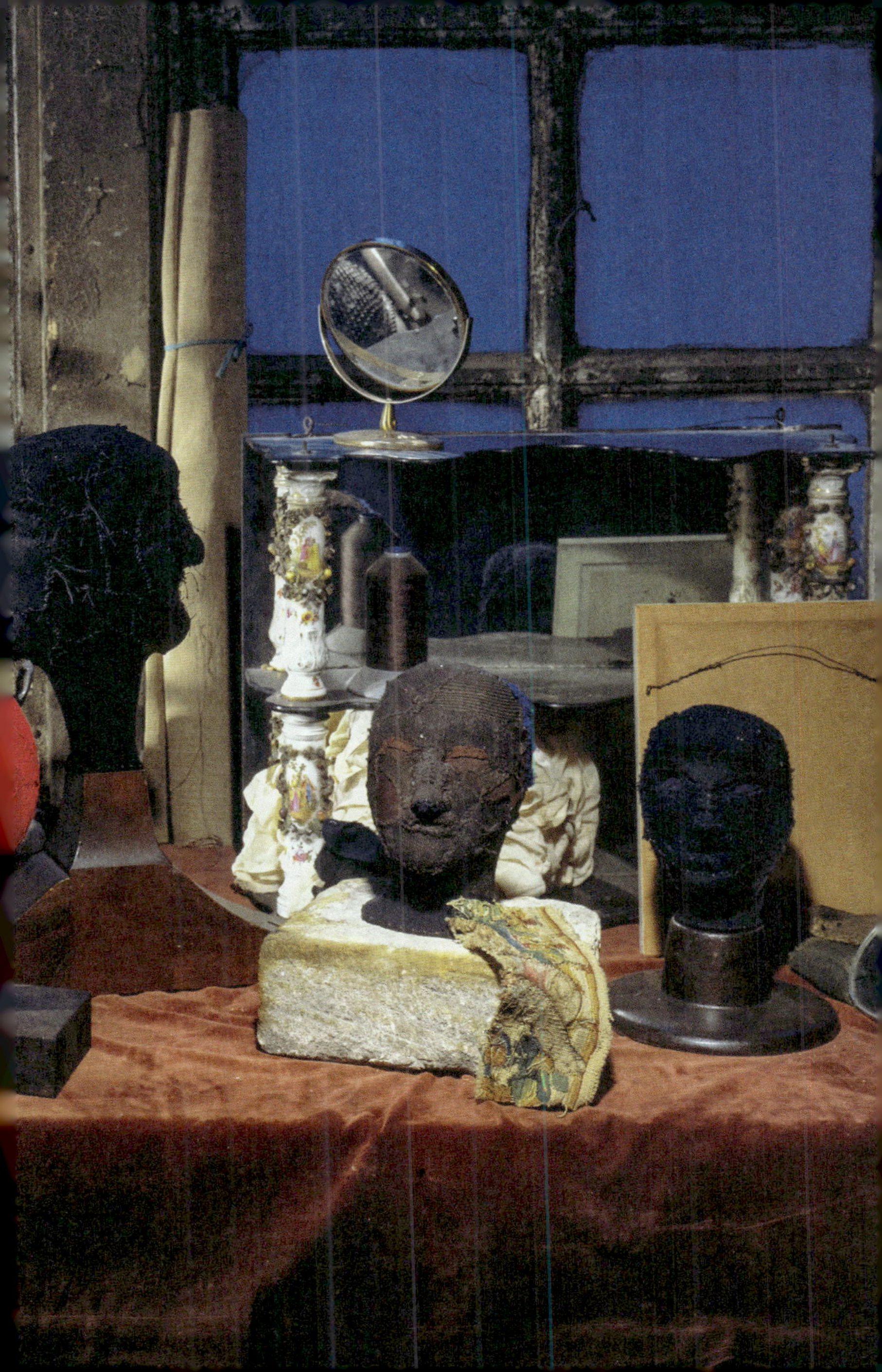

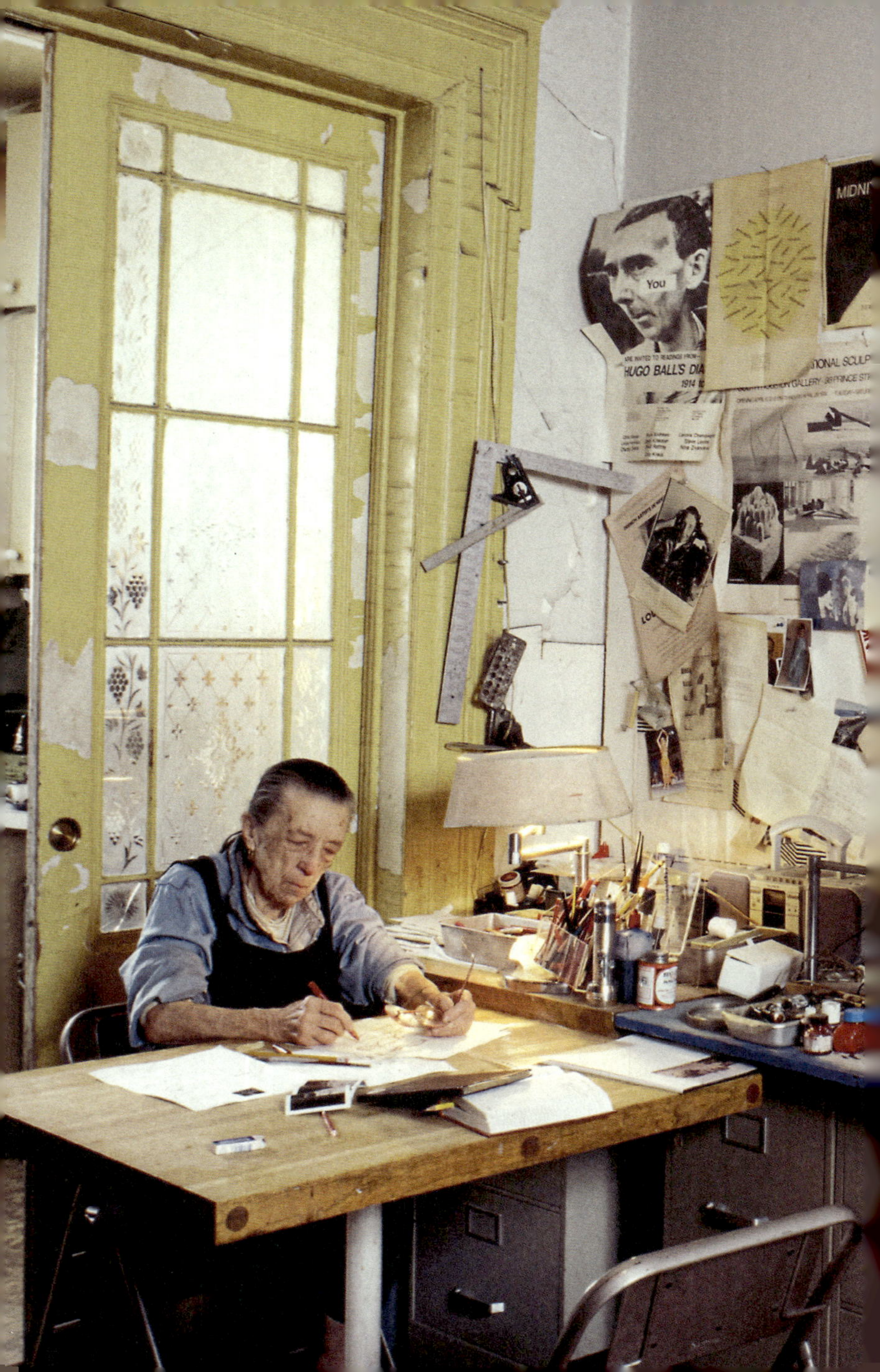
You
HUGO BALL'S DIA

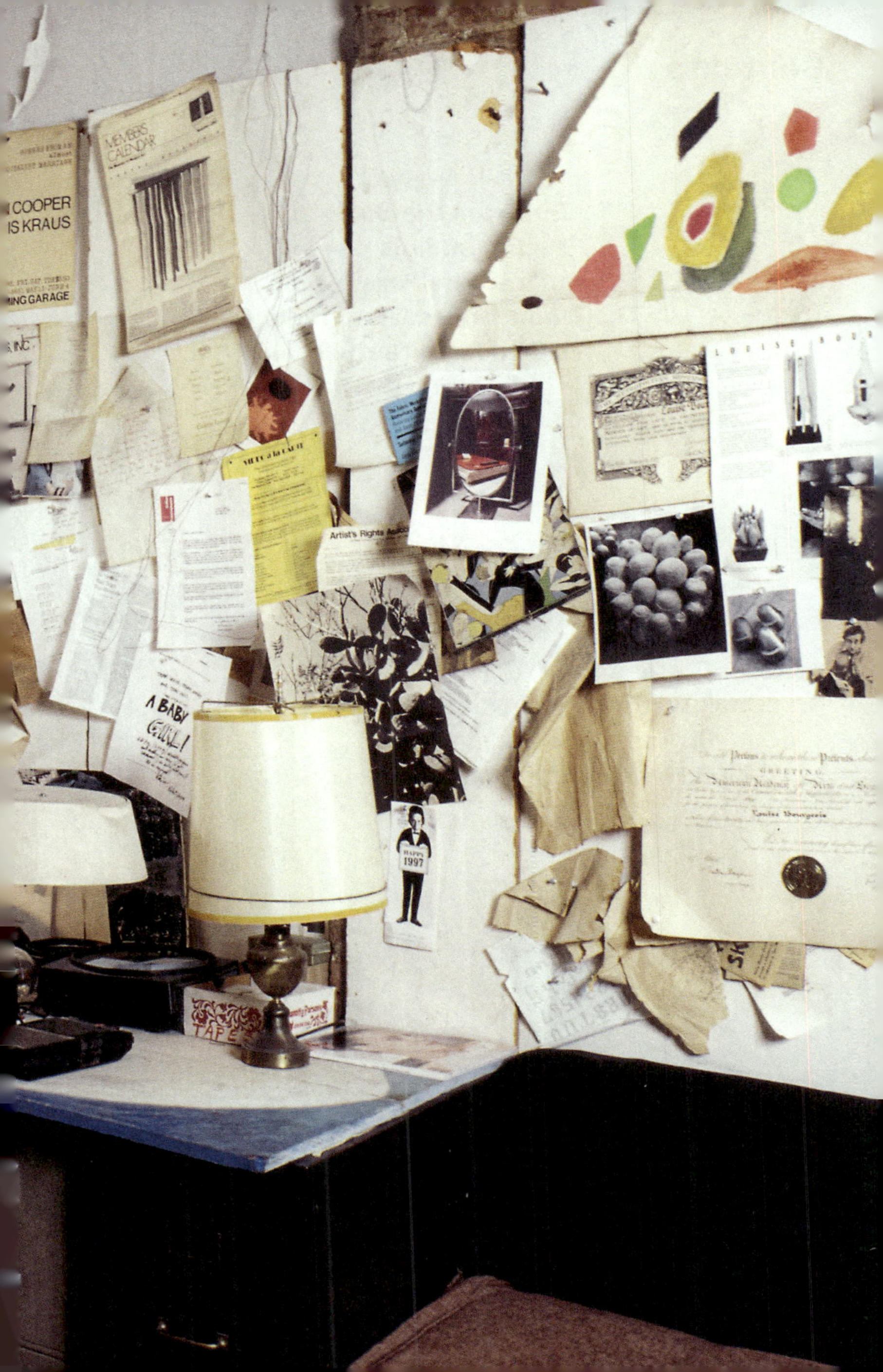
MEMBERS CALENDAR
COOPER
IS KRAUS
MING GARAGE
Artist's Rights
A BABY
HAPPY
1997
GREETING
TAPE

Contents

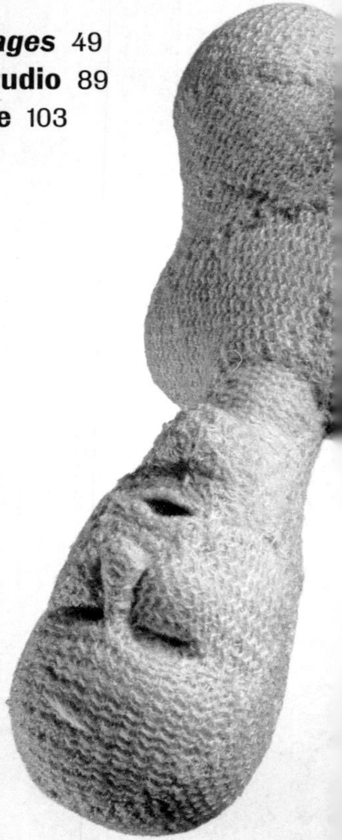

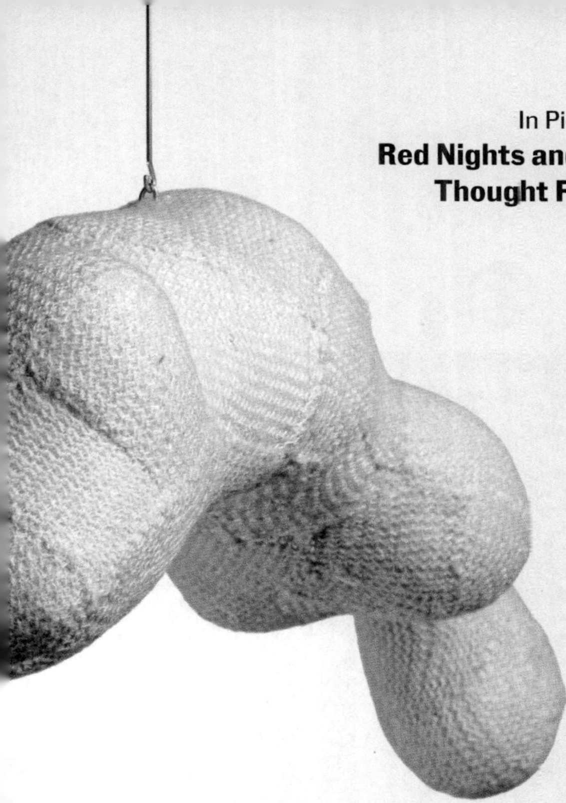

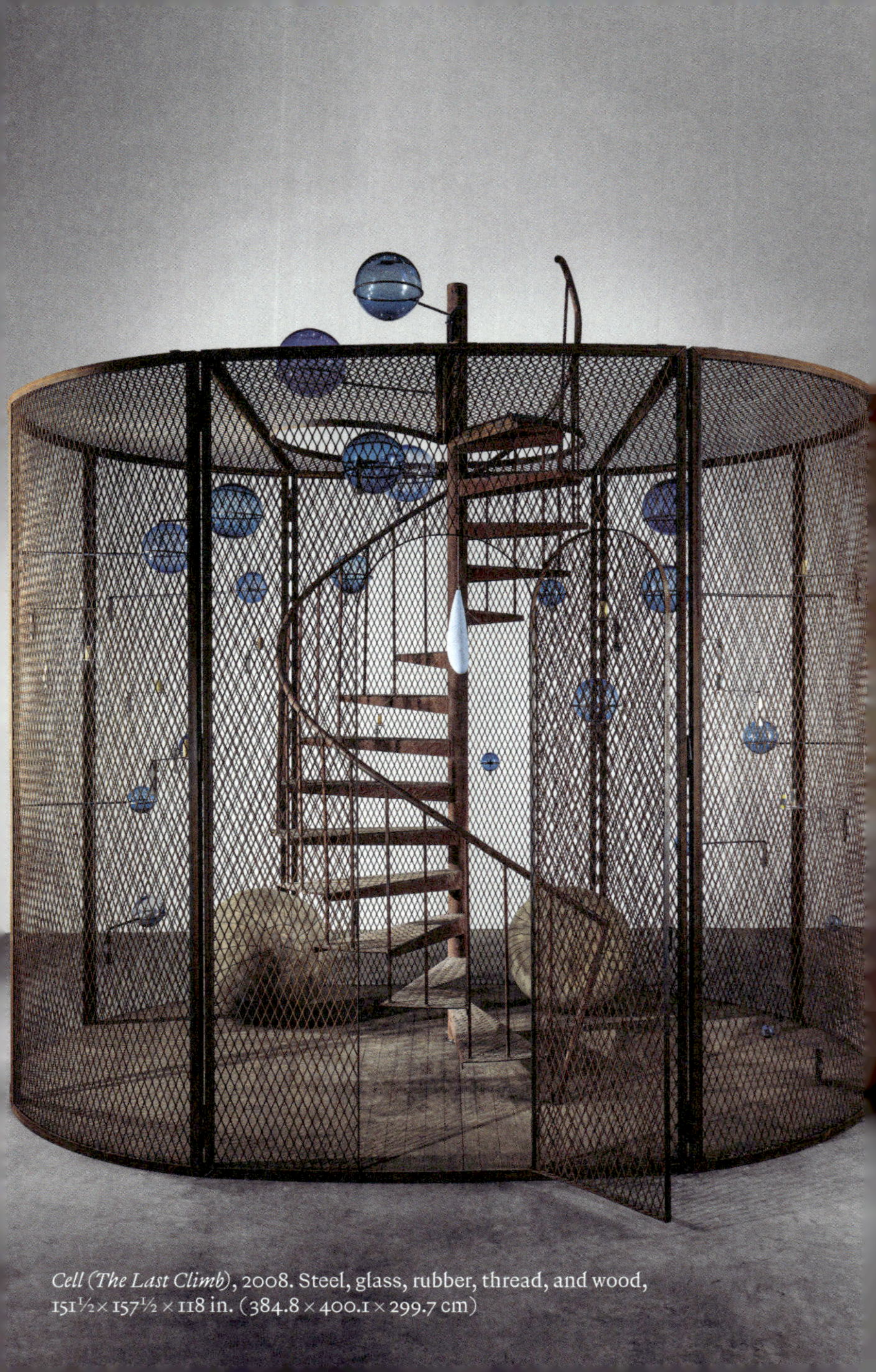

Cell (The Last Climb), 2008. Steel, glass, rubber, thread, and wood, 151½ × 157½ × 118 in. (384.8 × 400.1 × 299.7 cm)

Entering the Spell

The door to the steel-mesh enclosure is open. Step close and look inside. A staircase spirals up and out through the ceiling, orbited by globes of blue glass as it rises. Two wooden spheres sit on the floor beneath a pendulous sky-blue rubber form, which is pierced by twelve needles that are threaded, in turn, to spools on the perimeter walls. A silence prevails in this poetic space—the silence before something happens. The wooden spheres have a listening presence. The twelve threads tremble—a fragile clock.

This austere yet ethereal structure, from 2008, is Louise Bourgeois's penultimate *Cell*. It is also the then ninety-six-year-old artist's tribute and farewell to her Brooklyn, New York, studio as a refuge, a storehouse, and a power source. The spiral staircase, which Bourgeois had designed some twenty-five years earlier, was salvaged from the studio when she was forced to vacate it in 2005. She had climbed the staircase almost every day during her years of wildest sculptural productivity. The blue rubber teardrop, a symbolic self-portrait, also comes from a kind of recycling, having been cast from one of the saclike forms she carved in wood in the late 1940s. The twelve threads connect this object to Bourgeois's family history of textile repair; they also seem to measure out the hours of a final day. *Cell (The Last Climb)* is a vision of the studio as a strange machine that the artist is in the process of exiting, leaving behind her, in those stairs, one of her most-loved shapes—a spiral.

It's a jolt to realize that, for much of her career, Bourgeois did not have a conventional studio. She made art because she needed to, and she did so wherever she could.

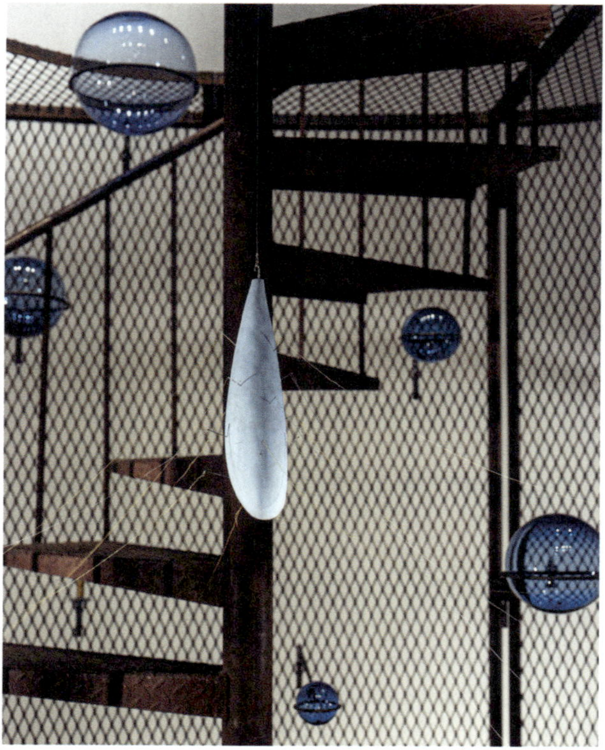

Cell (The Last Climb) (detail), 2008. Steel, glass, rubber, thread, and wood, 151½ × 157½ × 118 in. (384.8 × 400.1 × 299.7 cm)

She worked on tiny printing plates at the kitchen table and made sculptures on the rooftop of the apartment building where she lived with her young family. She worked in a small spare room of the apartment, at a weekend home in Easton, Connecticut, and later in the art-crammed basement of her brownstone in the Chelsea district of Manhattan. Only in 1980, aged sixty-eight, did she acquire the vast industrial studio in Brooklyn. In the mid-2000s, she returned to making art at home, working prodigiously from the small butcher-block table in her parlor. Her studio history reflects a career that never "developed" conventionally or consistently. Rather, it moved with thrilling unpredictability—circling back, leaping forward, waning, intensifying, always searching, never satisfied. From slender, haunting totems to visceral *Lairs*, from metamorphic marbles to vast steel *Cells*, from the spider sculptures for which she's best known to the thousands of drawings she called "thought feathers," she created a kingdom (as writer Chris Kraus put it) whose dimensions seem to change whenever we reenter it.

Through all this, the studio was her emotional axis and imaginative home—a real location that was also a place of solace, memory, truth, and discovery. "My work in the studio is everything to me," she said. "It is where I function and it is where I find purpose in life." Fears, regrets, and existential anxieties shadowed Bourgeois from childhood. But as her longtime friend and assistant Jerry Gorovoy has said, she was never calmer or happier than in the studio, working with resistant materials to give physical form to the powerfully conflicted feelings that drove her. Bourgeois hastened to add that this state of deep concentration was not like falling into a dream. Instead, it involved entering what she memorably called "the spell"—a state of open and active communion with her innermost motivations and the possibilities of her materials.

Our sense of Bourgeois is shaped in part by the many portraits made of her in later life—none greater than Robert Mapplethorpe's image of the artist grinning regally with the lumpy, phallic form of *Fillette* (1968) under her arm. (The photograph was cropped for propriety when it was reproduced in the catalogue of Bourgeois's retrospective at the Museum of Modern Art [MoMA], New York, in 1982.)

The image testifies to her charisma, her mischief, her droll intelligence, her anxious pride, and her considerable style. But to get close to Bourgeois in the studio, in the state of the spell, we need to turn to her art.

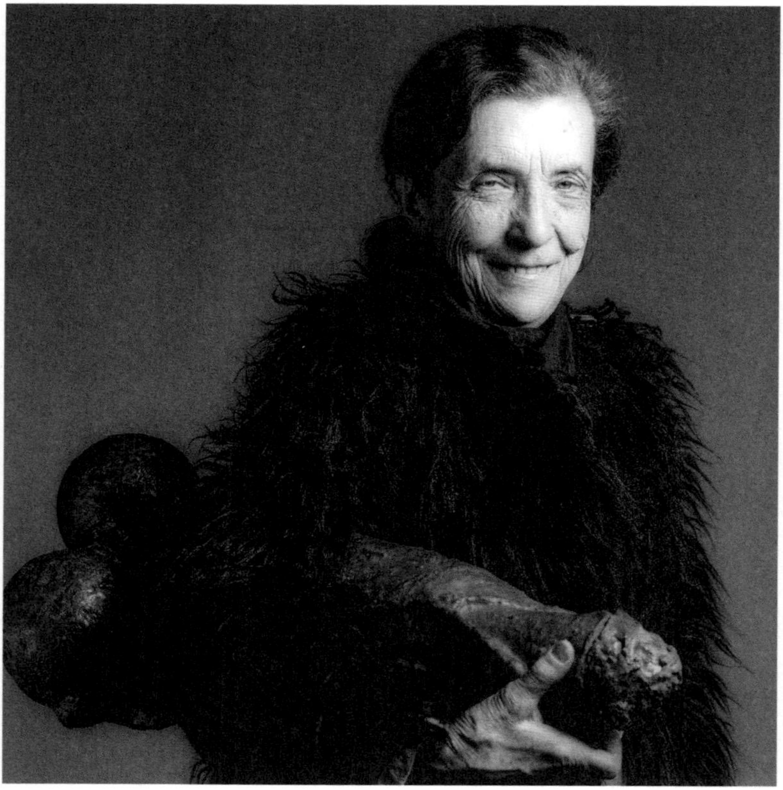

Robert Mapplethorpe, *Louise Bourgeois*, 1982

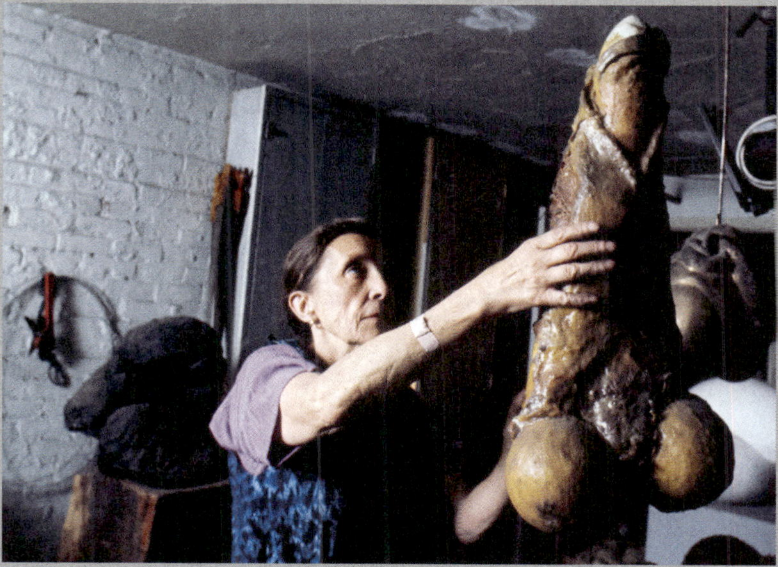

Bourgeois with *Fillette* (1968) in her home studio, New York, 1974

Fillette (1968)
A vital organ that looks cooked or flayed. Larger than life, but terribly vulnerable. Not set on a plinth, but hooked like a carcass. Painful to look at, but also hard to tear your gaze from. To discuss it is to reveal yourself. One writer called it "dirty," another "comic." The artist described it as a tribute to the men in her family, yet named it *Fillette* ("little girl"). Looking again, aren't the testicles like breasts, or bulbous legs at the base of a torso? And how should we read the splitting, shroudlike quality of the latex skin? Almost sixty years since it was made, *Fillette* is still a shock to encounter in an art museum—a sculpture that feels both too raw and too ancient for the polite environs of the white cube. It demonstrates Bourgeois's formidable gift for going right to the crux, delivering objects so vivid and potent they make our descriptions seem inadequate.

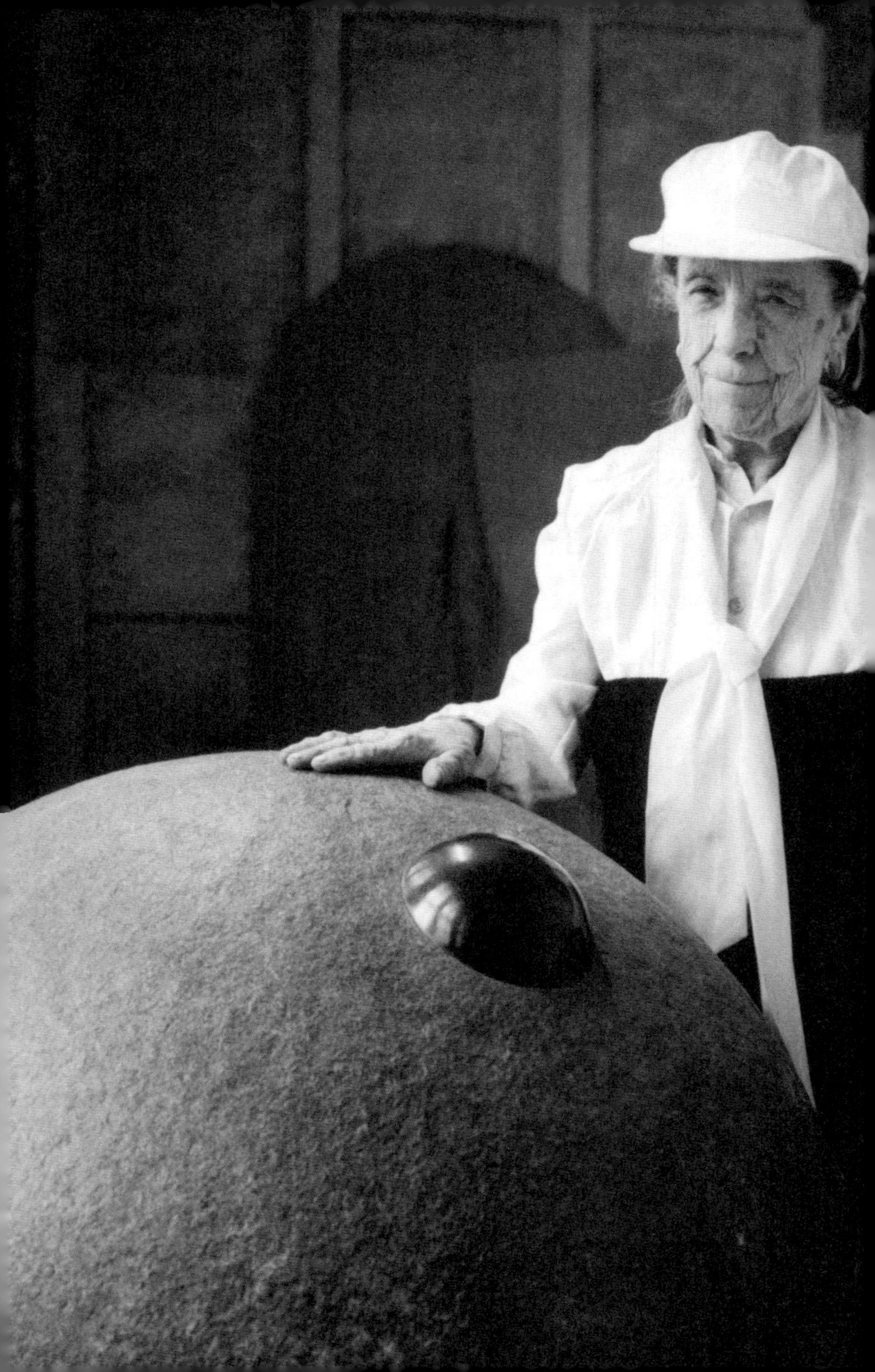

“It is not conscious motivation.
It is unconscious motivation.
After a work is finished,
then you say, Ah my God!
This is what I meant.”

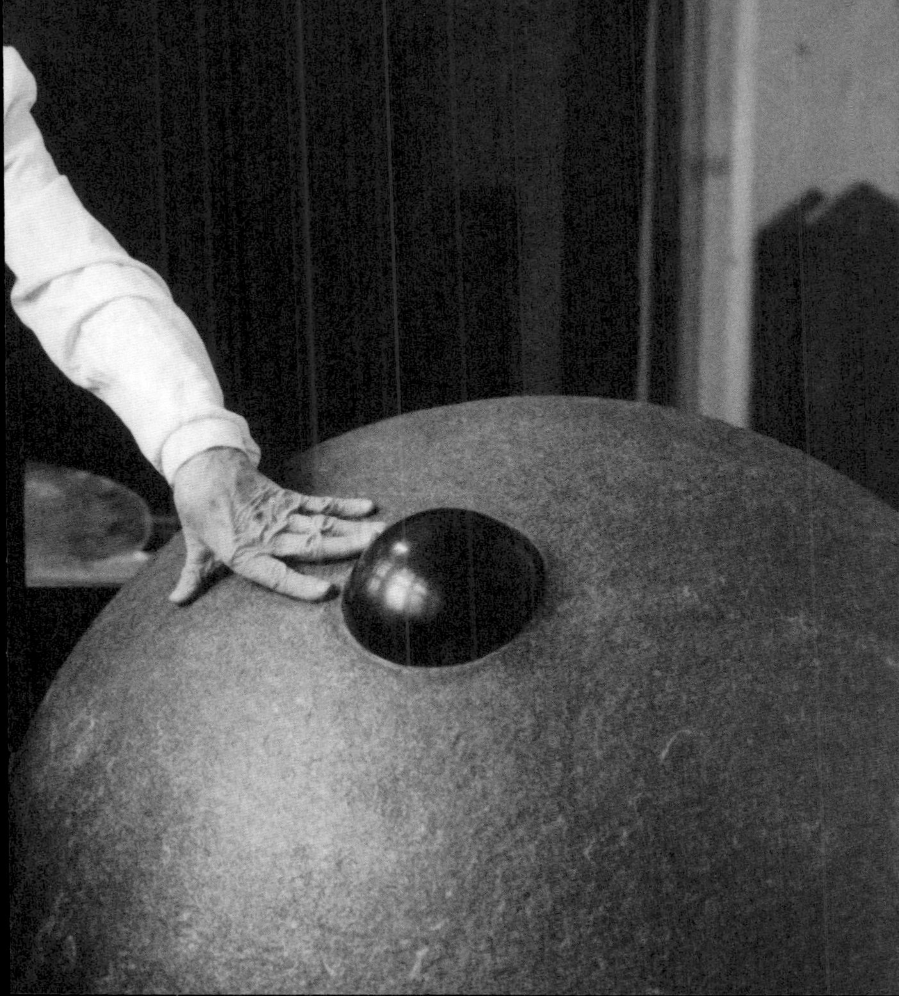

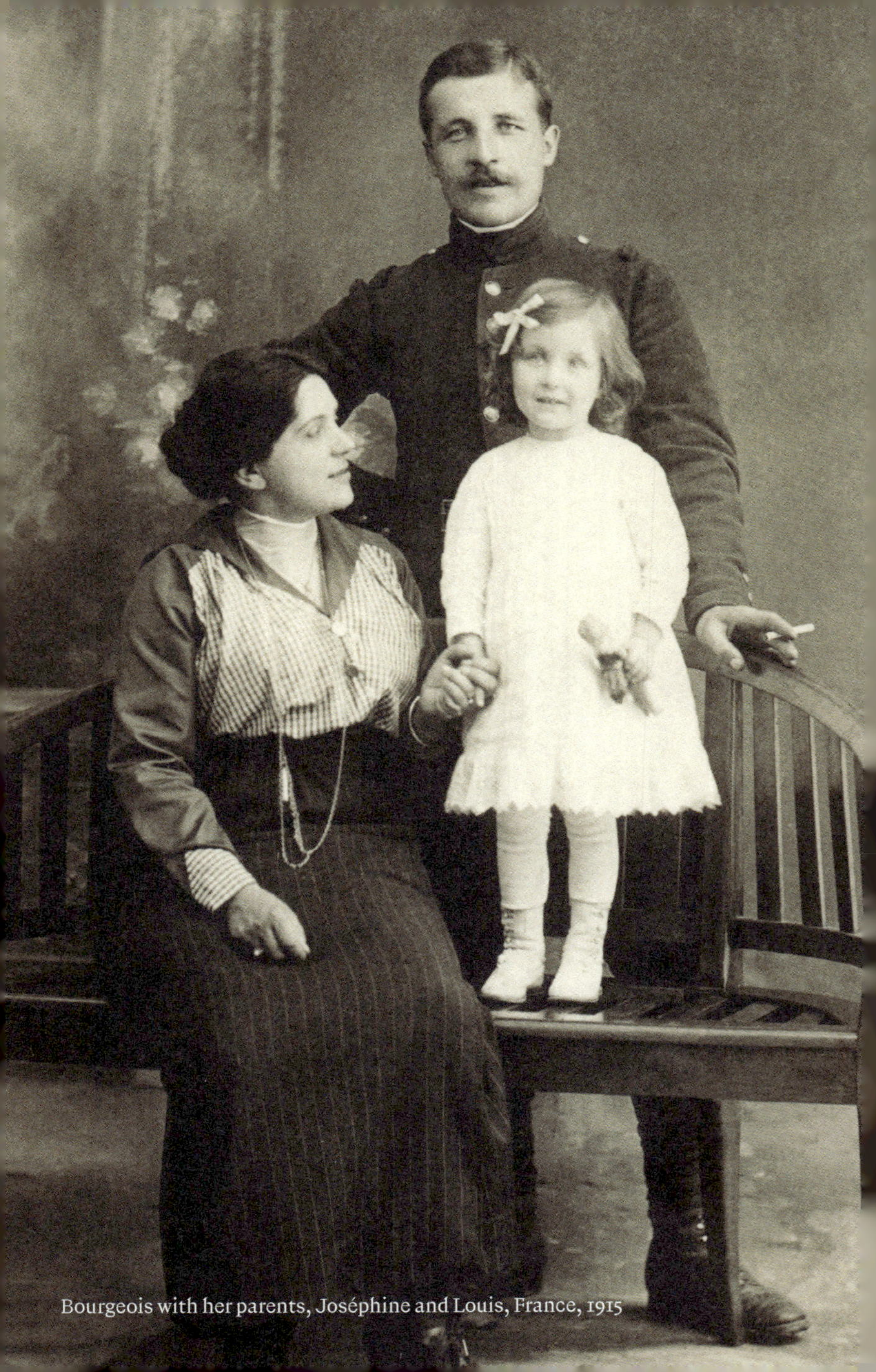

Bourgeois with her parents, Joséphine and Louis, France, 1915

Beginnings

Photographs of Bourgeois's girlhood in France portray a lost and seemingly charmed world of well-appointed domesticity and stylish vacations. But the past was never truly *past* for Bourgeois. It consoled, angered, and inspired her. She returned increasingly to its fears and wonderments across her long life as an artist. At times, one feels that memory was her medium, as surely as fabric or marble.

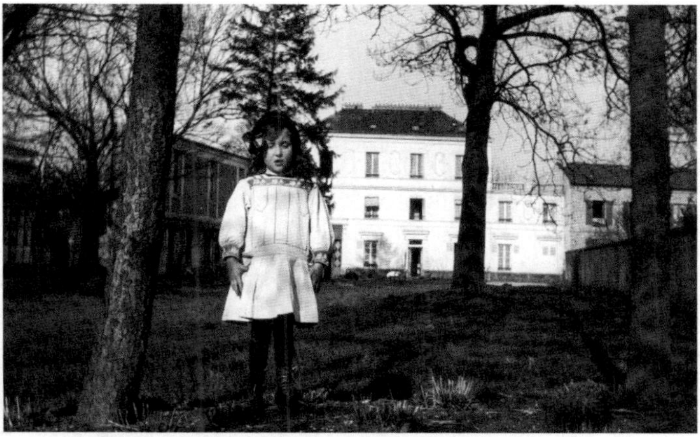

Bourgeois in the garden of her family home, Choisy-le-Roi, France, 1917

In Bourgeois's account of her beginnings, even her birth was a disruption. She arrived on Christmas Day in 1911, interrupting the doctor's "oysters and champagne." Her parents, Louis and Joséphine, ran a prosperous tapestry restoration business—her charismatic father sourcing old tapestries and her steadfast mother overseeing their restoration. The family home and grounds in Choisy-le-Roi, just outside Paris, and later in nearby Antony, furnished Bourgeois with a trove of physical memories, from the smell of honeysuckle and boxwoods to the wringing and washing of wool in the Bièvre River and the sight of stars above the garden at night.

It was also a world of materials and making, of canny salvage and repair. Decades later, Bourgeois could recall in extraordinary detail the techniques of the tapestry workshop. She also remembered her happiness as a child on being enlisted as a *dessinateur*, responsible for drawing lost forms back onto damaged tapestries in readiness for reweaving (the lower sections were often the most worn, and Bourgeois became adept at sketching legs and feet). Her lifelong sense of the studio as a place of working solace took root in these moments. The fabric book *Ode à la Bièvre* (2002)—stitched together at the far end of her life from oddments gathered over the course of it—is a recollection (and a letting go) of this memory-drenched landscape.

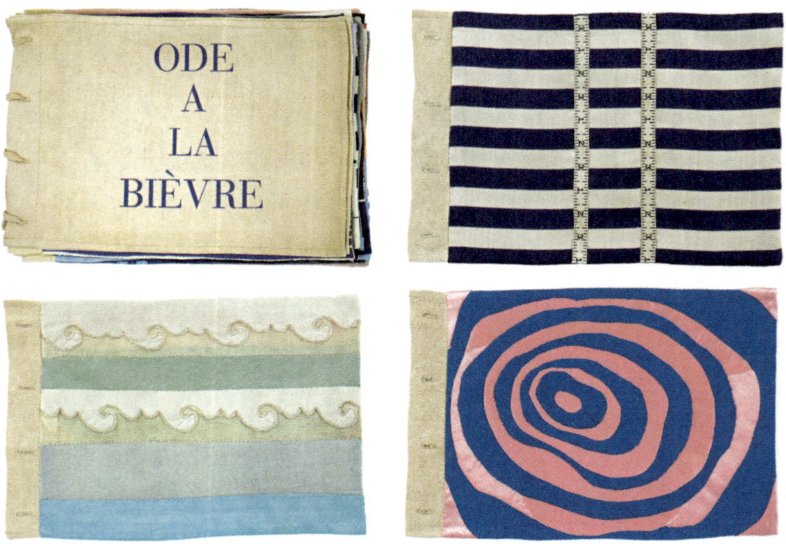

Ode à la Bièvre (details), 2002. Fabric and lithograph book, 25 pages, each 11 × 15½ in. (27.9 × 39.4 cm)

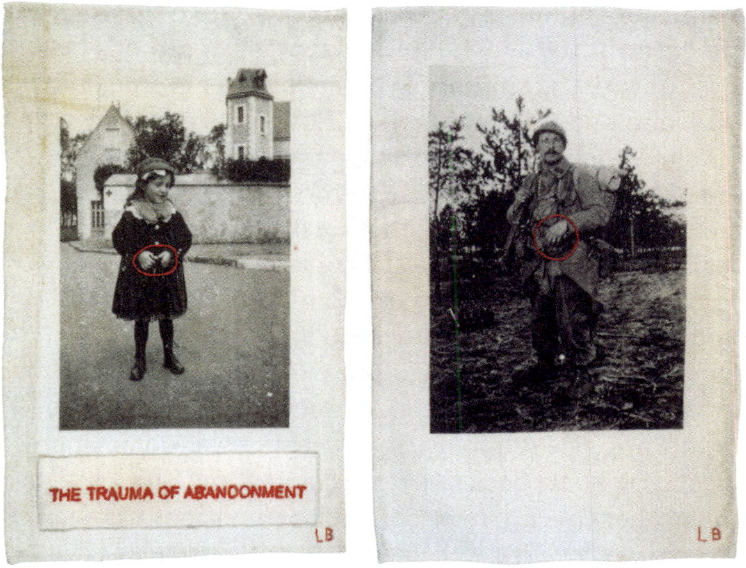

The Trauma of Abandonment (details), 2001. Digital prints on fabric with thread additions, 12 pages, each 10 × 6 in. (25.4 × 15.2 cm)

Bourgeois was the brightest of three siblings, later studying at the elite Lycée Fénelon in Paris. She was also her parents' favorite and, despite the presence of a younger brother, an honorary son in the eyes of her father. Like many favored children, she was hypersensitive to the balance of her parents' approval and to the fluctuating tensions between them. The stability that Bourgeois cherished was undone by World War I; her uncle died in the war's first week, and her father, after enlisting, was wounded. Bourgeois recalled the chaos this unlatched in her mother, who bundled the children off to their grandparents in central France and followed Louis anxiously from camp to camp, sometimes with the young Louise. In the red-stitched fabric book *The Trauma of Abandonment* (2001), Bourgeois zeroes in on these early dislocations as the source of lifelong fears.

This wartime trauma is bound up in Bourgeois's story with a betrayal and a loss. First, there was her father's long affair with the children's young English governess, Sadie Richmond. (The tale, which Bourgeois narrated in a slideshow for her MoMA retrospective, was ceaselessly repeated by fascinated commentators.) But the major rupture in Bourgeois's early emotional life was the death of her mother in 1932. Joséphine contracted lung disease during the postwar influenza pandemic and later was nursed for several years by Bourgeois, by then in her late teens. The black stone sculpture *Ventouse* (1990) is a heartbreakingly tomblike recollection of this experience, incorporating glass cupping jars like those she would apply to Joséphine's bare back to relieve congestion. The loss of her mother engendered a complex of emotions that Bourgeois would work with and worry at for decades. Among them were guilt for not having done enough to save Joséphine, fury at her father for his many infidelities, and anger at her mother for having stoically tolerated them.

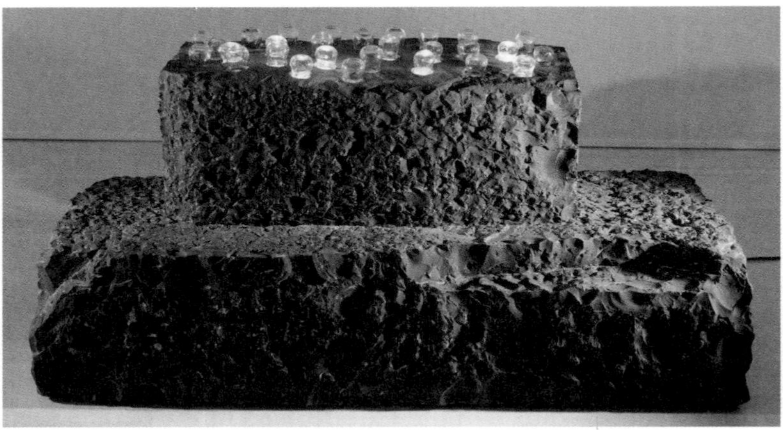

Ventouse, 1990. Marble, glass, and electric light, 34 × 78 × 32 in. (86.4 × 198.1 × 81.3 cm)

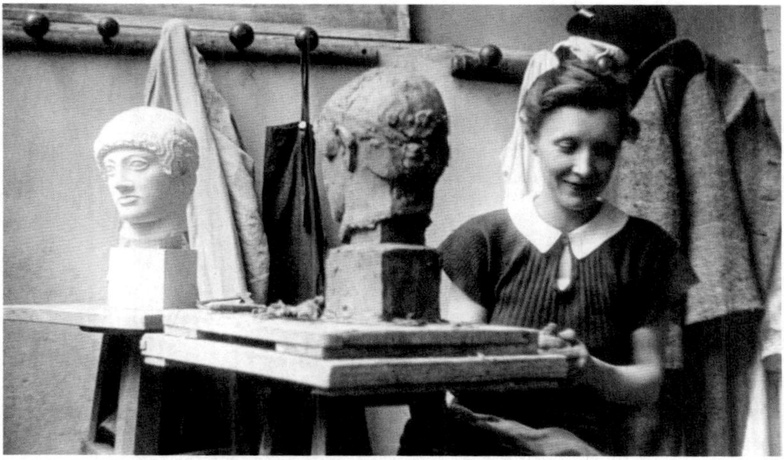

Bourgeois at the Académie de la Grande Chaumière, Paris, 1937

In the wake of her mother's death, Bourgeois was a young woman shaking free of a family dynamic she found oppressive, while also seeking a stabilizing order. At first, she turned to mathematics, a subject whose rules and reliability had always comforted her, taking classes in calculus and solid geometry at the Sorbonne. But by 1933, she had thrown herself decisively into the study of art in Paris's schools and academies. "Art is a privilege, a blessing, a relief," Bourgeois reflected many years later, and the tenacity with which she pursued her studies suggests she felt this from the outset. She loved the "total, friendly silence" in which students drew all day in the ateliers. And she soaked up the guidance of a run of teachers, including Fernand Léger. Bourgeois attributed her "passion for the third dimension" to an improvised lesson from the burly modernist, who suspended a wood shaving under a shelf and invited her to observe its movement. Her drawings of the form prompted Léger to declare "Louise, you are not a painter, you are a sculptor."

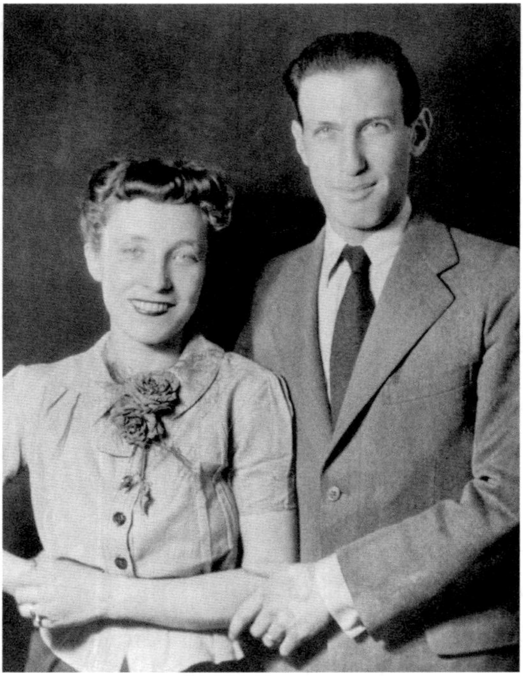

Bourgeois and Robert Goldwater, New York, 1938

In retrospect, Bourgeois appears to have been getting ready for something. Her preparations culminated unexpectedly in the summer of 1938. Bourgeois had opened a small art gallery in her father's tapestry salesroom in Paris. Here, she met Robert Goldwater, a young art historian from New York who was emerging as a leading scholar of modernism and non-Western art. Calm, kind, and intellectually formidable—the opposite of her impetuous father, Bourgeois observed—Goldwater offered both stability and escape: emotional anchorage and the promise of elsewhere. "I had found a diamond," she recalled. Hardly three weeks later, they were married, and four weeks after that "the runaway girl," as Bourgeois described herself, disembarked in New York City.

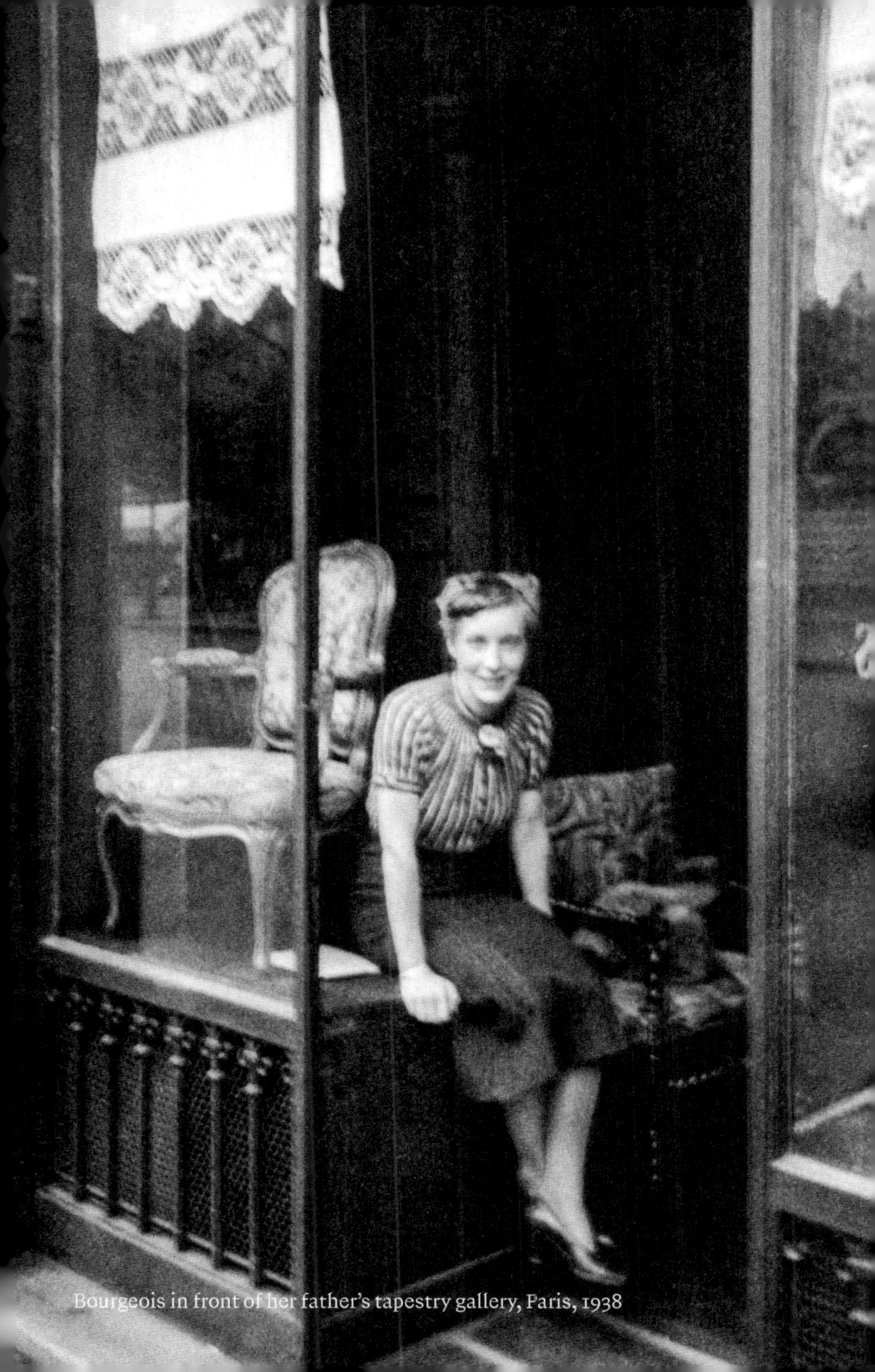

Bourgeois in front of her father’s tapestry gallery, Paris, 1938

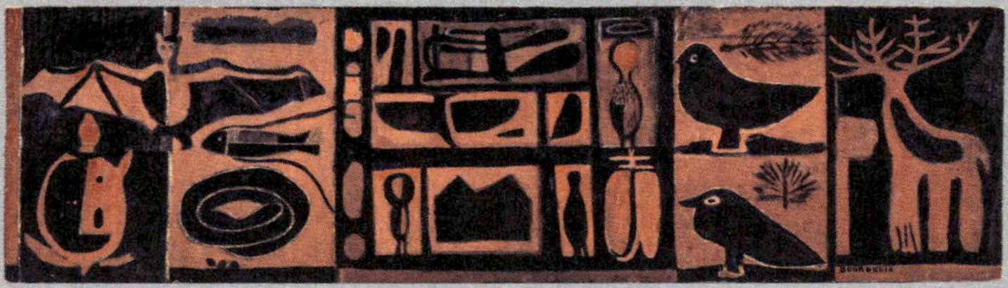

Connecticutiana, 1944–45. Oil on wood, 11 × 42 in. (27.9 × 106.7 cm)

Emotional Geometries

Bourgeois studied geometry for just a few months in the unsettled period following her mother's death, but its lessons and rules—eternal, reliable—consoled and inspired her for the rest of her life. Geometry lay at the origin of her love of sculpture; both are disciplines for imagining form in space. More than that, geometry introduced her to the possibility (as she put it) that "chaos could be licked." With representational images—a blade, a body—she could cut to the emotional quick. But geometry gave her a way to settle and structure volatile feelings. In this symbolic realm, where every shape is charged with emotional significance, a triangle (two points in tension with another) often means trouble, while circular subsets inside a parent circle might diagram family comfort (or claustrophobia). Spirals are tension incarnate: releasing outward or cranking inward. Parallel lines are reliable but desolating (think of Bourgeois's stiffly paired *Personages* [pp. 49–53]) because they run together but can never touch. These shapes are theoretically pure and unchanging—that was their attraction initially for Bourgeois—but the poetry lies in how they're humanized, made fallible, when Bourgeois draws, paints, sews, or sculpts them. *Connecticutiana* (1944–45) provides an early example with its elemental, imperfect grid, while the fabric book *Ode à l'Oubli* (2002) is a late and gorgeous compendium of her “emotional geometries,” among them wavering stacks, stitched sets and progressions, and soft grids of beautifully faded fabrics. As Bourgeois said, “The Euclidean is comforting because nothing can go wrong . . . but it is not the geometry of pleasure.”

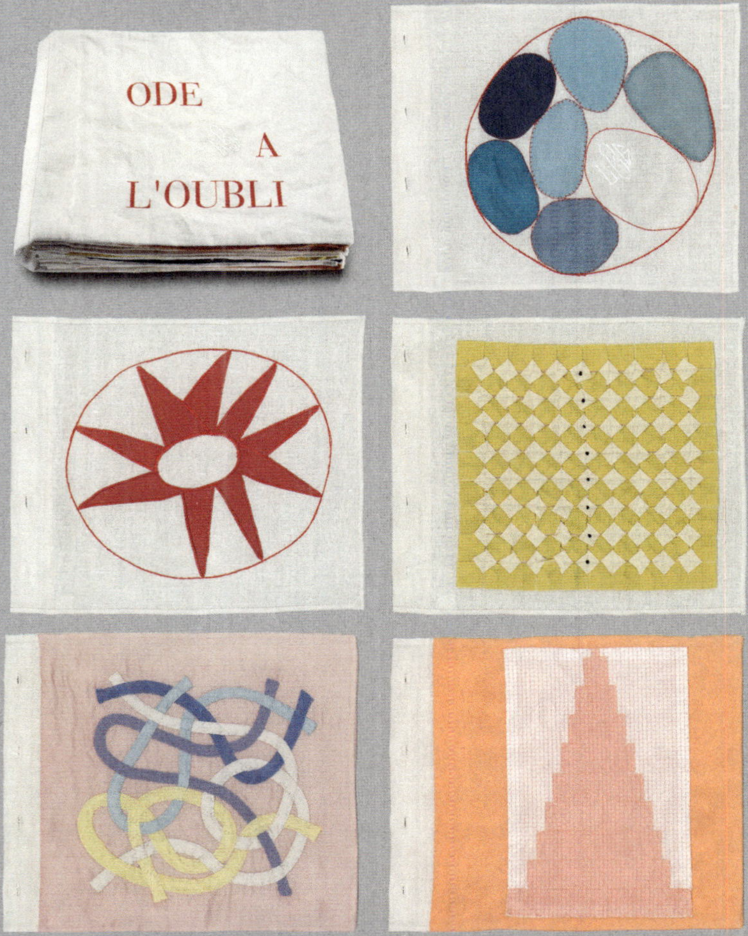

Ode à l’Oubli (details), 2002. Fabric and lithograph book, 35 pages, each 11 × 15½ in. (27.9 × 39.4 cm)

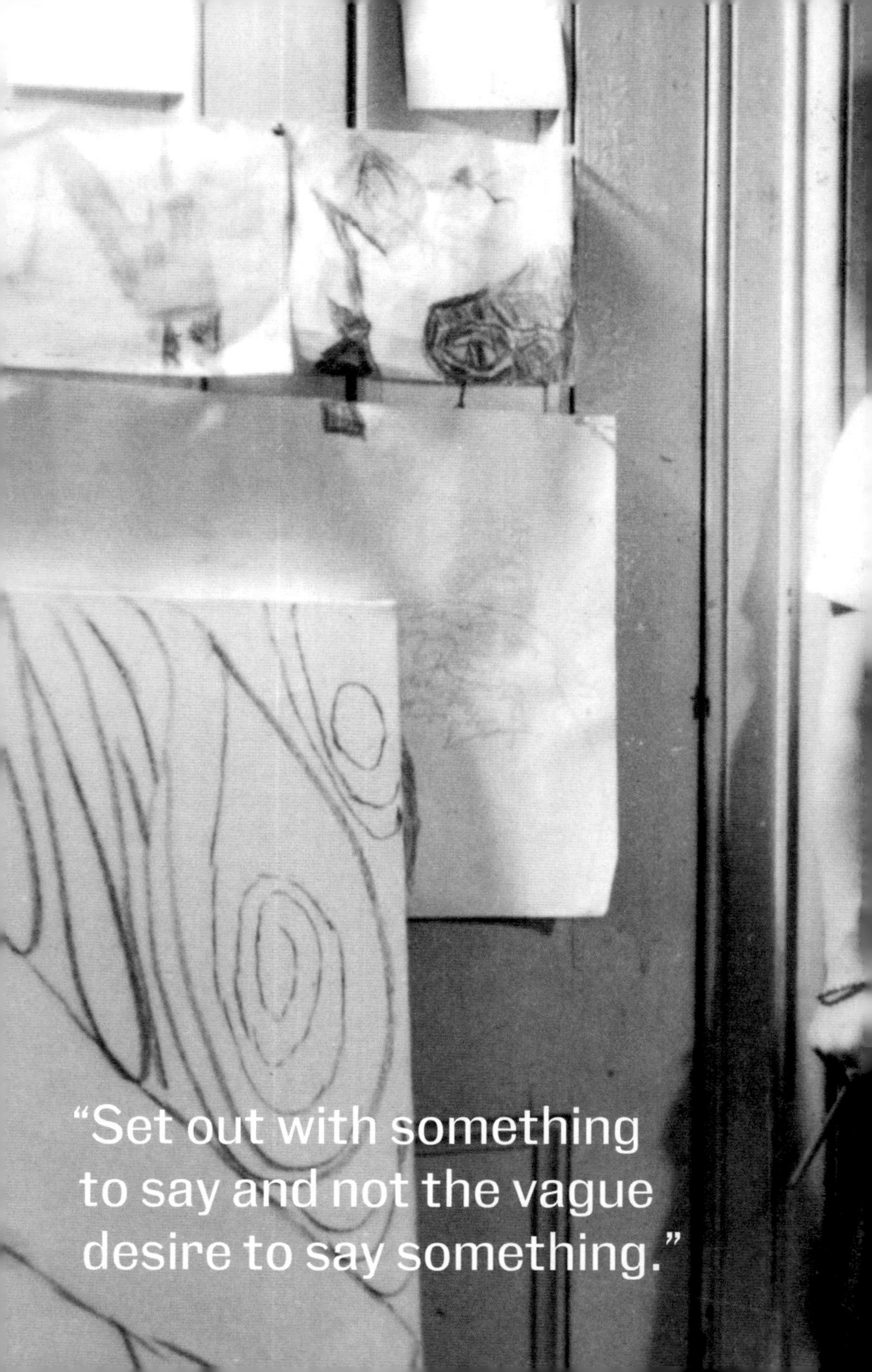
“Set out with something
to say and not the vague
desire to say something.”

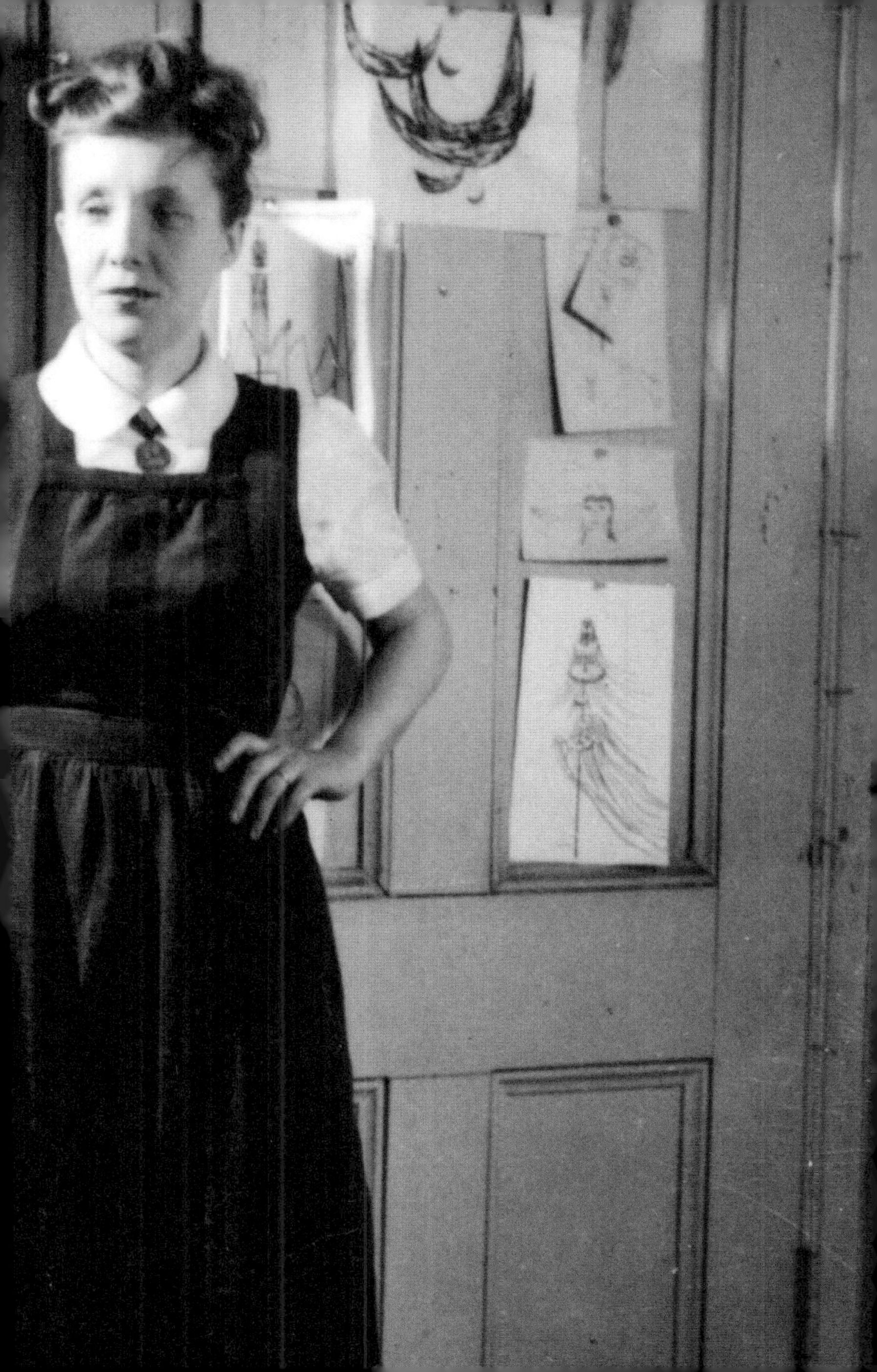

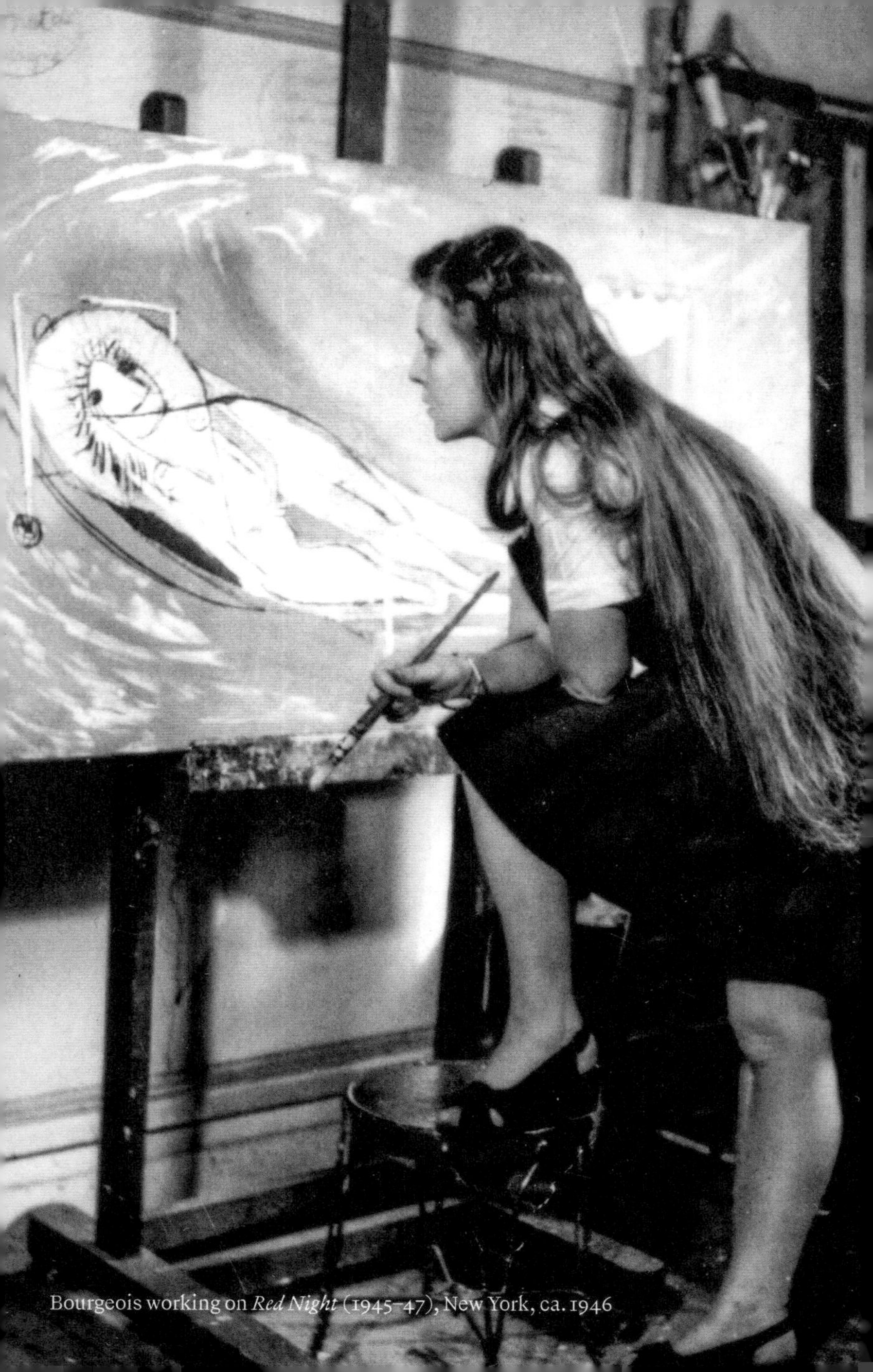

Bourgeois working on *Red Night* (1945–47), New York, ca. 1946

Red Nights and Roof Songs

Bourgeois's flight from France to New York was the event around which her life turned. It opened possibilities and brought on responsibilities that shaped her and her art forever. In *The Runaway Girl* (ca. 1938), which she made soon after her arrival in New York, Bourgeois paints herself as a long-haired young woman crossing an ocean, valise in hand, with her home and past life receding behind her. The journey is difficult; rocks threaten from below, and a lone swimmer pursues her. Rather than striding, she seems drawn along by a force she is not quite in charge of; for the first time, we see the helpless, dangling feet that appear in so many of Bourgeois's sculptures. The childlike simplicity of the image distills (or perhaps nervously downplays) the magnitude of the move.

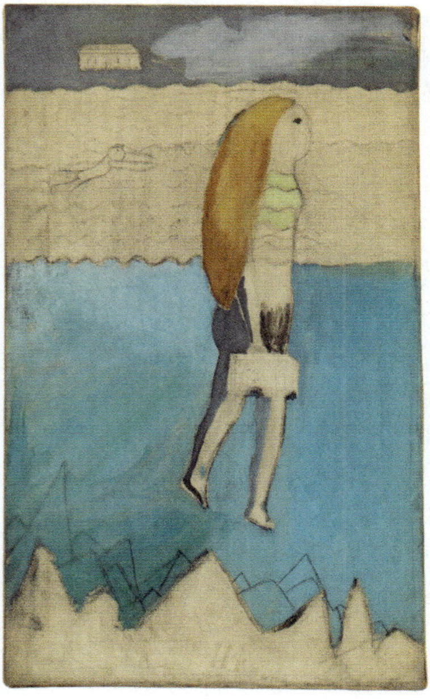

The Runaway Girl, ca. 1938. Oil, charcoal, and pencil on canvas, 24 × 15 in. (61 × 38.1 cm)

Bourgeois thrilled to the visual severity and artistic vitality of New York, writing to her father of "the hustle and bustle and the intense energy which flows in the city's arteries." Simultaneously, she reckoned with new obligations as the mother of three young sons (one adopted, two born soon after) and the wife of an esteemed professor and critic. Amid these demands, the studio was her haven more than ever—a place in which to rediscover her innermost motivations. At its barest, the "studio" might be an improvised space "between the bed and the window" where Bourgeois worked on paintings, or a corner of the kitchen table where she made drawings or etchings, diluting the acid for the children's safety. Her first dedicated space for making was a room in Stuyvesant's Folly, the apartment building at 142 East Eighteenth Street where the family lived from 1941 to 1958. Far from constraining her, the smallness of the space was comforting; she knew her boundaries. "I do not need much to work with," she wrote in her diary in 1949. "Keep the house + the studio a small size so that you feel at home in them like a snail in her shell."

Bourgeois also found imaginative sustenance and respite from domesticity in art schools and communal studios, enlisting in classes at the Art Students League immediately after her arrival in New York and, from 1947 to 1949, making prints at Stanley William Hayter's Atelier 17 studio. Though intensely private as an artist, she valued the hands-on knowledge and artistic companionship found in Hayter's experimental workshop, where she met the Spanish luminary Joan Miró and made the bleakly poetic engravings for her book *He Disappeared into Complete Silence* (1947; p. 49). Nonetheless, the prime site of Bourgeois's creativity was her "shell" in the Eighteenth Street apartment. Here, she created most of the hundred-plus paintings that define her first decade as an artist. Modestly scaled, scratchily worked, full of deep reds and odd hieroglyphs, these paintings are a seedbed of the forms and feelings that would come to define Bourgeois's art.

Red Night (1945–47)

The bed is a boat in a storm of red. A gust makes the curtain fly up. The mother and children who ride the bed appear lashed in to stop them from tumbling. The mother's black eyes and electric-shock hair tell of a night of chronic wakefulness. A baby is tucked under each of her arms and another between her legs—as if being born while they lie there. The children's blithe, cheerful faces only heighten the sense that the mother is alone with her struggle, though one notices, looking closer, that another body seems to lie in the bed alongside her. A photo of Bourgeois at work on *Red Night* (p. 40) reveals how she simplified the image, muffling certain details to ratchet up the feeling of emotional chaos. It is one of the first—and still among the most anguishing—of Bourgeois's many images of conflicted maternity.

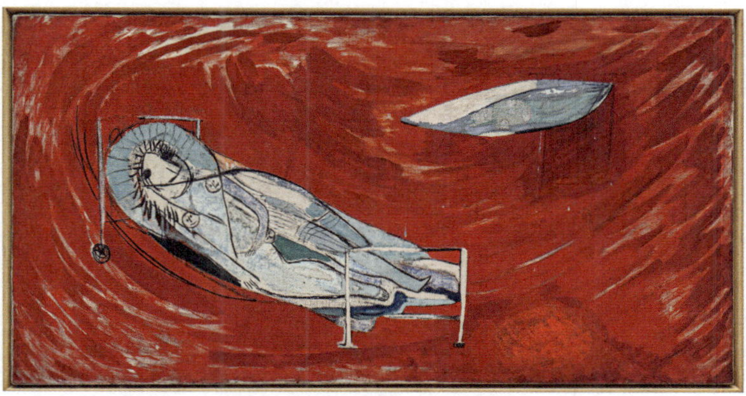

Red Night, 1945–47. Oil on linen, 30 × 60 in. (76.2 × 152.4 cm)

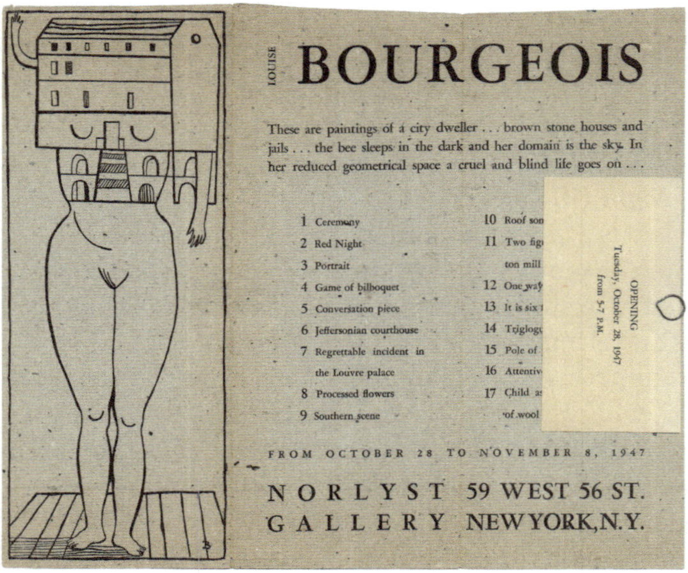

Announcement for *Louise Bourgeois: Paintings*, Norlyst Gallery, New York, 1947

Femme Maison (1946–47)

No wonder the woman leaps in shock—her body has been subsumed by a building. More than that, her sex is exposed, and a door stands open in her torso. Houses, like bodies, are meant to be private: protection for the selves within. But this woman seems not so much sheltered by architecture as trapped and silenced inside it. The painting is one of four Bourgeois made of the *femme maison*—a woman whose body has merged disquietingly with a house or apartment building. The "woman houses" in the other paintings seem poignantly unaware of their predicament; one greets a friend, and another waves hello, as if nothing is amiss. This one, however, with her three upthrown arms, projects a kind of giddy panic, as if she's trying to break free of a structure that has already claimed her.

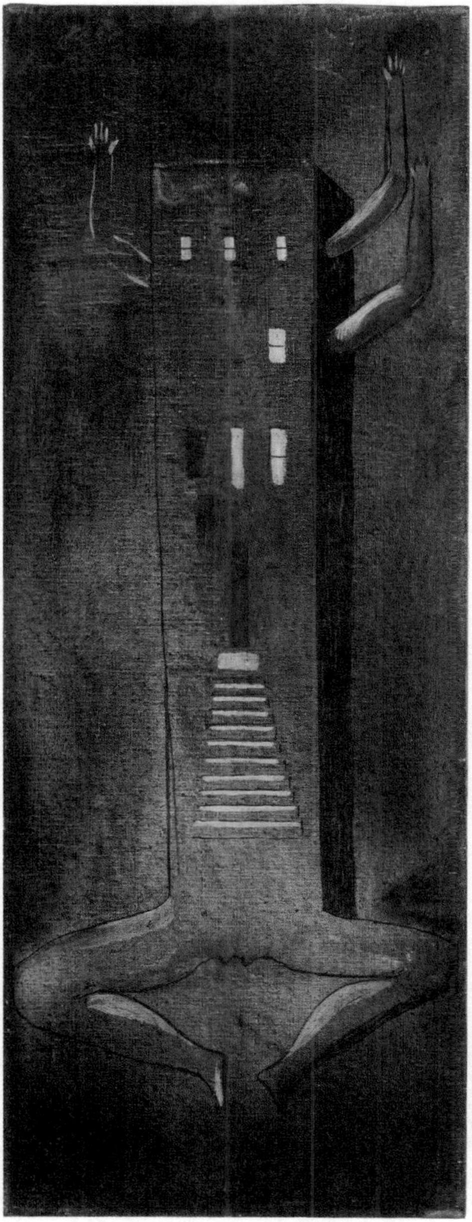

Femme Maison, 1946–47. Oil and ink on linen, 36 × 14 in. (91.4 × 35.6 cm)

***Roof Song* (1947)**

Where *Red Night* portrays a mother trapped with her fears, *Roof Song* depicts a moment of freedom—a woman, escaped from her home and responsibilities, exulting on her rooftop. Bourgeois loved the roof of her apartment building and made sculptures there in the mid-1940s: "Suddenly I had this huge sky space to myself, and I began creating these standing figures." Her surrogate in the painting seems electrified by the presence of the spiky totem she has created. With her moonlike smile, wings of hair flung wide, and breasts that read also as eyes, she is simultaneously on a high and on the edge—a manic, ecstatic angel. The long coil of smoke is one of the earliest of many spirals that Bourgeois would create over her career—suggesting, within the world of this painting, that the house downstairs is on fire.

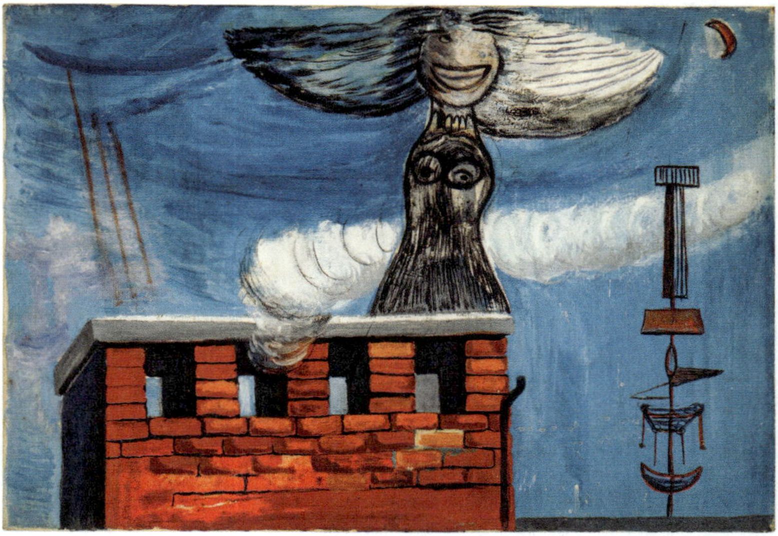

Roof Song, 1947. Oil on linen, 21 × 31 in. (53.3 × 78.7 cm)

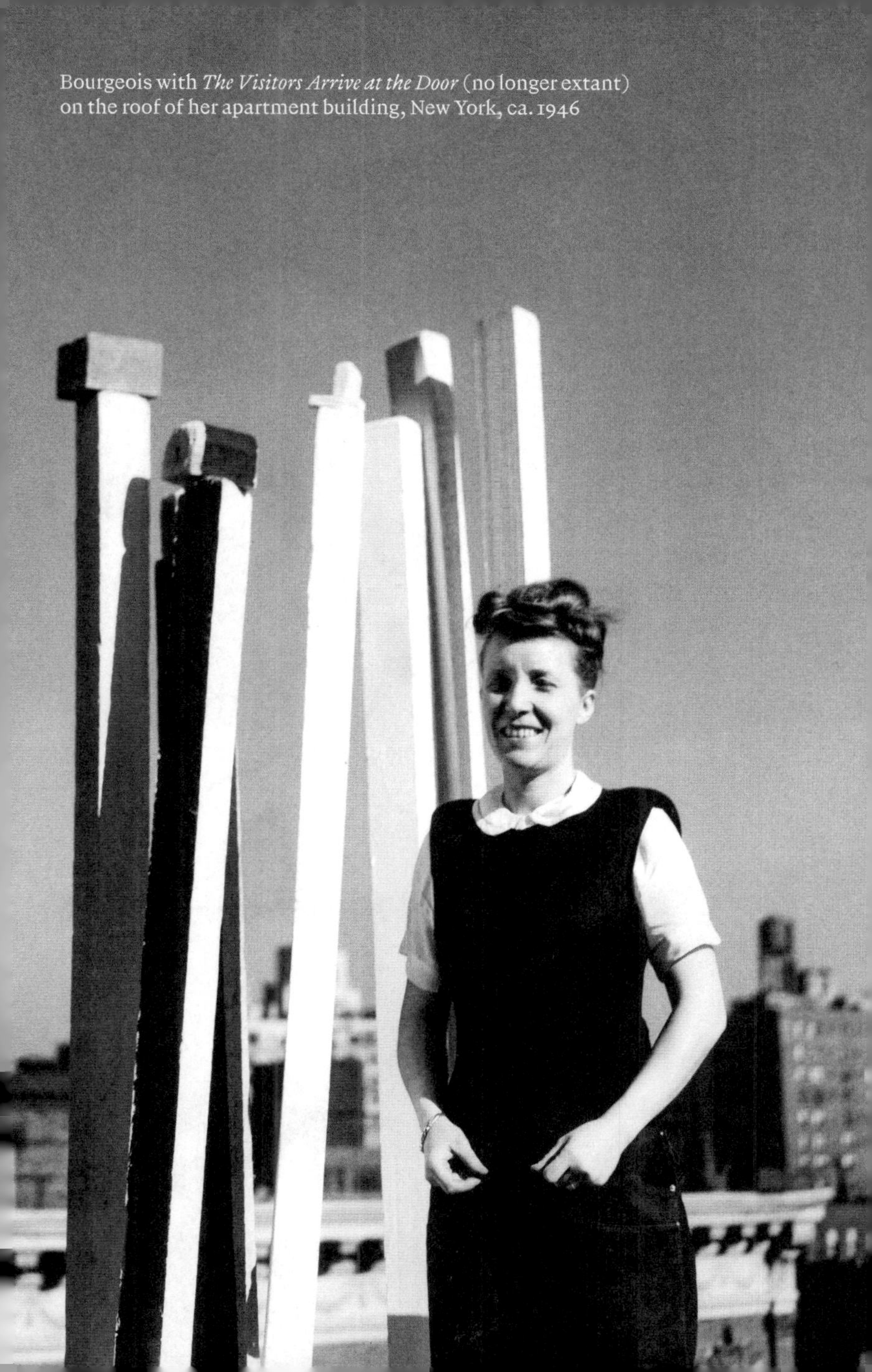

Bourgeois with *The Visitors Arrive at the Door* (no longer extant) on the roof of her apartment building, New York, ca. 1946

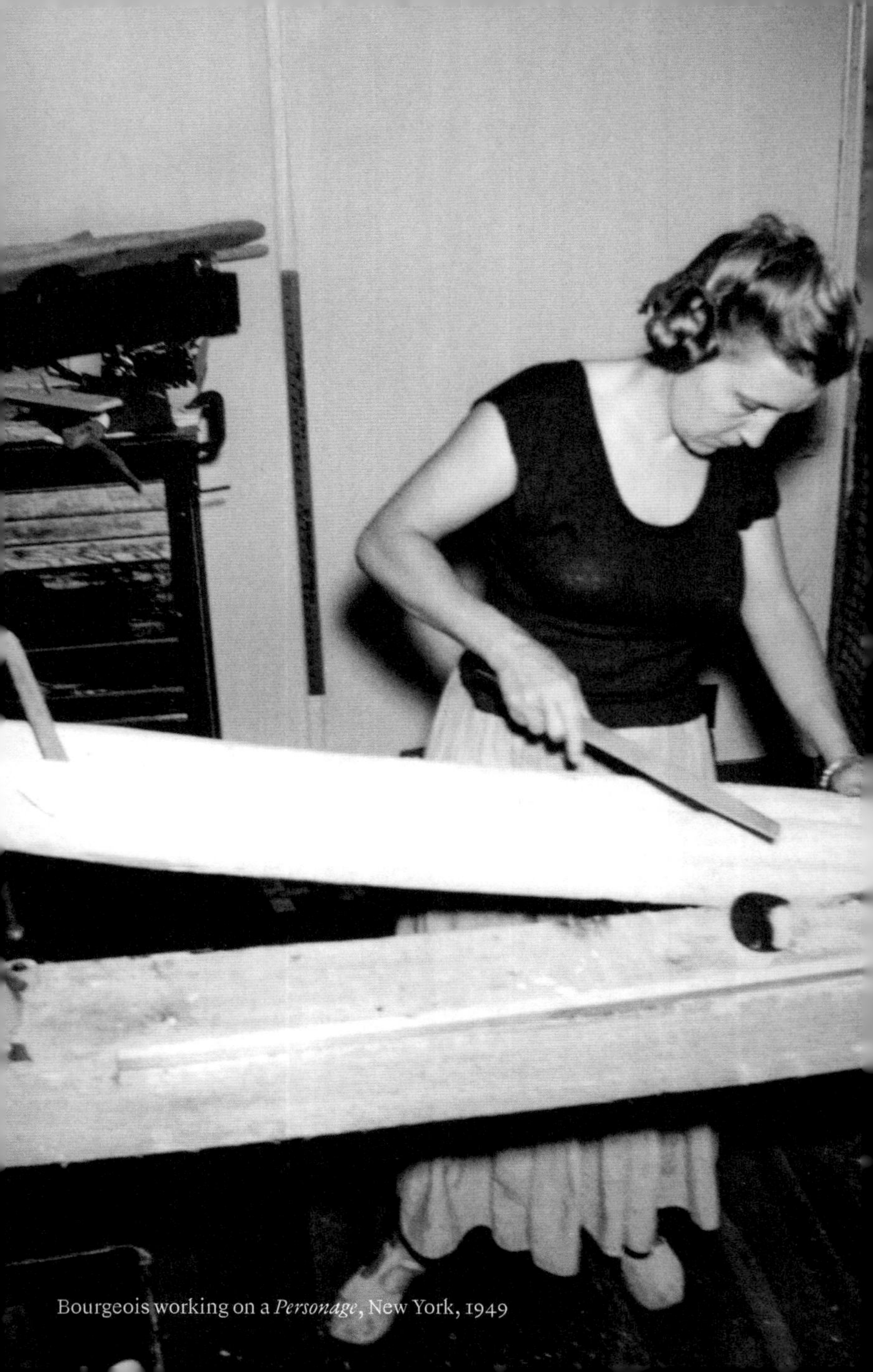

Bourgeois working on a *Personage*, New York, 1949

Presences: The *Personages*

Even as Bourgeois pressed forward ambitiously, staging her first solo exhibition in 1945, she thought constantly of her family in France and the life she had left behind. Her guilt and homesickness were compounded by World War II, which made travel back to France impossible. Simultaneously, her distance from that formative world made it vivid and mysterious. We see her holding and turning this past in many paintings of distant houses and lonely figures. A blue-tinted painting of a young woman presenting flowers at a mausoleum, *Reparation* (1945), is an act of contrition for missing her grandmother's funeral. Feelings of panicked abandonment and devastating remoteness move through her prints from this time, especially the nine engravings in *He Disappeared into Complete Silence*. But her great contemplation of the distances that separate people is the group of sculptures collectively known as the *Personages*.

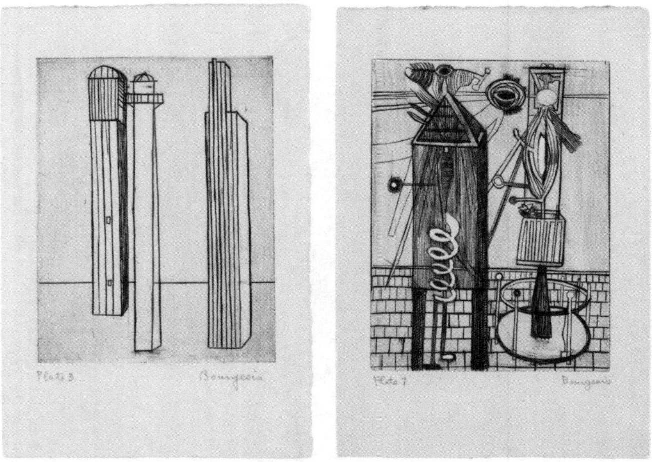

He Disappeared into Complete Silence (details), 1947. Illustrated book of nine engravings and letterpress text, each 10 × 14 in. (25.4 × 35.6 cm)

Between 1946 and 1954, Bourgeois made more than eighty of these spearlike sculptures, working in a small room of the family's apartment at Stuyvesant's Folly, or on the building's roof, and sometimes at their weekend home in Easton, Connecticut. Arthur Drexler, a painter and later the director of MoMA's Department of Architecture and Design, recalled visiting the studio and finding "this very small, intense woman—extremely svelte, handsome—wielding a huge cleaver with which she worked on balsa wood." In a photo from this time (p. 48), Bourgeois holds a rasp rather than the unforgettable cleaver, but we sense what she had gained in her move from painting to sculpture—namely, a satisfying actuality. Gouging into a length of balsa or paring back a plank of salvaged cedar, she was making bodies, not just diagramming or picturing them. "The reason was a psychological one," Bourgeois recalled. "These pieces were presences—missed, badly missed presences."

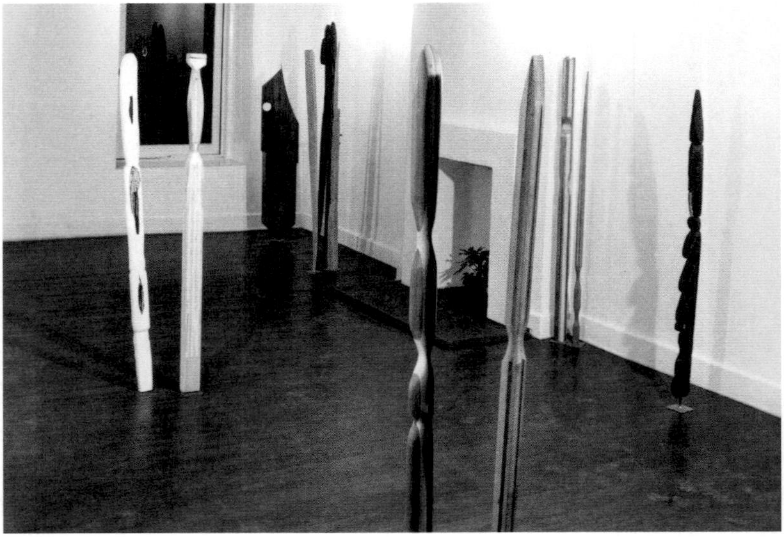

Installation view, *Louise Bourgeois: Sculptures*, Peridot Gallery, New York, 1950

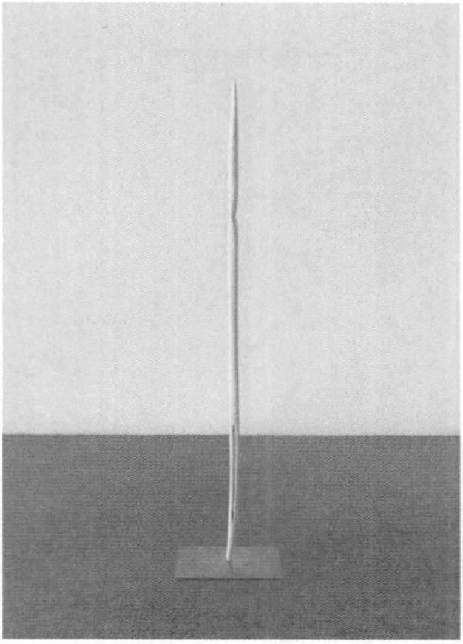

Needle Woman, 1947–49. Painted bronze and stainless steel, 56½ × 12 × 12 in. (143.5 × 30.5 × 30.5 cm)

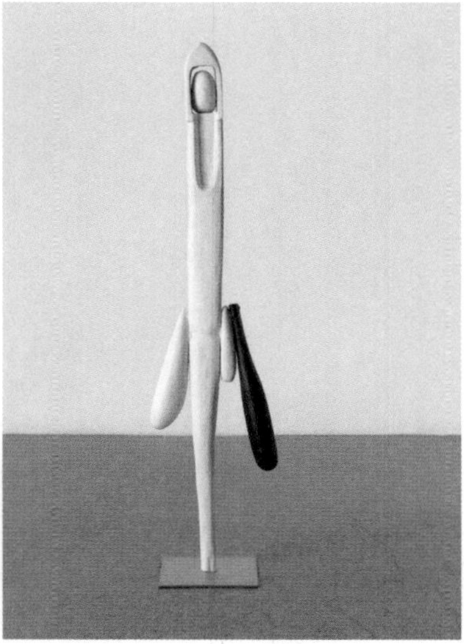

Woman with Packages, 1949. Painted bronze and stainless steel, 65 × 18 × 12 in. (165.1 × 45.7 × 30.5 cm)

Though Bourgeois claimed that the *Personages* stood the same height as she, or as individual family members, almost nowhere does she make explicit connections between these works and specific people. As with totemic objects, the goal is not resemblance but potency. Many of the *Personages* give sharp physical shape to tensions in families and relationships; consider *Dagger Child* (1947–49; p. 52), in which the child is worn as a weapon on the hip of an adult. Other figures are given the form of objects from Bourgeois's family history; *Needle Woman* (1947–49) is sharp but whittled down to nearly nothing, with a long, narrow cut in her body. *Woman with Packages* (1949) is an abstracted portrait of Bourgeois with her children: a stoic, armless maternal pillar bearing her three remarkable burdens. Poised anxiously on their tips, the *Personages* often seem

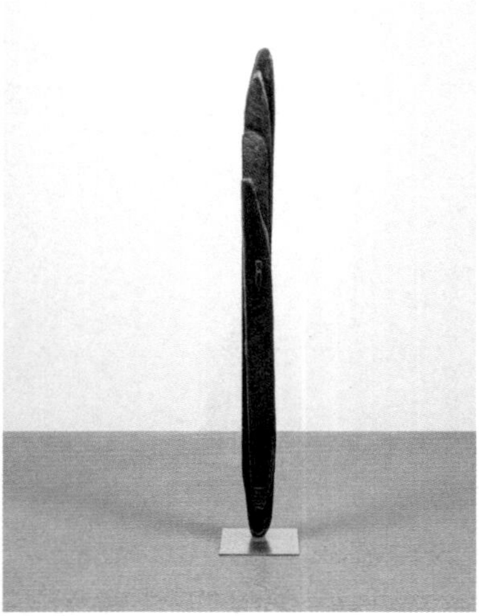

Dagger Child, 1947–49. Painted bronze and stainless steel, 75⅝ × 12 × 12 in. (192.1 × 30.5 × 30.5 cm)

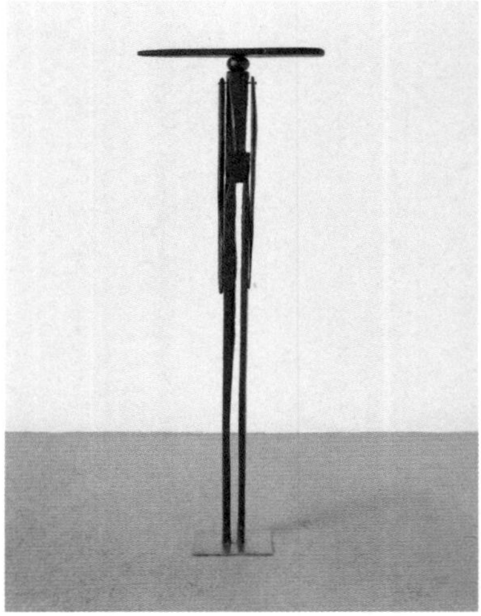

Observer, 1947–49. Bronze, dark patina, and stainless steel, 76 × 28 × 12 in. (193 × 71.1 × 30.5 cm)

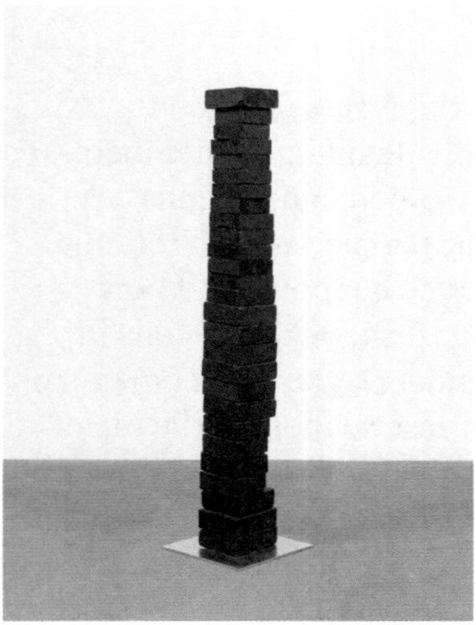

Memling Dawn, 1951. Painted wood and stainless steel, 67¼ × 15 × 15 in. (170.8 × 38.1 × 38.1 cm)

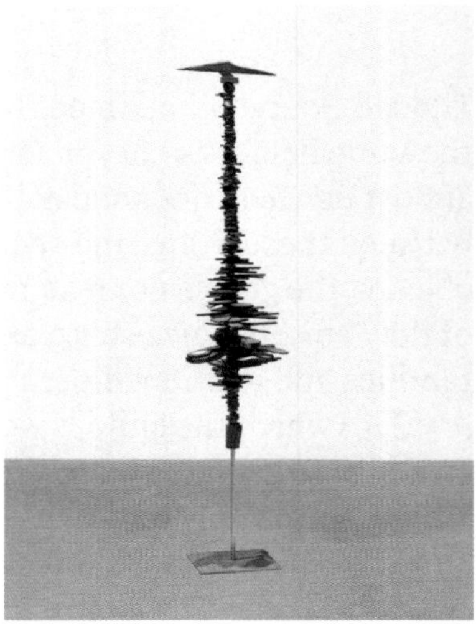

Femme Volage, 1951. Painted wood and stainless steel, 73 × 18 × 13 in. (185.4 × 45.7 × 33 cm)

to have withdrawn into themselves, with high windows and notches suggesting lookouts from which a reclusive self might cautiously peer.

The psychological power of the *Personages* as a group became evident when Bourgeois first presented them, in exhibitions at New York's Peridot Gallery in 1949 and 1950. What viewers encountered on each occasion were sculptures without bases or plinths, their tips bolted into the floor so that each stood—albeit precariously—on its own. Together, they formed a tense crowd of figures that Bourgeois likened to a cocktail party—a social field that also constituted a pioneering example of installation art. Spacing the sculptures through the gallery with an irregularity that invited wandering, Bourgeois made visitors into participants in a gathering defined by distances and fragile alliances. Some of the sculptures leaned close to each other, as if attempting to kindle some kind of warmth. Some existed in psychic zones of their own, like the stilled and ominous *Observer* (1947–49).

The *Personages* bodied forth feelings and tensions that recur in Bourgeois's art—the challenge of persisting, the fear of falling, the push and pull between love and aloneness. In the early 1950s, their apprehensive rigidity gave way to a new volatility, as Bourgeois began to stack dozens of wooden forms rather than carve singular ones (this was also a period of emotional upheaval, triggered by her father's death in 1951). *Memling Dawn* (1951) is a mute, solemn tower of black blocks that can twist independently on their axis. *Femme Volage* (1951), with its skirt of outflung wooden tongues and blades, seems to spin on the spot like a dervish—a woman charged with so much agitating energy that she threatens to fly apart.

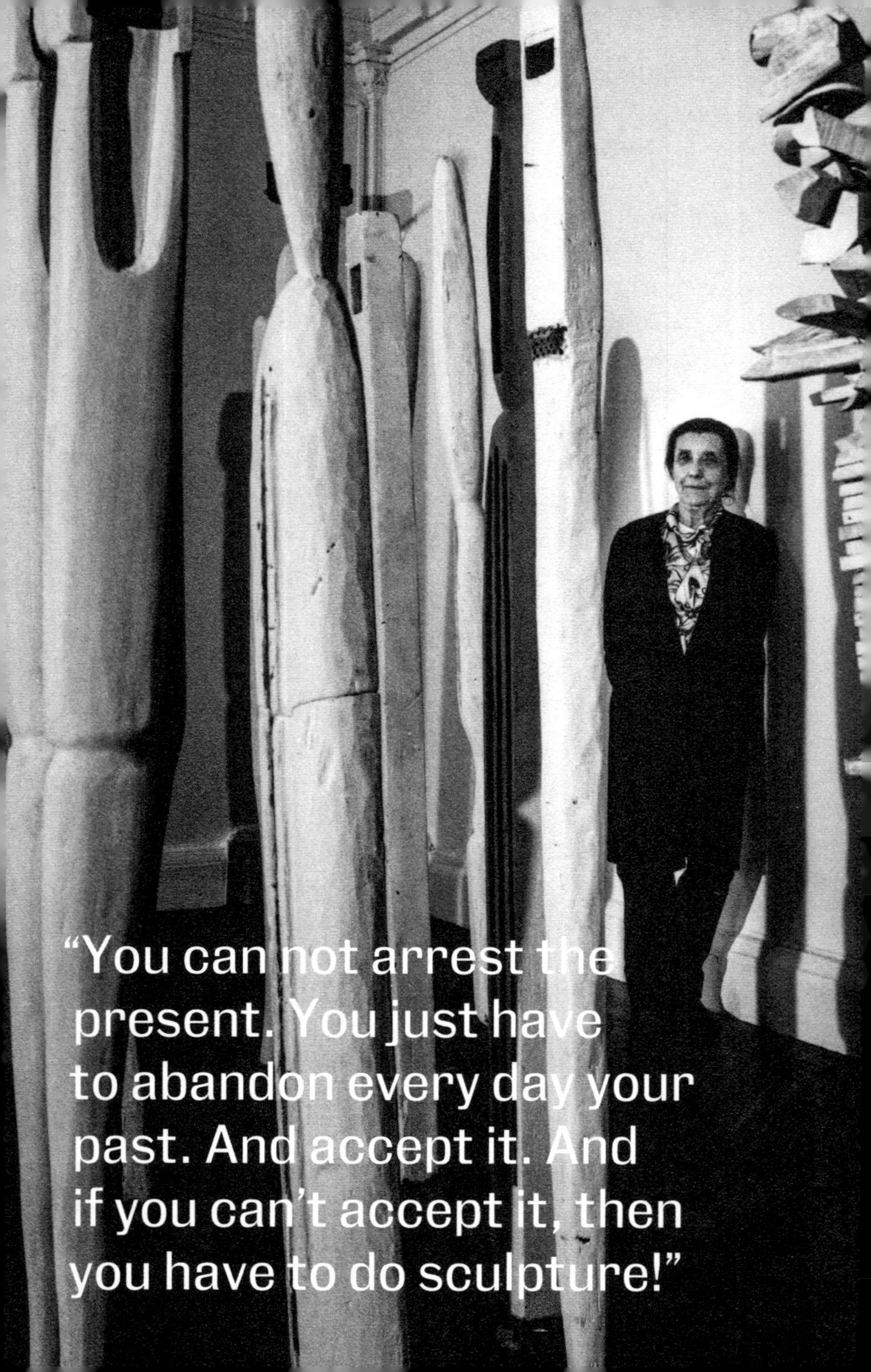

"You can not arrest the present. You just have to abandon every day your past. And accept it. And if you can't accept it, then you have to do sculpture!"

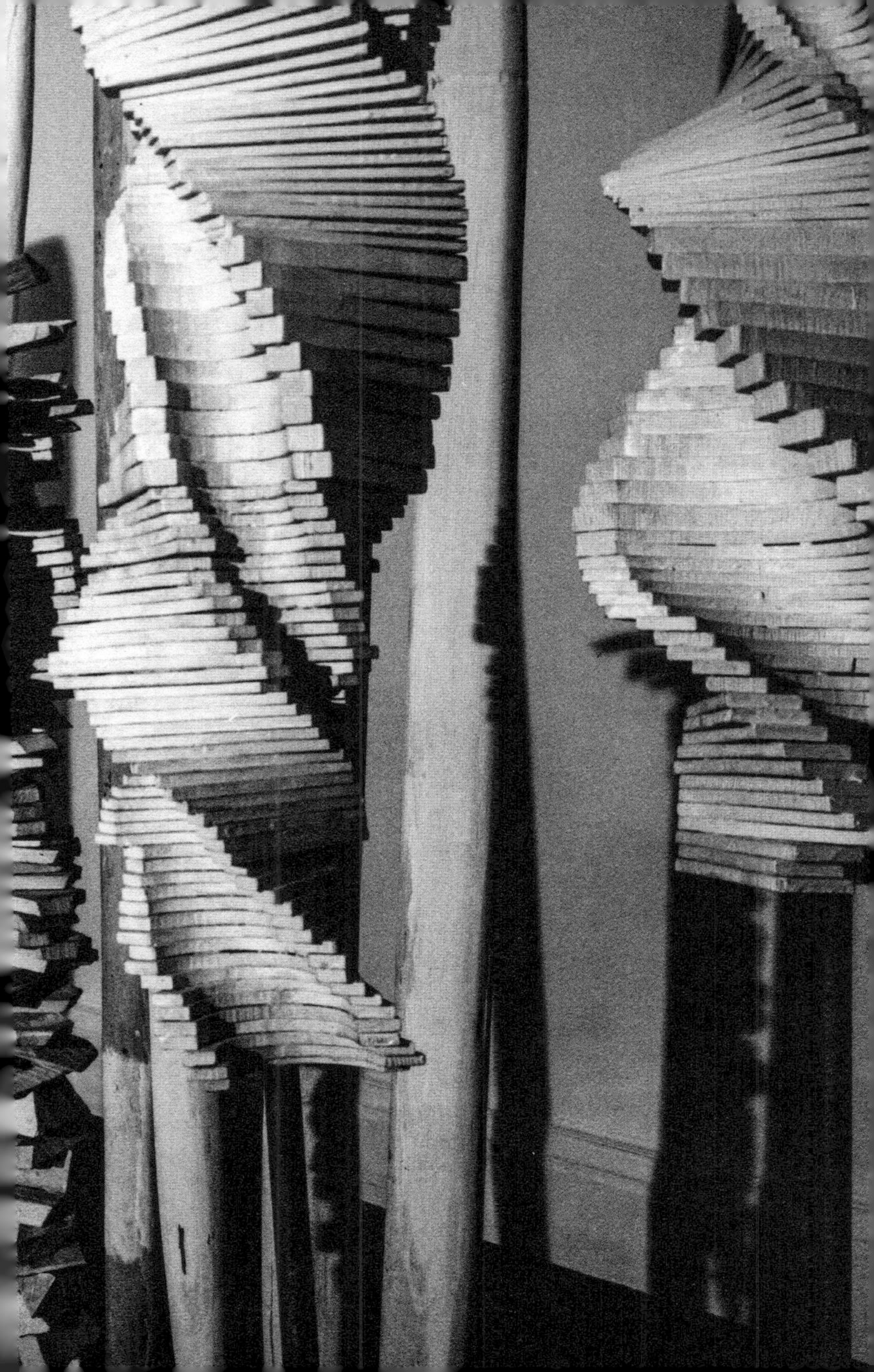

Thought Feathers

Bourgeois called drawings "thought feathers": ideas seized in mid-flight. She produced them at all times of day and often in the sleepless hours of the night. Whimsy and trepidation mingle in many early drawings; tiny figures navigate giant landscapes or peer out from inner places. Then there are the hundreds of drawings where black ink lines seem to surge and flex their way toward sculpture. In others, space is brought to order with calming, repetitive strokes. Much later, Bourgeois made *The Insomnia Drawings* (1994–95; p. 59) in red ink, ballpoint, and pencil on many kinds of non-art paper, floating these nighttime productions from her second-floor landing down the stairs in readiness for Jerry Gorovoy, her assistant, to collect in the morning. The drawings catch not the outward look of the world, but the shapes of memories, impulses, and feelings, giving urgent yet fragile form to the anxious flutter of nocturnal consciousness. "Feathery" is too soft a word for these ludic, often feverish works, which remind us of other senses of the verb "draw": to draw out memories, to draw up from the depths.

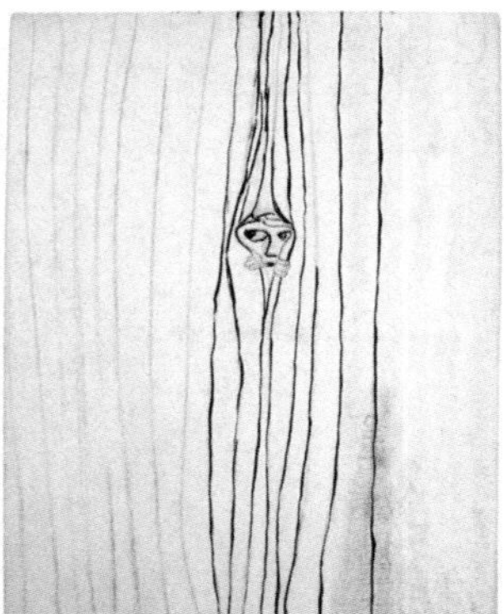

Untitled, 1950. Ink and charcoal on paper, 14 × 11 in. (35.6 × 27.9 cm)

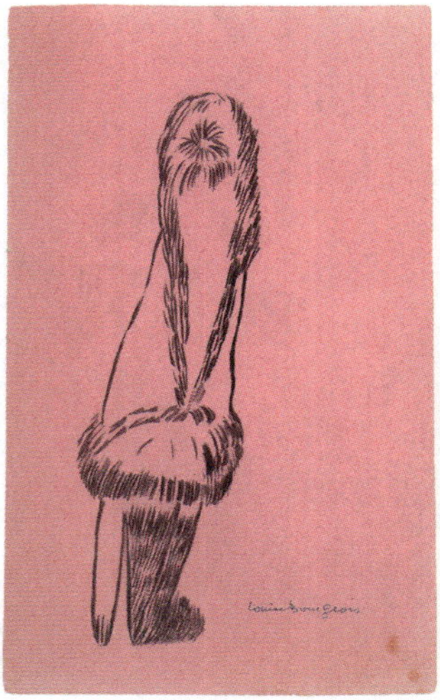

Untitled, 1946. Ink on pink paper, 10 × 6¼ in. (25.4 × 15.9 cm)

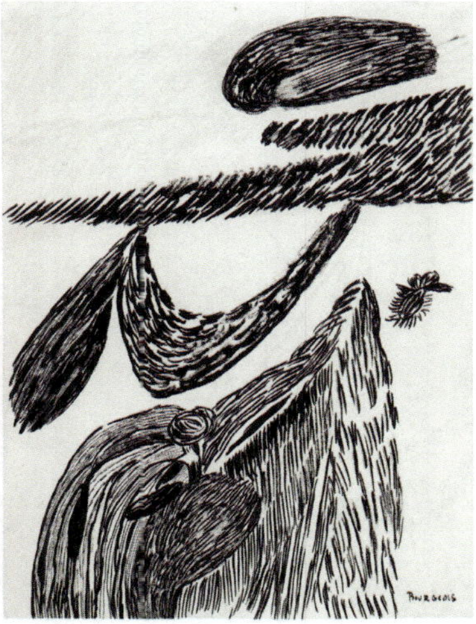

Untitled (Inner Life), 1953. Ink on paper, 11 × 8½ in. (27.9 × 21.6 cm)

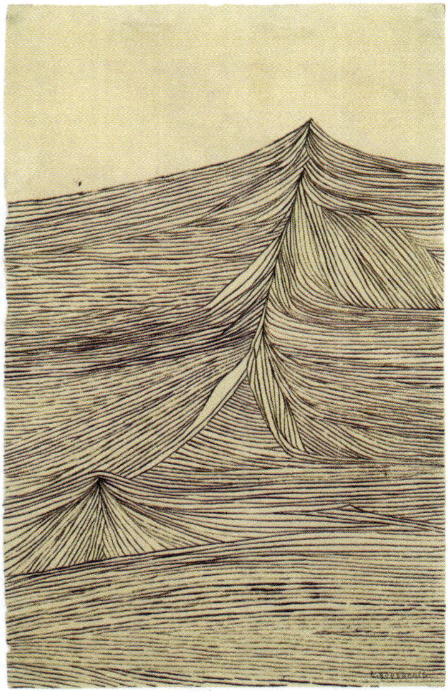

Untitled, 1944. Ink on paper, 19 × 12½ in. (48.3 × 31.8 cm)

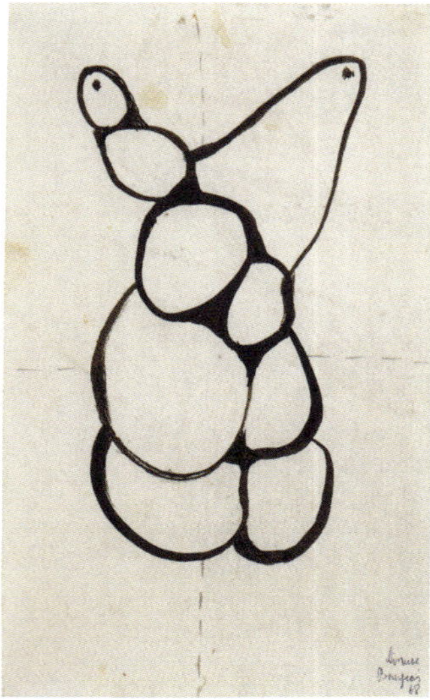

Untitled, 1968. Ink and pencil on paper, 8 × 5 in. (20.3 × 12.7 cm)

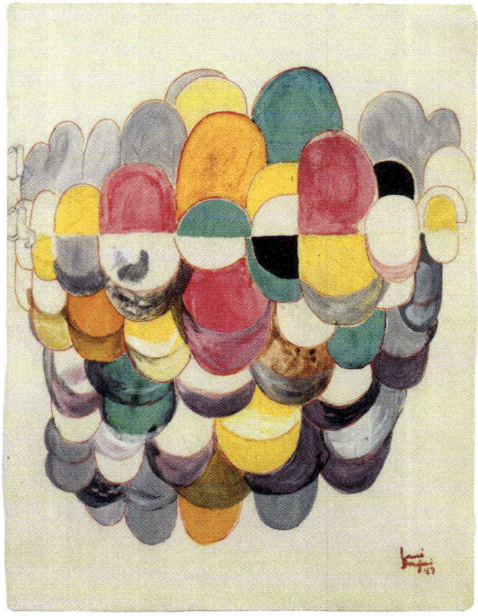

Untitled, 1967. Ink and gouache on paper, 14 × 11 in. (35.6 × 27.9 cm)

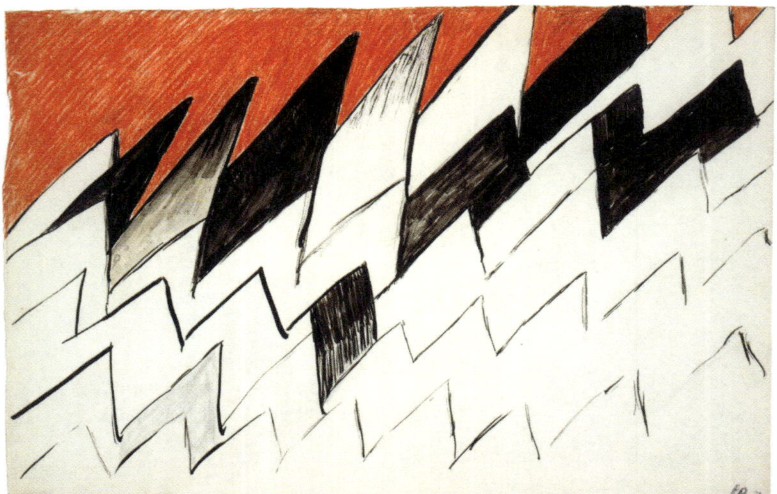

Untitled, 1970. Ink, charcoal, and crayon on paper, $7^{1}/_{8}$ × $11^{1}/_{4}$ in. (18.1 × 28.6 cm)

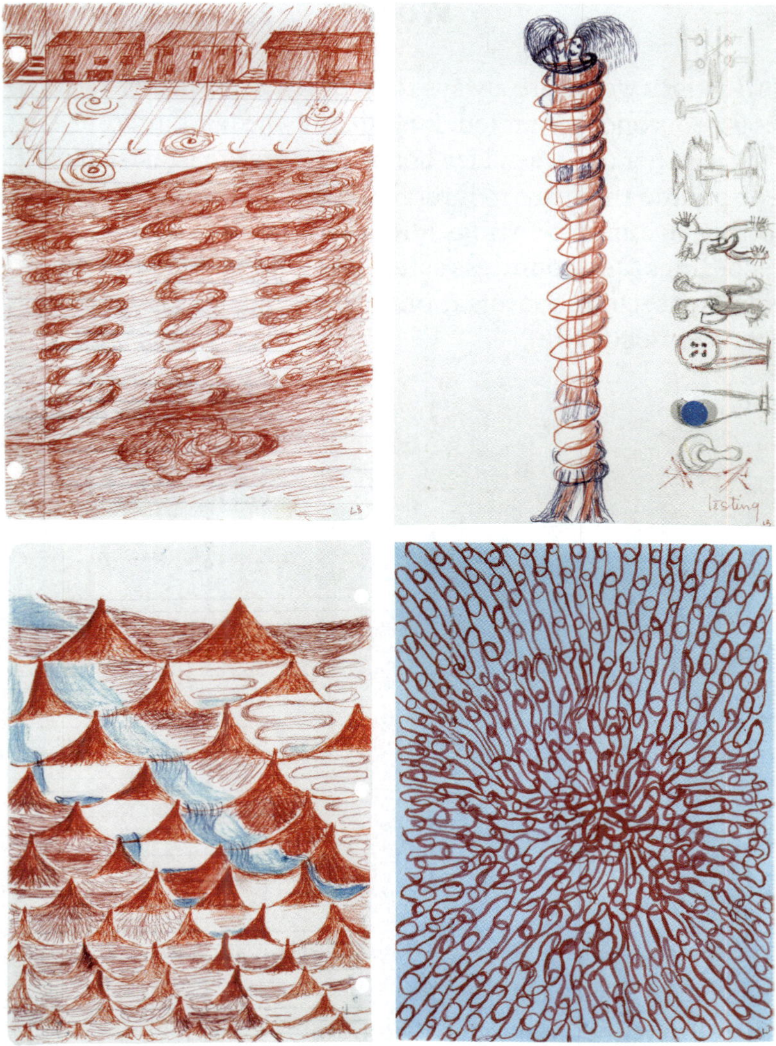

The Insomnia Drawings (details), 1994–95. Mixed media on paper, 220 sheets

Words

“An artist’s words are always to be taken cautiously,” Bourgeois once remarked. It is wise advice but hard to follow in her case, because her own words are irresistible. She poured them out in interviews, diaries, notebooks, letters, insomniac jottings, dream recordings, audio recordings, and countless scrap-paper notes—a lifelong, round-the-clock conversation with herself about life and art (but mostly life).

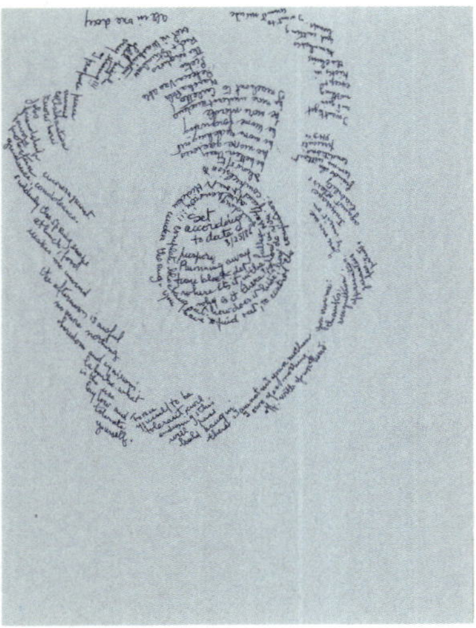

Loose sheet of writing, 1986. Ink on blue paper, 11 × 8½ in. (27.9 × 21.6 cm)

Art Is a Guaranty of Sanity, 2000. Pencil on pink paper, 11 × 8½ in. (27.9 × 21.6 cm)

There are tender messages to Robert (“I dreamt about you, we were running one after the other in a street full of skyscrapers”), stoic assertions of purpose (“I want to be the owner of my own trouble”), ecstatic memories of place (“The sound of a pebble falling in the black and distant water of a well”), miniature fables of folly and need (“ashamed like a fox caught by a hen"), startling self-portraits ("I am a collection of wooden pearls never threaded"), and sudden declarations of need ("I don't want to understand, I just want to be cradled").

Her daunting intelligence, powers of recall, and glinting humor are especially evident in film footage from the 1980s and 1990s, where the tiny artist ("she looked like a peacock feather could knock her over," recalled writer Gary Indiana) commands the screen with her teasing asides, fits of destruction, and transports of memory. In the unforgettable orange-peeling sequence from the documentary *The Spider, the Mistress, and the Tangerine* (2008), Bourgeois narrates a childhood humiliation by her father with such intensity that she seems to reenter the traumatic scene.

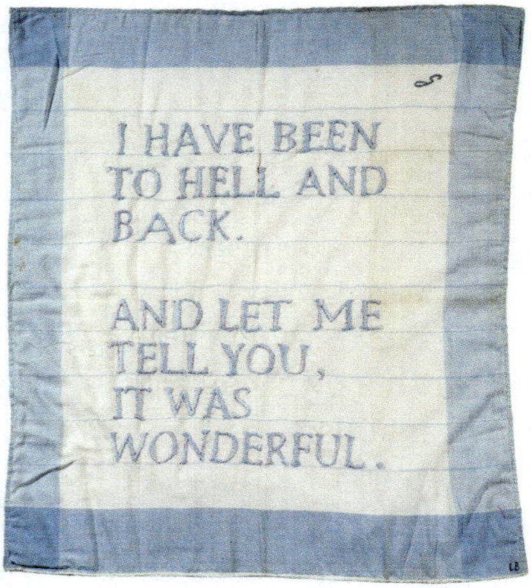

Untitled (I Have Been to Hell and Back). 1996. Embroidered handkerchief, 19½ × 18 in. (49.5 × 45.7 cm)

Language was a lifeline for Bourgeois in the difficult decade of the 1950s, when her father's death in Paris spun her into a long and incapacitating depression. Though encouraged tenderly by Robert, she produced art intermittently through this period, eventually clawing her way back to a provisional equilibrium through psychoanalysis and writing. Hundreds of loose sheets of writing rediscovered among the many papers in her home in the 2000s are harrowingly honest records of what curator Philip Larratt-Smith called Bourgeois's "season in hell." At the same time, their very existence and the vehemence of the images they excavate ("she talks with a hatchet—when he talks it smells of semen") testify to her will to know and live.

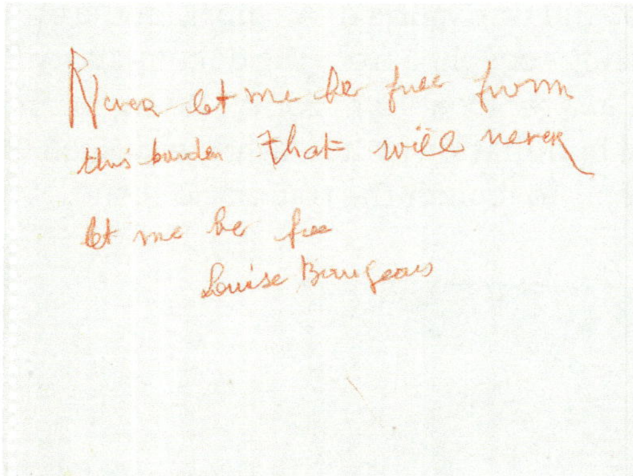

Loose sheet of writing, ca. 2008. Red pencil on paper, 9 × 12 in. (22.9 × 30.5 cm)

In the 1990s, Bourgeois began using her own words as found materials, folding her bleak aphorisms and existential koans—"Mercy merci," "Art is a guaranty of sanity," "Fears make the world go round"—back into her fabric works, print projects, and *Cell* sculptures. Bourgeois trusted objects, with their reassuring concreteness, more than she trusted language. But there are single sentences in her writings that catch, as decisively as any sculpture, the challenge and privilege of artmaking (and of living): "Never let me be free from this burden that will never let me be free."

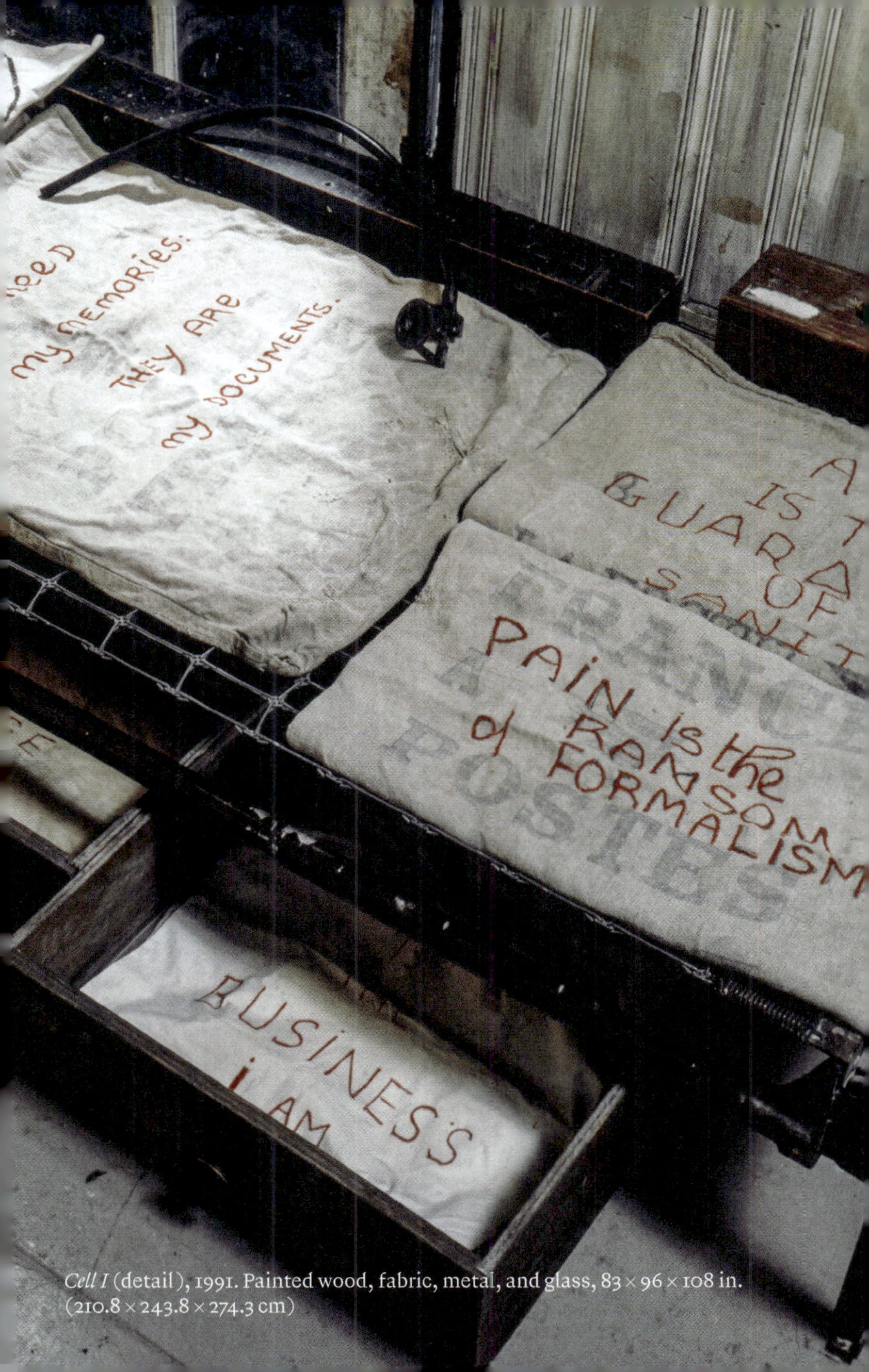

Cell I (detail), 1991. Painted wood, fabric, metal, and glass, 83 × 96 × 108 in. (210.8 × 243.8 × 274.3 cm)

“Cooking Up Forms + Ideas”

Bourgeois kept a diary from her early teens until her final years. The selections here, drawn from a lifetime of diaries and related loose sheets of writing, address the challenges and rewards of daily life in the studio—and the life the studio led in her dreams and imagination.

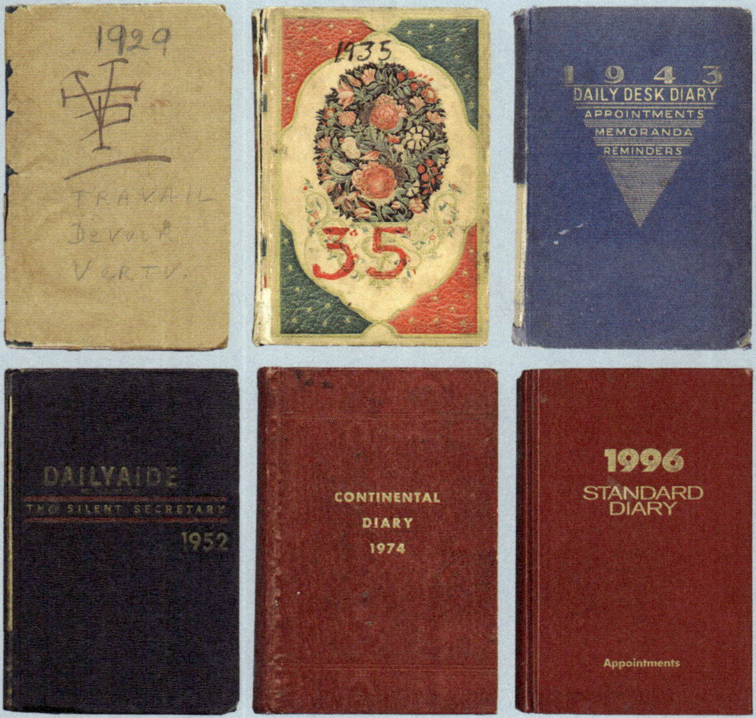

Bourgeois’s diaries from 1929, 1935, 1943, 1952, 1974, and 1996

October 26–27, 1949
Keep in mind that apart from silence
I do not need much to work with.
Keep the house + the studio a small size
so that you feel at home in them like
a snail in her shell.
You work in the morning even before
getting dressed—sometimes for 3 days
you are in a liquified mood just
going from one room to another
cooking up forms + ideas, this can be
done only in warmth + intimacy—you then
do not need to project yourself but to fold and
if you had a private entrance +
silence and enough room you
should keep the family together—
also be in the village.
the care of an oil burner is not much
work.

May 3, 1963
Saturday night
Lots of people come in and out of my
studio, they have keys and don't even notice
I'm not there, they make comments and use
my things, but I survive and I'm not
angry or revolted. I have to move out
soon and they have things to do—all men.
In a house-cum-studio with several floors,
someone closes the door to the cellar [. . .]
and I find myself locked in.
I loosen a few stones from the wall to the width
of my shoulder, and crawl out
of the cellar—ok

June 6, 1974

I recreated the living room exactly
as it was when Robert was here intimate
waxed, shiny—he loved it, it was his
favorite room
I loved the bedroom best with its
cochineal red heart, bedspread, mysterious
and warm
The challenge of Robert being immortal
Bateson obsession, all his books, students
friends he is not gone
The challenge of my being alone + dispossessed:
I am an artist with the whole house as a
studio, I am not weak or crushed. I do
not need a family, Robert would be
proud of me and that is enough.

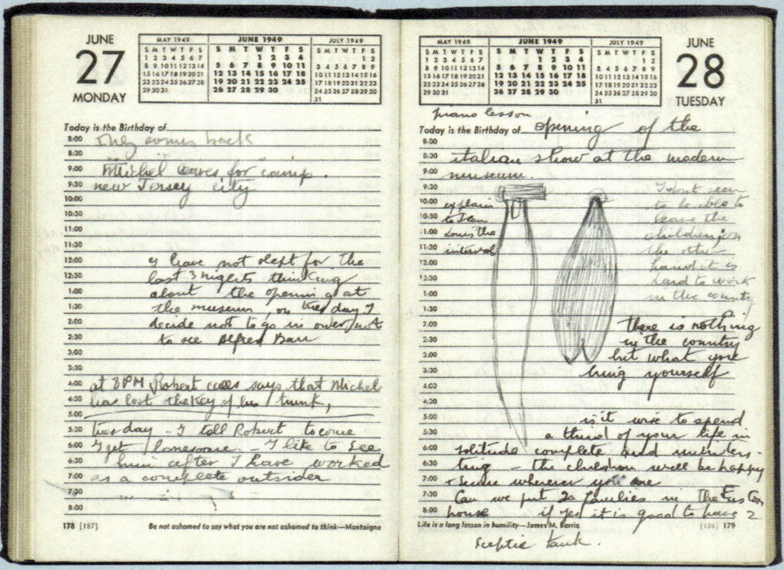

Diary entries, June 27–28, 1949. 7¾ × 10 in. (17.7 × 25.4 cm)

February 10, 1985

chaotic and useless as it
appears to be this form has to [be] kept in a set
to fit—
the notches are bad—
Nothing can replace the marks
of time, the failures, the starting over
in the wood
the fabricators are the thugs of art
crafty old foxes (little)
Fix a failure, repair a
construction, reinforce a house
beg forgiveness or simply
excuse yourself, pay one's dues or
right to an association or even
pay one's taxes is an attitude
and requires a certain education
I don't have the necessary tools
to build this piece—band
saw, only—little by little I feel like
I've arrived.

March 29, 1990

my will is an open wound.
The sacrifices made to have the permission to . . .
I enter my studio like a church.
I don't deserve it; to be a woman, to be a mother,
to be a friend
I don't deserve the attention, to be chosen,
to be selected,
that's the mystery. Why don't I deserve to be
loved—because I don't deserve it. I want something
that I don't deserve.
but that's why I want it because I don't deserve it

I wish someone would break the rule for me,
what a challenge
I don't deserve it because I don't love myself,
I don't love myself because
I'm afraid of myself. Sam said it. self-destruction.

January 14, 1994

The <u>euphoria</u> of saying no: of freedom, to
create euphoria, euphoria, euphoria, euphoria
that crashes after 2 hours or one hour
the joie de vivre, to understand, revelation of
of success followed by confusion and
a certain fear, fear of what.
Every time I changed homes I
regained, hope
Rue de Seine, Rue Royer Collard, avenue
d'Orleans, Rue Mazarine [. . .]
Nothing done there. 63 Park. 333 E 41. 142 E 18
335 W 22. 347 W 20. 518 Van Duzer.
475 Dean. Broken Promises.
I paid my debts I can leave: euphoria.

March 23, 1994

The studio is the
work of <u>art</u>
I am just the intermittent
visitor.
you understand the
thread <u>of my</u> thoughts.

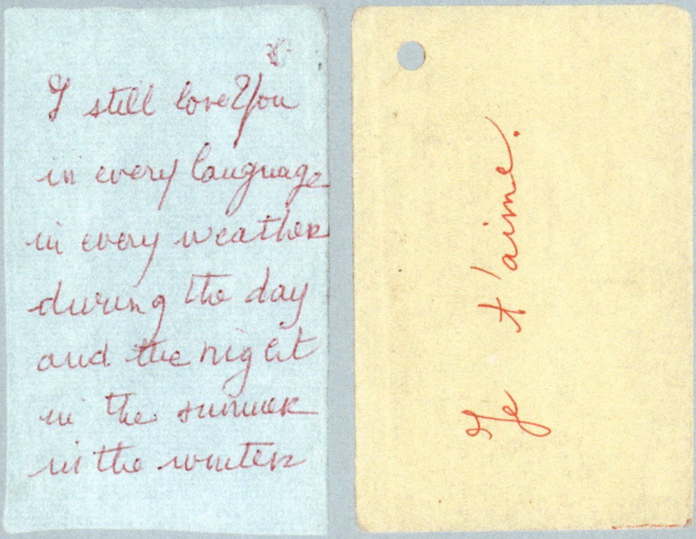

Note to Robert Goldwater, ca. 1960s. Red ink on blue paper and envelope, 4½ × 2¾ in. (11.4 × 7 cm)

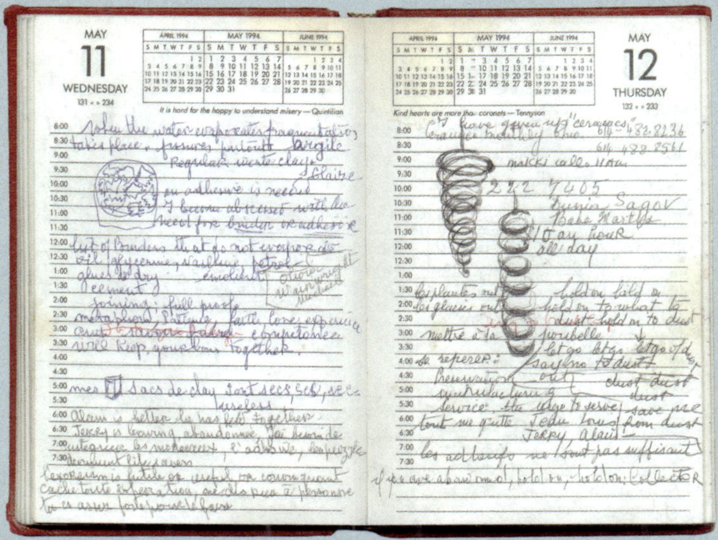

Diary entries, May 11–12, 1996. 9 × 12 in. (22.8 × 30.4 cm)

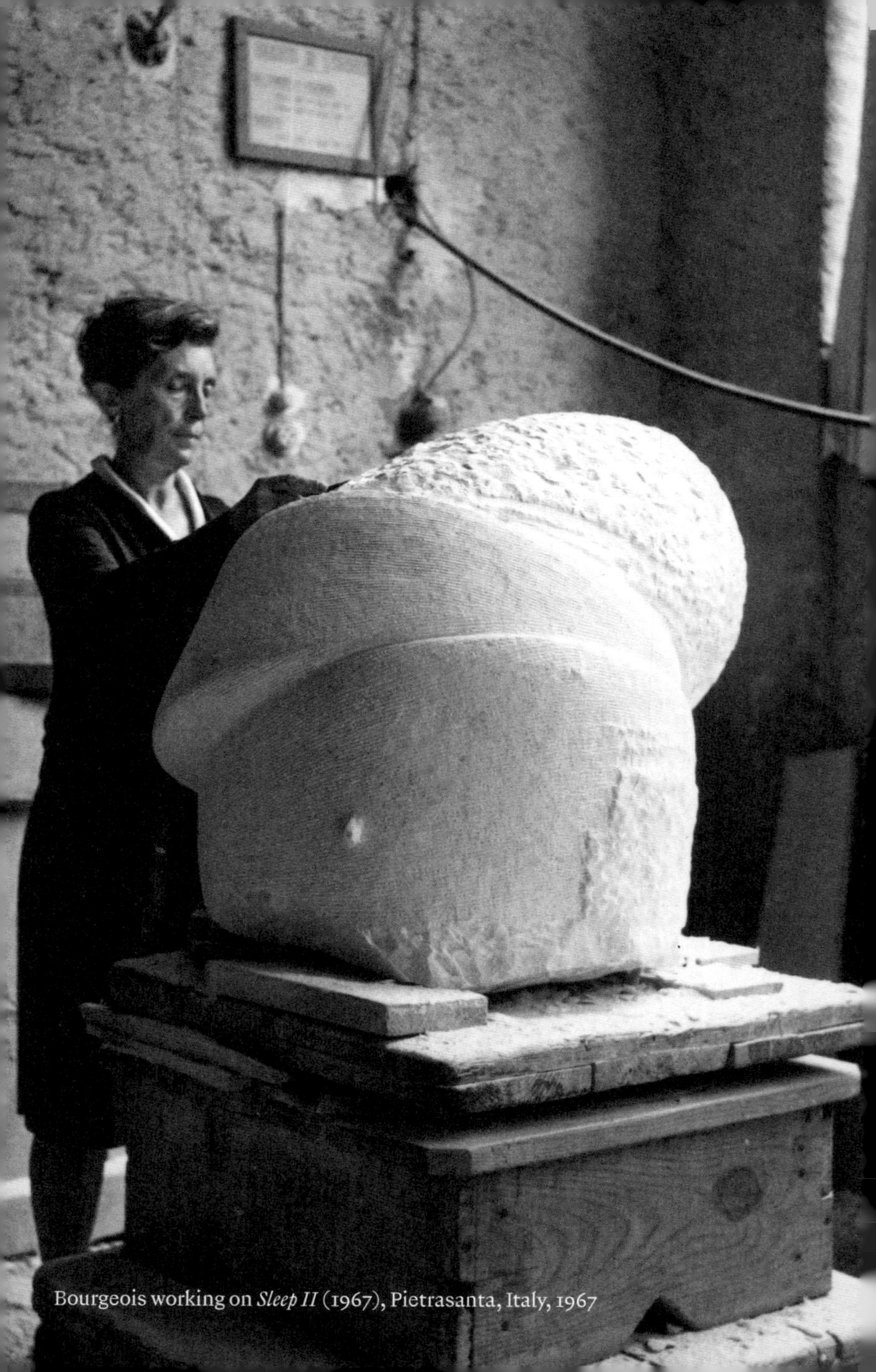

Bourgeois working on *Sleep II* (1967), Pietrasanta, Italy, 1967

Metamorphoses

Self-doubt and punishing depression shadowed Bourgeois through the 1950s. Reemergence is the unavoidable word for what took place in the following decade. In 1962, Bourgeois and Goldwater moved to a brownstone on West Twentieth Street (by now their children had left home), and Bourgeois's studio in its basement became a site for primal sculptural experiments. Working plaster with her hands, she made sculptures like nests and colonies. Pouring latex and resin, she collaborated with gravity to create oozing "unconscious landscapes." The defining forms in this fertile period are unquestionably her *Lairs*, which range from coiled towers and coagulated mounds to a hanging carcass punctured with tunnels (*The Quartered One* [1964–65; see cover]). Made in the wake of her intense engagement with psychoanalytic therapy and writing, the *Lairs* show Bourgeois pushing past language to a wordless form of self-examination, excavating forms from inside herself that she can then hide in vicariously. With its staring slit and dank interior, *Le Regard* (1966; p. 72) exemplifies this dredged-up quality, while *Torso, Self-Portrait* (1963–64; p. 72) is a powerfully strange projection of a self blindly trying to protect itself. Breasts, buttocks, spine, sex, and ribs all seem present in this shieldlike object, but they are moved and transposed in such a way that none can be named with certainty.

Works from this period were revealed to the world at New York's Stable Gallery in 1964, Bourgeois's first solo exhibition of new work in eleven years; they were also included in *Eccentric Abstraction*, a watershed group show curated by art writer and activist Lucy Lippard at Fischbach Gallery, New York, in 1966. Here, for the first but not the last time, Bourgeois appeared as the vital contemporary of much younger artists (Bruce Nauman and Eva Hesse among them), all of whom were countering and complicating the Minimalism of the time with more impure and suggestive forms of abstraction.

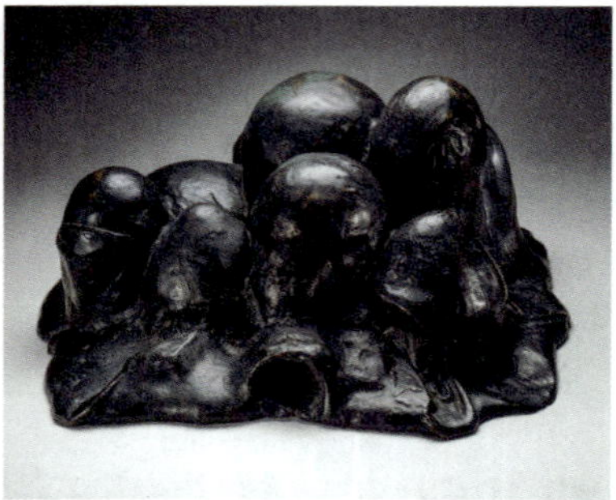

Unconscious Landscape, 1967–68. Bronze, black patina, 12 × 22 × 24 in. (30.5 × 55.9 × 61 cm)

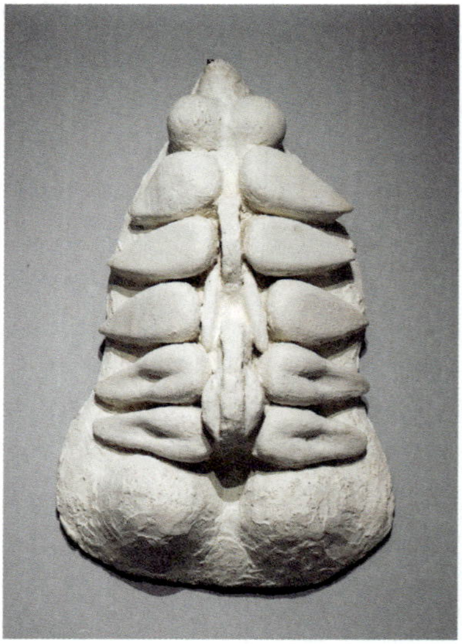

Torso, Self-Portrait, 1963–64. Plaster, $24\frac{3}{4}$ × 16 × $7\frac{7}{8}$ in. (62.9 × 40.6 × 20 cm)

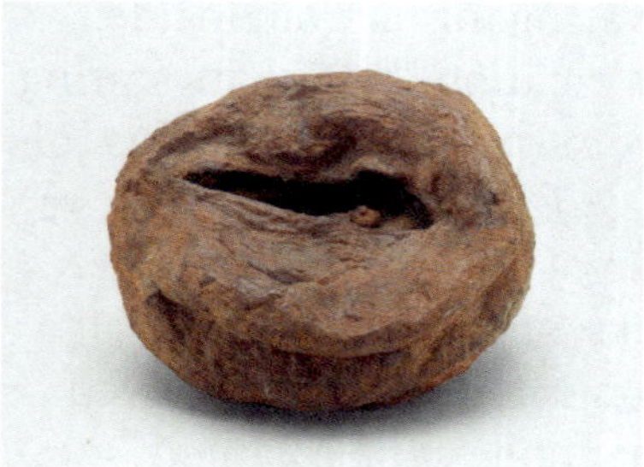

Le Regard, 1963. Latex over fabric, 5 × $15\frac{1}{2}$ × $14\frac{1}{2}$ in. (12.7 × 39.4 × 36.8 cm)

The flow of "eccentric" forms in Bourgeois's basement studio points to a larger impulse—the drive toward metamorphosis that led her, in the later 1960s, to the marble and bronze studios of Carrara and Pietrasanta in Italy. Though perversely old-fashioned in the context of avant-garde New York practice, marble and bronze were the mediums through which centuries of Western sculptors had explored bodily metamorphosis. As a guide at the Louvre in the late 1930s, Bourgeois had moved among such sculptures. She even made, in 1967, a tactile homage in bronze to the Baroque master Bernini, telling an interviewer at the time that "it is really in this statuary of the past that I find great stimuli." As for marble, she loved the oscillation from violence to tenderness that the medium permitted: first, the aggressive attack on the cube; next, the finessing and polishing. Similarly, she took delight in how hard stone could be shaped to appear soft and flourishing. In *Sleep II* (1967; p. 70), the phallic marble seems to forget its own rigidity as it slumbers. In *Cumul I* (1969), shy, swelling forms peep from the drapery that covers them.

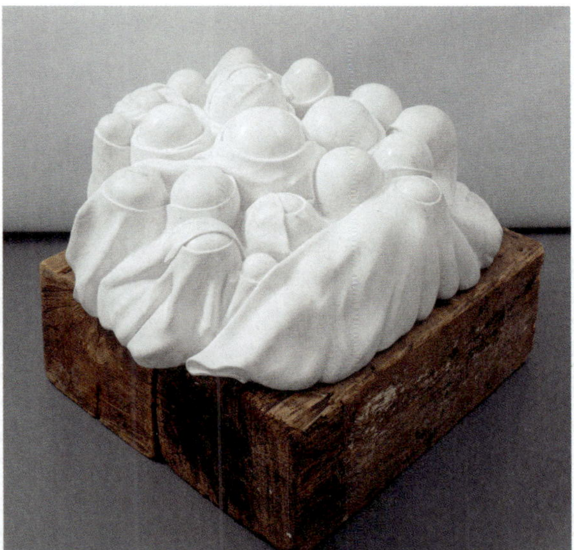

Cumul I, 1969. Marble and wood, 20¹⁄₁₆ × 50 × 48 in. (51 × 127 × 122 cm)

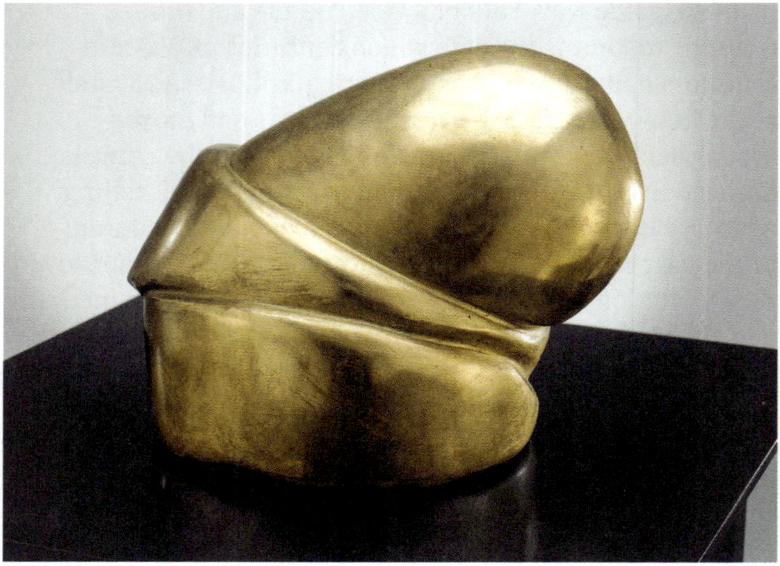

Untitled (Sleep II), 1968. Bronze, polished patina, 5½ × 7 × 6 in. (14 × 17.8 × 15.2 cm)

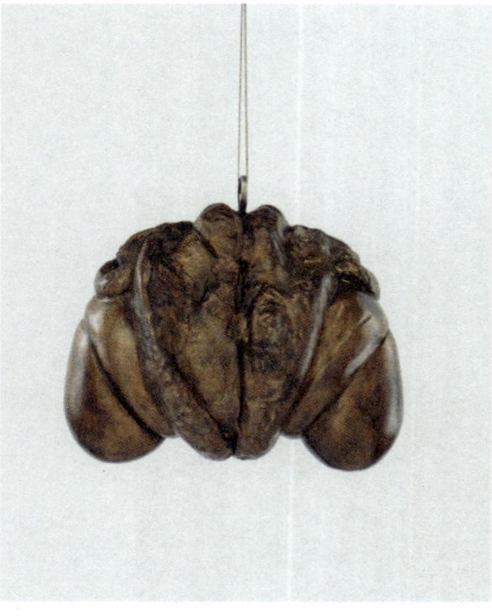

Janus Fleuri, 1968. Bronze, gold patina, 10⅜ × 12½ × 8⅜ in. (25.7 × 31.8 × 21.3 cm)

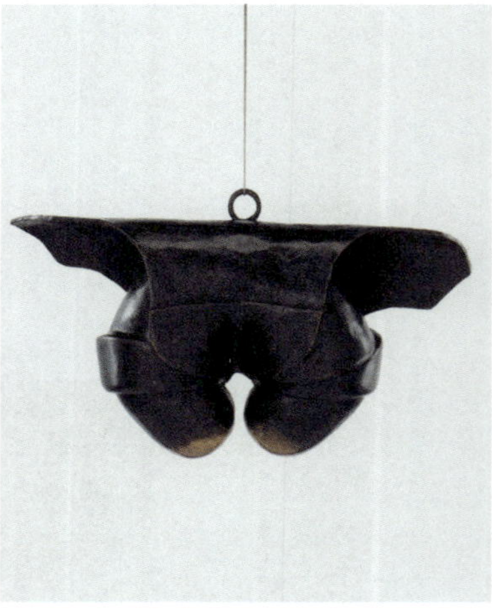

Hanging Janus with Jacket, 1968. Bronze, dark and polished patina, 10⅝ × 20⅝ × 6⅜ in. (27 × 52.4 × 16.2 cm)

A related feeling of bodies gathering stirs among the protuberances in *Clamart* (1968), a sculpture imbued with the lonely, solemn quality of a memorial (Clamart is the name of the village near Paris where Bourgeois's parents and grandparents are buried).

Bourgeois's metamorphic impulse is evident above all in her lifelong habit of cannibalizing and recombining her own sculptures. *Untitled (Sleep II)* (1968), for instance, is a low-lying bronze that resembles a plump, drowsing penis. By doubling and fusing a version of this form and the fleshy overspill of cast metal at its base, Bourgeois arrived at the suspended bronze *Janus Fleuri* (1968). In this new incarnation, the penislike forms take on the character of hanging breasts, and the center becomes a blooming ("fleuri") image of the female sex. The *Janus* form (Bourgeois named the series for the two-faced Roman god of beginnings) goes on to lead other lives in four related sculptures, sometimes tensing as if tickled or aroused, sometimes stilled in its black "leather jacket."

Through all this, Bourgeois reserved the right to change and mingle her mediums; she restlessly declined to abide by the modernist ethos of "truth to materials." But to follow her work in stone, particularly, is to see her singular imagination flexing. A deeply idiosyncratic maker is taking what she needs from tradition, reanimating the language of the classical fragment with distortions and shocks of detail. At times, she seems to be populating an alternative museum of figurative sculpture, where news from the "volcanic unconscious" surges up through immutable forms. Consider *Untitled (with Hand)* (1989), in which a child's arm extends from a polished sphere above the chiseled words "I love you I love you." Or *Nature Study (Velvet Eyes)* (1984), in which vast, pensive eyes are carved out from a heavy block of marble. As Bourgeois said of marble in a 1988 interview, "I take it over with my fantasy, my life force."

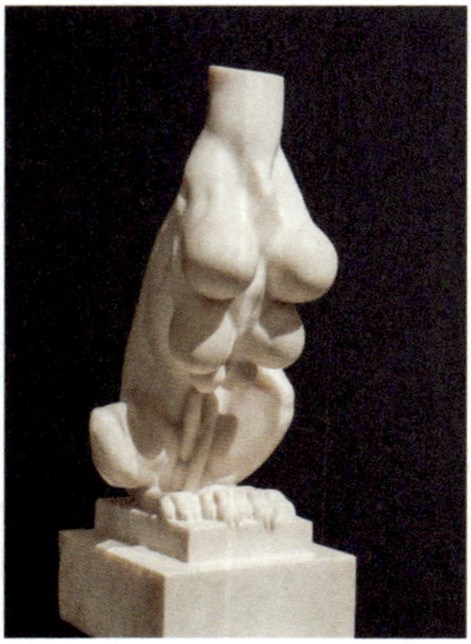

Nature Study, 1984–94.
Marble, 36 × 16 × 12¾ in.
(91.4 × 40.6 × 32.4 cm)

The most fertile of these "takeovers" is *Nature Study* (1984–94), a work in pink Portuguese marble that Bourgeois also created in red wax, blue rubber, and polished bronze (she returned to Italy in the 1980s but worked with stonemasons in New York thereafter). *Nature Study* originated, like many of her sculptures at this time, with a rescued object: a broken plaster cast of a hunting dog Bourgeois found in a dumpster. With its head removed, and breasts and phallus added, the offcast became a thrilling entity—a dog-goddess endowed with everything she needs to nurture and protect her family. Far from seeming outlandish, the creature's new attributes are calmly held within the form of the carving, whose smooth skin of pink marble looks as though it would yield if you pressed it. A sexual Sphinx, it incarnates the transforming desires Bourgeois brought to sculpture. "If I want," she once declared in a note to herself, "a thing becomes another thing."

Bourgeois working on *Nature Study* (1984) in her Brooklyn studio, New York, 1984

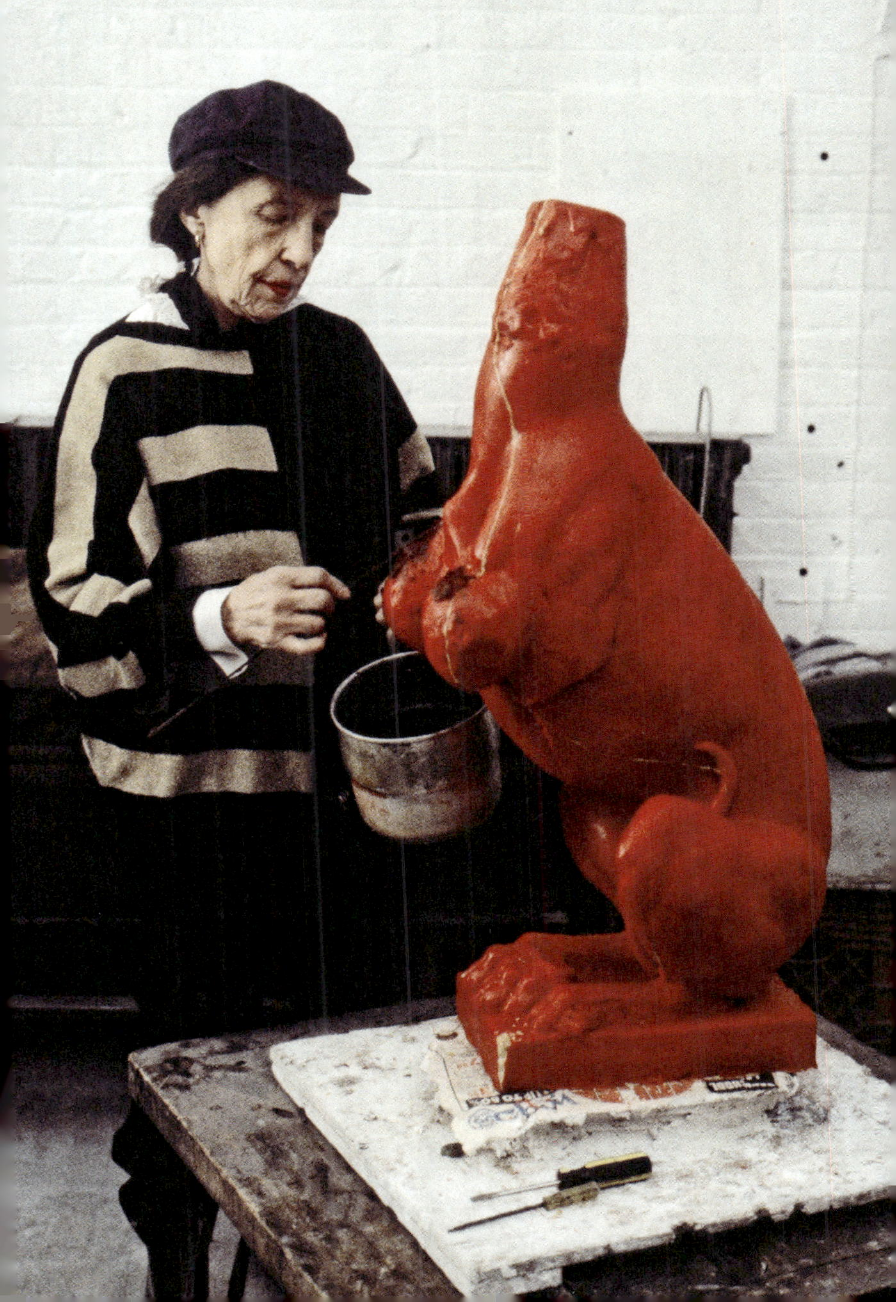

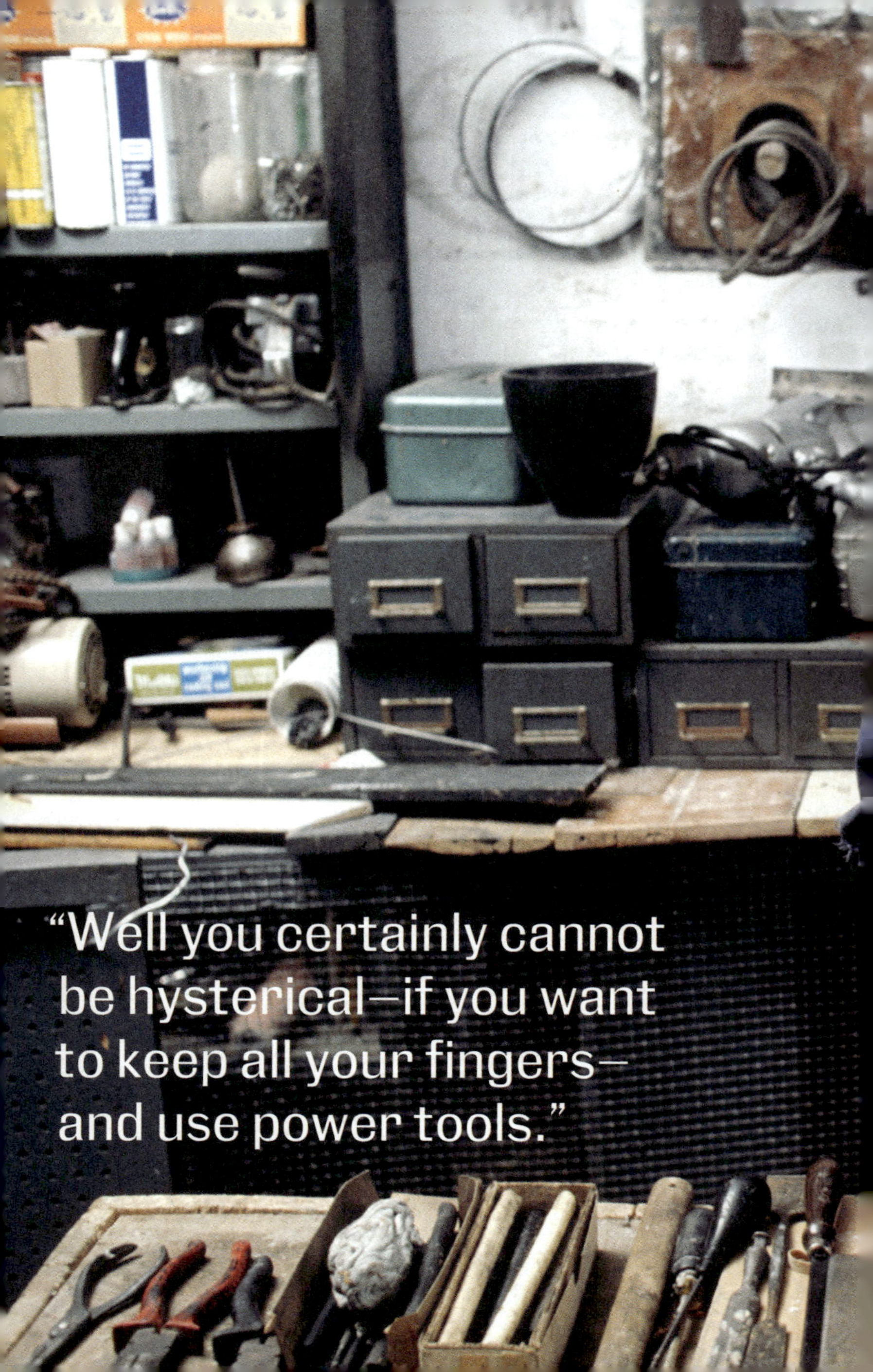

“Well you certainly cannot be hysterical—if you want to keep all your fingers—and use power tools.”

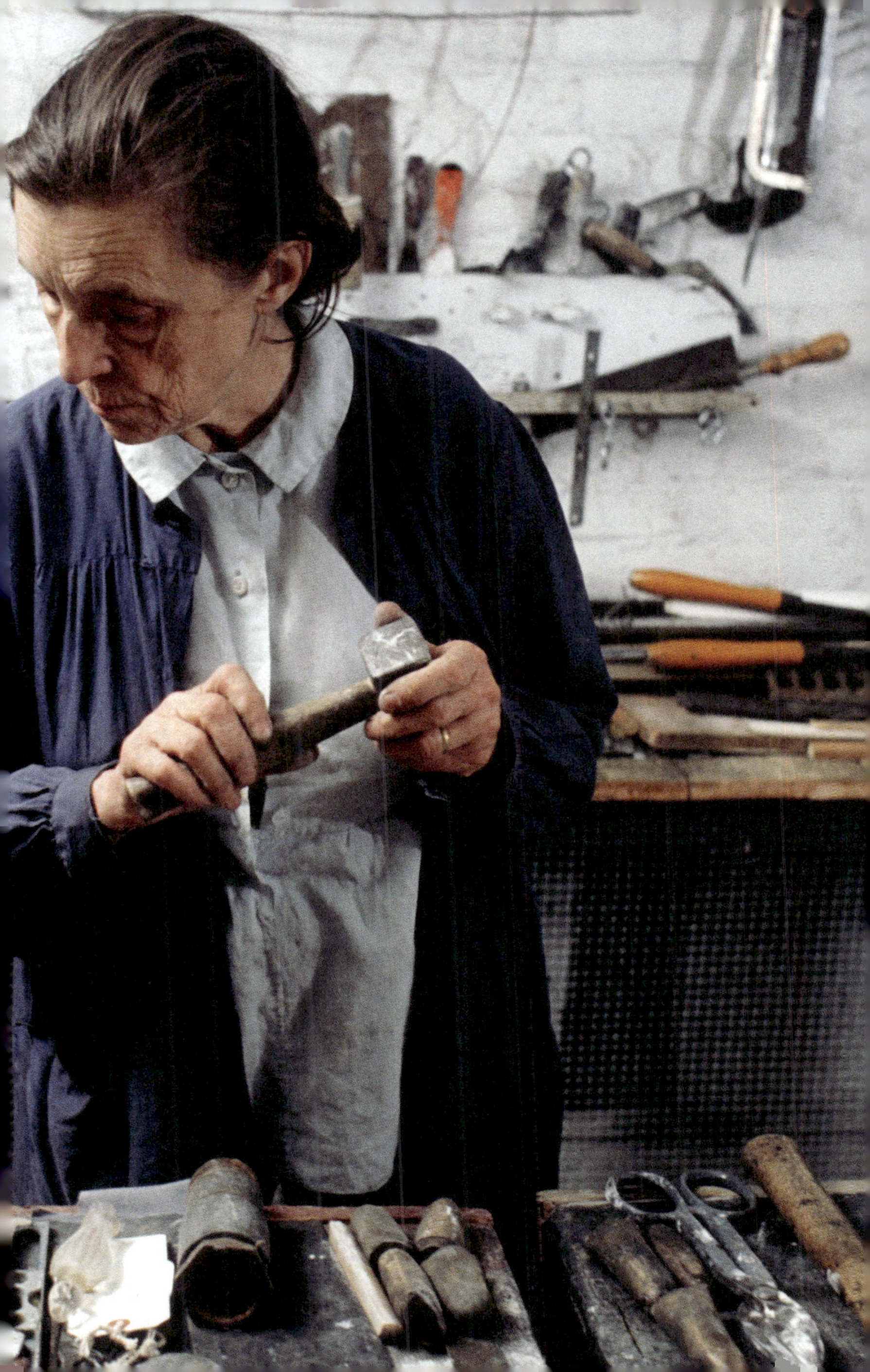

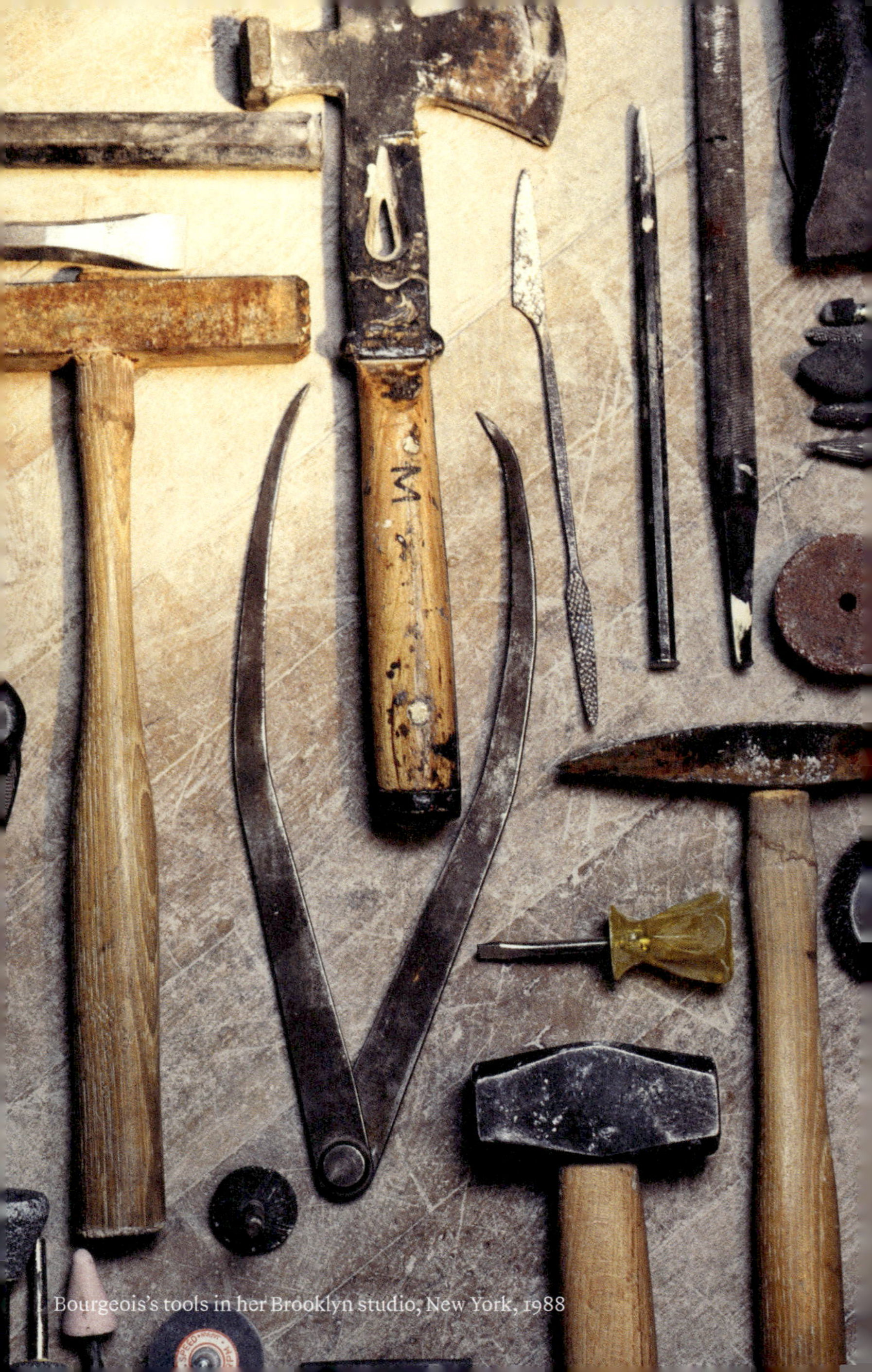

Bourgeois's tools in her Brooklyn studio, New York, 1988

Tools of Her Trade

Hammers, mallets, chisels, awls, scrapers, pincers, pliers, clamps, sewing needles, rasps, and six different kinds of saw—these are some of the items recorded by Bourgeois in a fascinating studio inventory from around 1963. The right tool was the one that got the job done, in what she called a "fight to the finish" with her materials. The inventory attests to her love of that fight: her passion for cutting, carving, and piercing. The pleasure and meaning of sculpture, for her, was the struggle with resistant materials. With tools in hand, she could take control and temporarily quell inner chaos. By giving fears a physicality, she could, as she said, "hack away" at them.

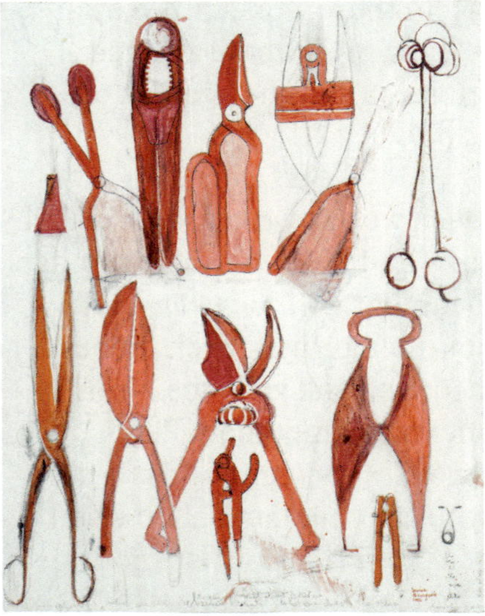

Untitled, 1986. Watercolor, ink, oil, charcoal, and pencil on paper, 23¾ × 19 in. (60.3 × 48.3 cm)

As well as using tools to make her art, Bourgeois portrayed them symbolically in her artworks. Looking at the scissors, clamps, and pliers in *Untitled* (1986), we realize they are human surrogates—“couples” that cannot snap together without causing hurt (written at the bottom of this drawing: “What one does to the other”). Bourgeois seems to identify with the mighty red shears in *Untitled (Scissors)* (1986), beneath which she wrote “I have to be strong to last through the day.” The essential presence among these emotional implements is the *femme couteau*, or “knife woman.” First seen in a beautifully insinuating marble (ca. 1969–70), and later reimagined in fabric, the *femme couteau* is a threatened woman who has stiffened into a tool of violent self-defense.

Real tools enter Bourgeois’s sculpture in the era of the *Cells*. A grim clatter of surgical instruments and kitchen utensils fills a side table in *Cell I* (1991), while the blade of an open paper cutter looms above an arched marble body in *Cell III* (1991). The implied aggression in these works hits a high pitch in *Cell (Arch of Hysteria)* (1992–93), where an aged bandsaw seems to have played its part in the agonies of the headless figure.

A “seems to” is a given in all such works, which are, after all, imaginative constructs. A funny and illuminating exchange on this point occurs in the documentary *Louise Bourgeois: No Trespassing* (1994), when journalist Nigel Finch probes Bourgeois on the question of cutting and violence. “You cut arms off, you cut heads off, you dismember,” Finch asserts, as Bourgeois mischievously revs the bandsaw in her basement studio. “Don’t you cut your lamb chop when you are ready to eat it? Is that a crime?” the artist shoots back, before demonstrating, more patiently, how two circles can be cut and slotted together to form a folding sphere. “It is not aggressive, it is not protective,” she concludes. “It is just inventive.”

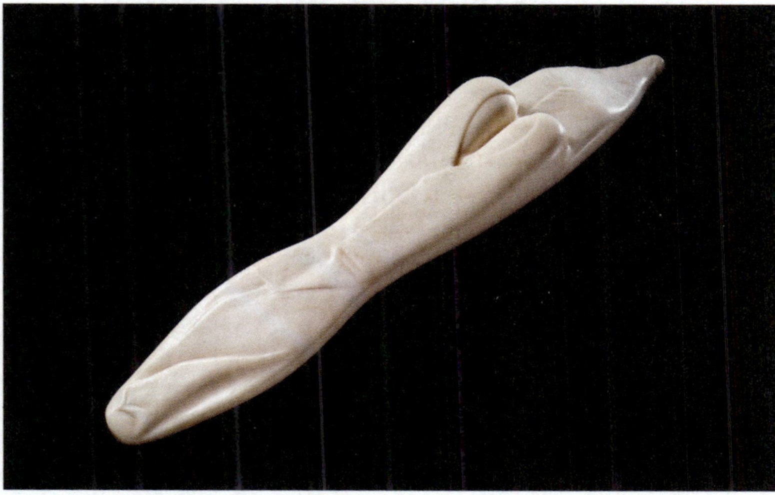

Femme Couteau, ca. 1969–70. Marble, $3\frac{1}{2} \times 26\frac{3}{8} \times 4\frac{7}{8}$ in. ($8.9 \times 67 \times 12.4$ cm)

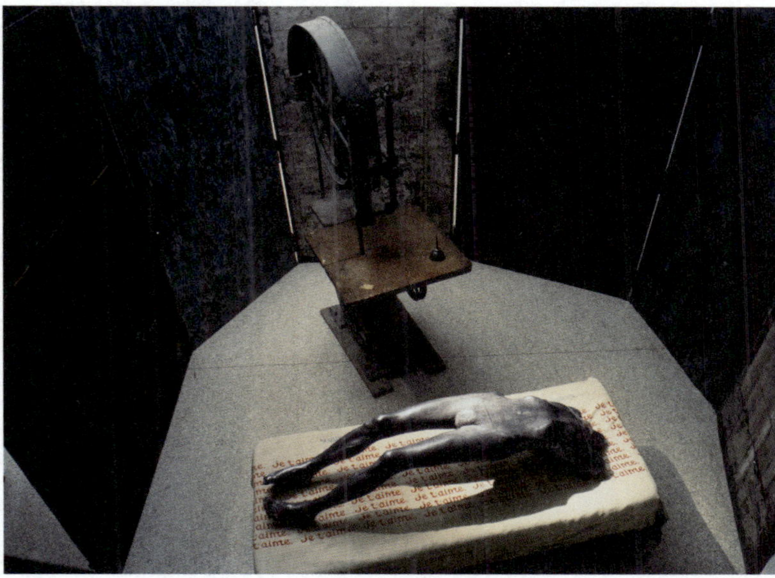

Cell (Arch of Hysteria), 1992–93. Steel, bronze, cast iron, and fabric, $119 \times 145 \times 120$ in. ($302.3 \times 368.3 \times 304.8$ cm)

On Tools and Rage

As well as recording daily events, Bourgeois's diaries and loose sheets of writing brim with associative chains, incantatory lists, and pungent descriptions of body, self, and process. Here, in language both precise and poetic, she examines two necessary elements in sculpture—the tools required to make the form and the furious focus required to wield them.

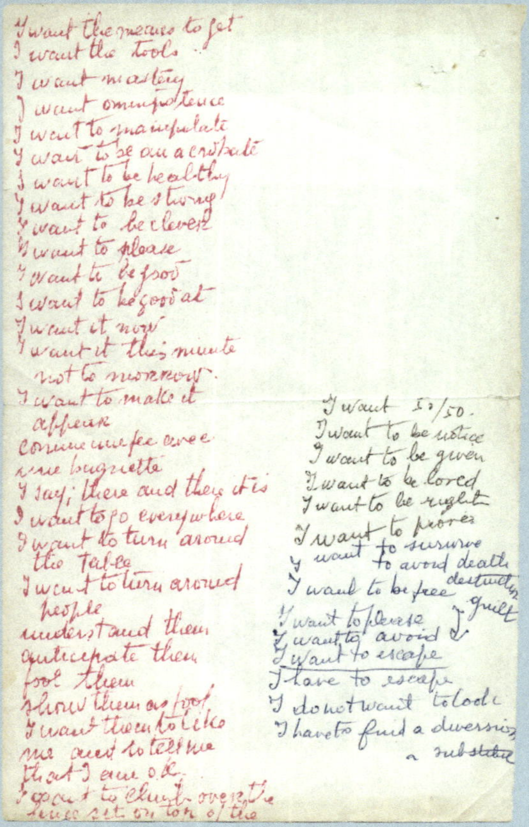
I want the means to get
I want the tools
I want mastery
I want omnipotence
I want to manipulate
I want to be an acrobate
I want to be healthy
I want to be strong
I want to be clever
I want to please
I want to be good
I want to be good at
I want it now
I want it this minute
not to morrow.
I want to make it
appear
comme une fee avec
une baguette
I say; there and there it is
I want to go everywhere
I want to turn around
the table
I want to turn around
people
understand them
anticipate them
fool them
show them as fool
I want them to like
me and to tell me
that I am o.k.
I want to climb over the
...
I want 50/50.
I want to be notice
I want to be given
I want to be loved
I want to be right
I want to prove
I want to survive
to avoid death
I want to be free destruction
guilt
I want to please
I want to avoid
I want to escape
I have to escape
I do not want to look
I have to find a diversion
a substitute

Loose sheet of writing, ca. 1962. Red, black, and blue ink on paper, 8½ × 5½ in. (21.6 × 14 cm)

ca. 1958

The tools
to have access to the tools,
look at them
try them
handle them
take them
put them back
examine them
put them away
clean them
brood over them—
using my tools
brutalize them
break them
repair them
replace them
protect them
have the key

ca. 1962

To <u>animate</u> a
<u>cube</u> it is not sufficient
to massacre it
  A shape can
become shapeless
without thereby
becoming another
shape
  generally what
one kneads has na
turally a shape
because of the hand
factor—
  With carving on
the contrary, the hand
only becomes the tool
of the willpower and the
willpower is more diffi
cult to handle. it
cannot
develop in
time (or in space)
and willful
attempts at sculpture
lead to shapelessness
or to incoherence
Sculpture can
integrate many a
blind and shapeless
aggression but it
requires more than
that—<u>aggression</u>
is necessary and
useful but it is
not sufficient.
As anger leads
to destruction, a
steady rage can be
productive.

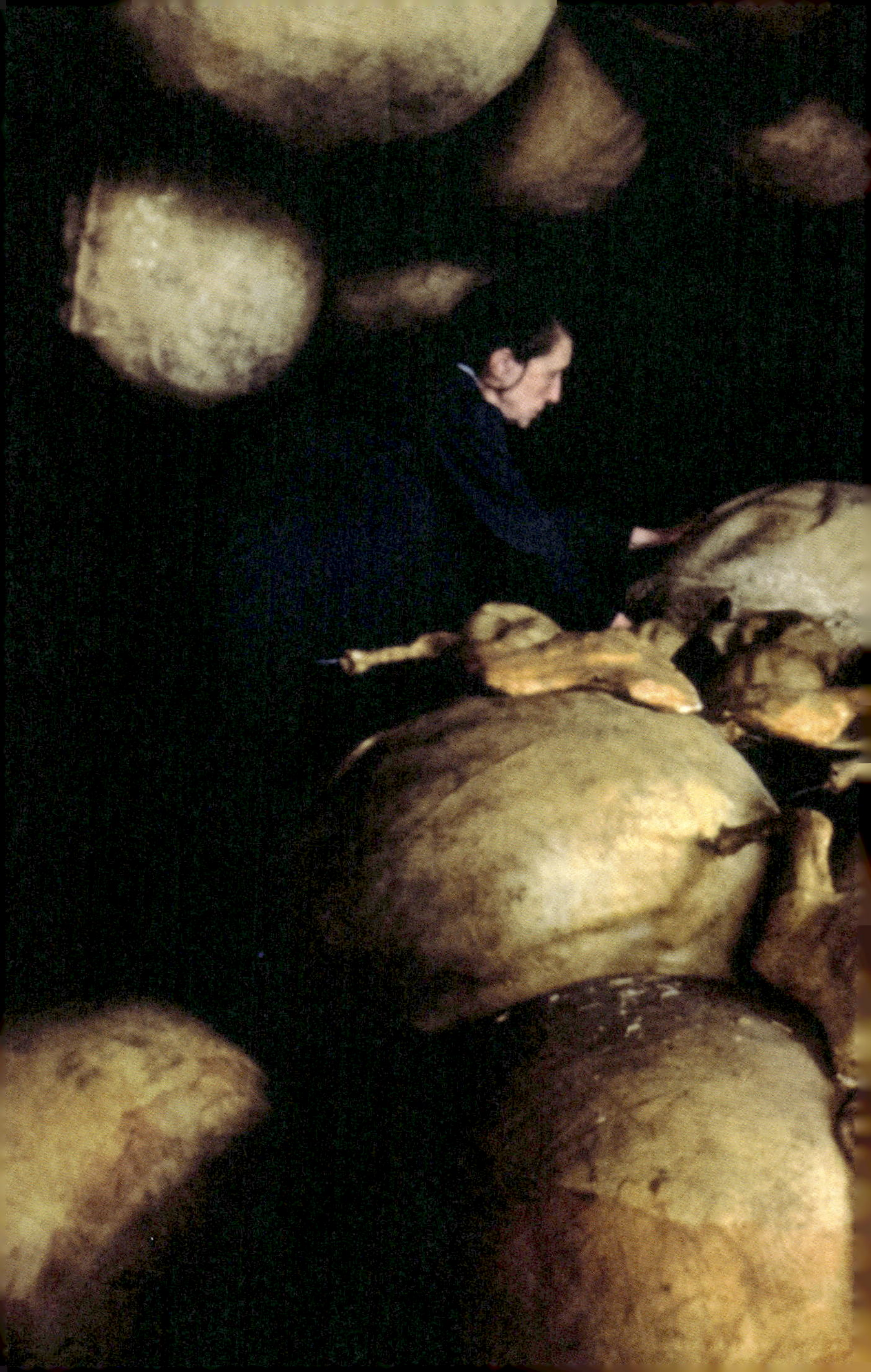

“I organize a sculpture the way we organize a treatment for the sick. You’d better know what you’re doing.”

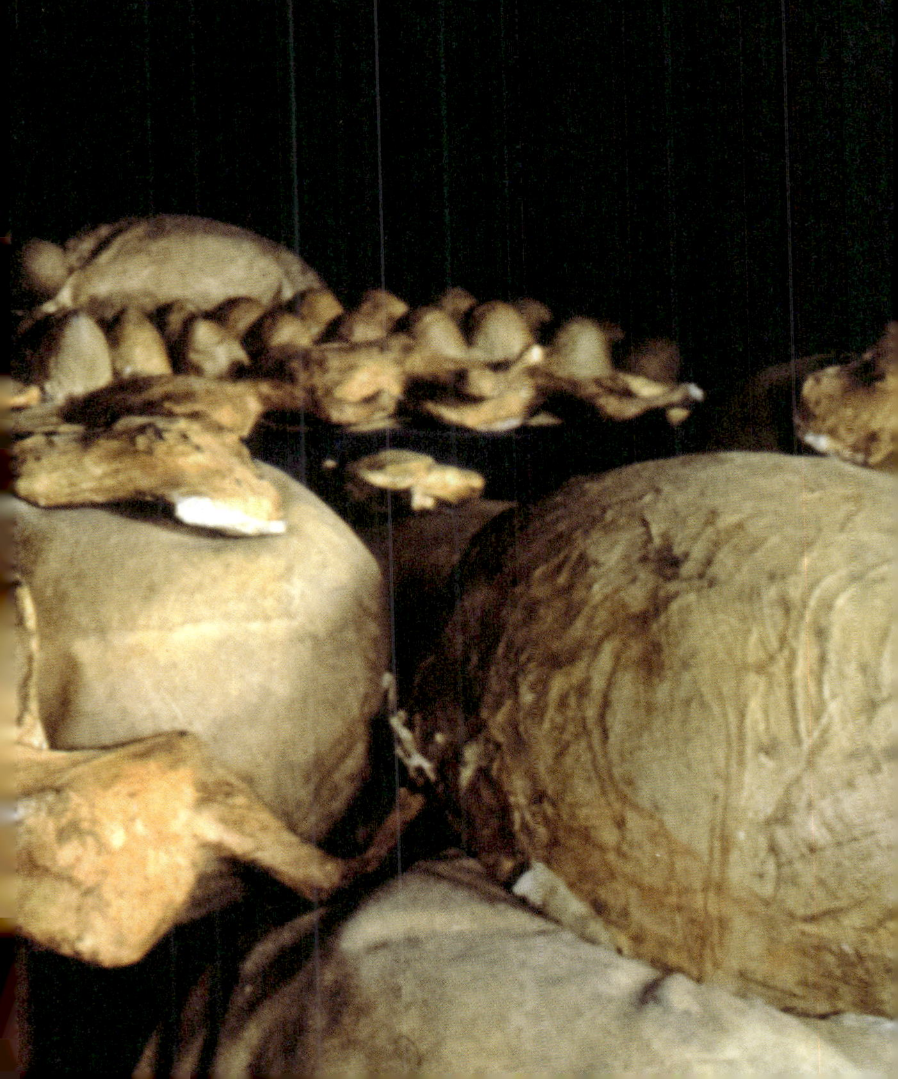

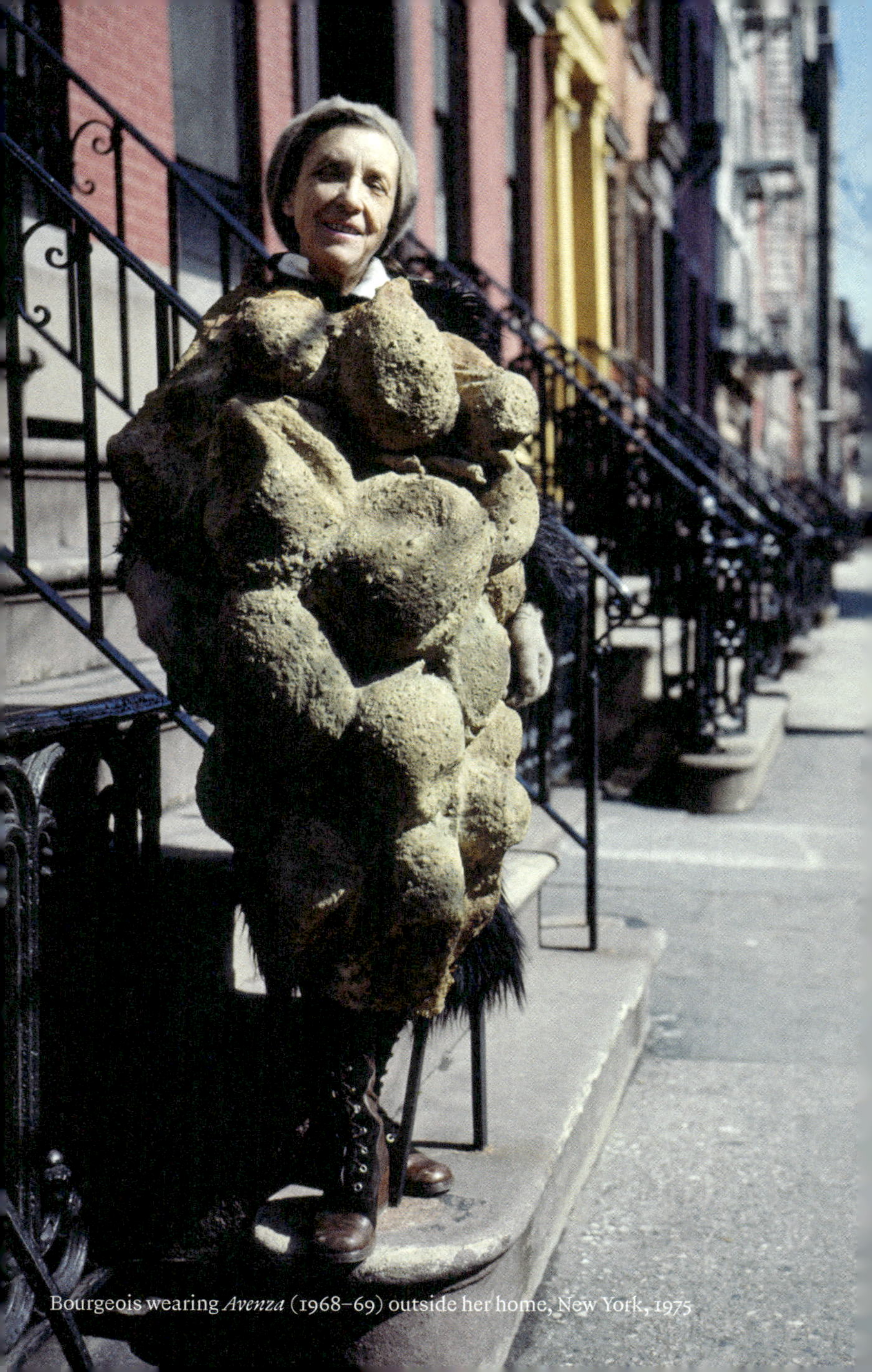

Bourgeois wearing *Avenza* (1968–69) outside her home, New York, 1975

The Whole House as a Studio

Further loss and a ferocious appetite for renewal define Bourgeois's life and art in the 1970s. In 1973, Robert Goldwater died unexpectedly, leaving Bourgeois by herself in their home; a diary entry addresses "the challenge of my being alone + dispossessed." She might have succumbed to grief and loneliness, or moderated her ambition. Instead, Bourgeois flung herself into a cathartic cleanup, replacing the family stove with a two-burner gas cooktop and rearranging the dining room on the parlor level as a space for artmaking. In her diary, she urged herself toward courage in defiance of despondency: "I am an artist with the whole house as a studio, I am not weak or crushed. I do not need a family, Robert would be proud of me and that is enough."

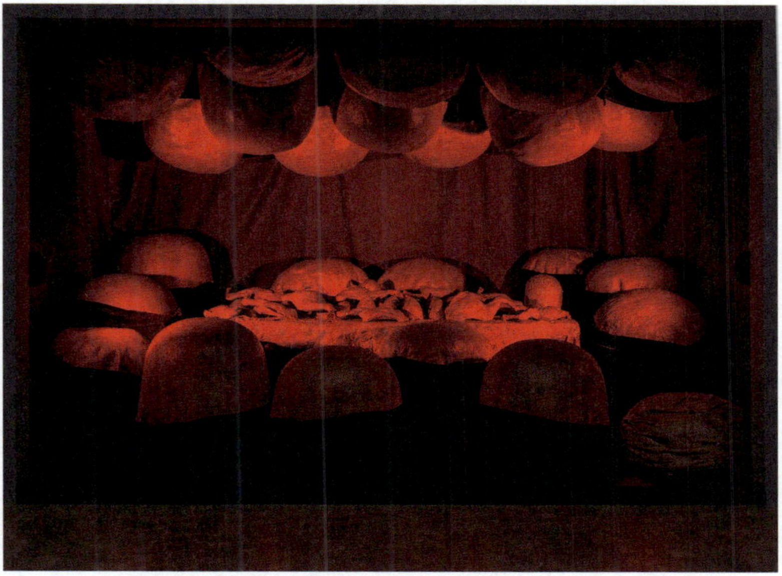

The Destruction of the Father, 1974. Latex, plaster, wood, fabric, and red light, 93⅝ × 142⅝ × 97⅞ in. (237.8 × 362.3 × 248.6 cm)

The fierceness of Bourgeois's resolve became apparent the following year, when she revealed *The Destruction of the Father* (1974; p. 89) in her first solo show in a decade. In photos of Bourgeois making this work in her subbasement, she resembles a peculiar explorer, fossicking among bumps and protuberances in an underground grotto (pp. 86–87). The final work is a red-lit cannibal banquet that looks like it might consume *us*. Forms recalling those in *Cumul I* (p. 73) gather in a shrouded interior, where body parts cast from chicken legs and lamb shoulders lie on a table or bed. Something has been violently dismembered; something is being consumed. A feeling of ceremony and malevolent comedy cuts across the violence. In interviews, Bourgeois glossed the installation with an irresistible narrative, of a family so tired of their bloviating patriarch that they tear him to pieces and devour him. Even if a viewer knows nothing of Bourgeois's story, or her complicated love for her father, the gusto in this work is unmistakable. Although *The Destruction of the Father* was made at a time of deep disenchantment with male authority of all kinds, it does not critique that authority so much as consume and absorb it. It is, in Bourgeois's words, "a very murderous piece"—a masterpiece that eats the master. When it was finished, she said she felt like a different person.

The aggression and psychological directness of this work resonated with younger artists and critics. Soon after its showing, *The Destruction of the Father* occupied the cover of *Artforum*, heralding an essay by Lucy Lippard. From its first sentences, Lippard's essay made clear that the old formalist frameworks weren't up to the task of describing Bourgeois's work: "Attempts to bring a coolly evolutionary or art-historical order to her work, or to see it in the context of one art group or another, have proved more or less irrelevant." The advocacy of Lippard and other feminist artists and critics set the stage for Bourgeois's 1982 retrospective at MoMA (Lippard was one of the signatories of a 1973 letter petitioning the museum's then-chief curator of painting and sculpture, William Rubin, to grant Bourgeois an exhibition). But Bourgeois was hardly waiting quietly for institutional endorsement. She opened her home to young artists, students, and collaborators, drawing out their emotional energy to supplement and fortify her own. Writer Chris Kraus, then in her twenties, later remarked, "This was an old woman who acted like a punk girl."

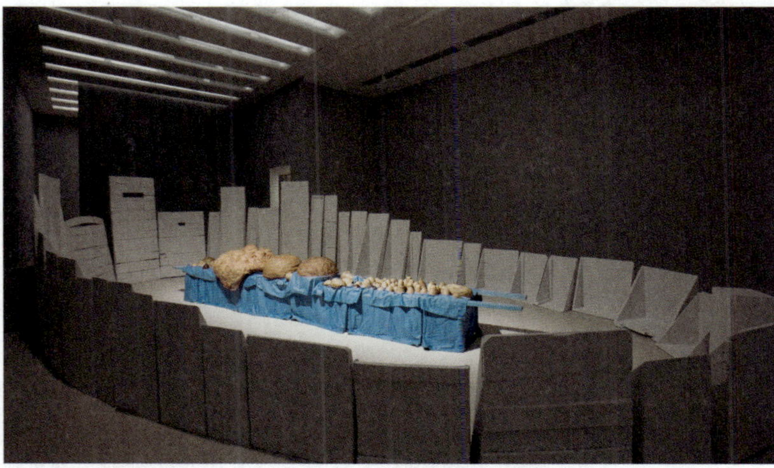

Confrontation, 1978. Painted wood, latex, and fabric, 86⅝ × 368 × 175½ in. (220 × 934.7 × 445.8 cm)

The climax of this unruly and fertile period was *Confrontation* (1978), an installation that filled the central exhibition space of Hamilton Gallery of Contemporary Art, New York, and is one of Bourgeois's largest. Here, the cavelike interior of *Destruction* has given way to a social arena, where a long blue platform spread with lumpish body parts

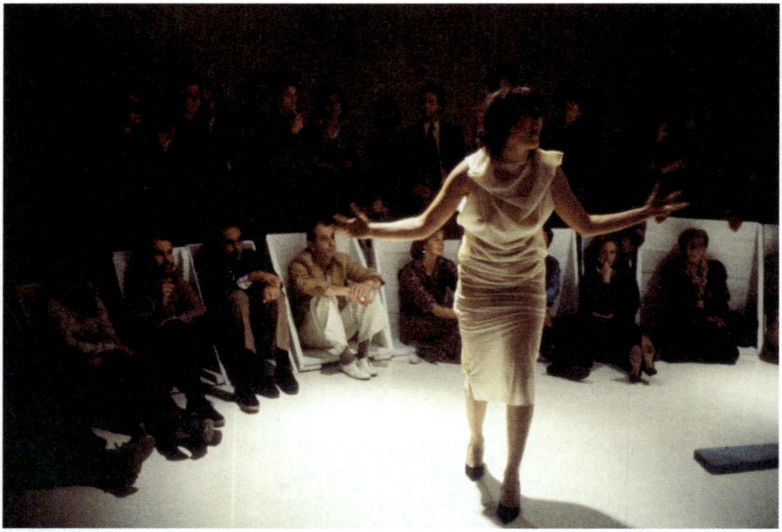

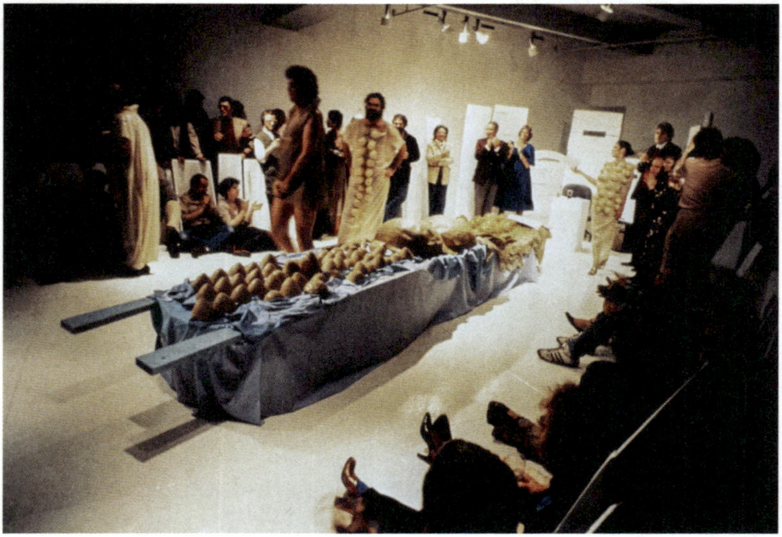

A Banquet / A Fashion Show of Body Parts, staged in *Confrontation* (1978), Hamilton Gallery of Contemporary Art, New York, October 21, 1978

is surrounded by an audience of painted wooden boxes standing like sentinels. This sculptural offering has served as a Rorschach test for writers, who have seen it variously as a meal, a wartime scene, a funeral, and a sacrifice. Pointing to the contrast between the full forms at one end of the table and their shriveled counterparts at the other, Bourgeois described *Confrontation* as the remains of a failed relationship—a romance between an older and a younger "creature" (her word) that has ended inevitably in death. But perhaps the best indication of the spirit of the work is the event that Bourgeois organized for the exhibition's last night, a punk-burlesque variety performance titled *A Banquet / A Fashion Show of Body Parts* (1978).

Assembling a multigenerational cast that included Goldwater's academic colleagues and Bourgeois's young collaborator Suzan Cooper, the artist treated her captive viewers (many sitting inside the installation) to a procession of reversals, revelations, and unburdenings. Sculptural garments created in latex brought skin and sexual organs to the outside. Men, wearing many-breasted robes, were rendered absurdly fecund. The punk-provocateur Cooper unleashed a song of maternal separation. In grainy footage of the event, Cooper's blazing performance cuts through the evening's archness, regrounding it in a primal "confrontation" with aging, loss, and abandonment. Bourgeois, hovering on the edges, is a gleeful ringmaster.

At the time, Bourgeois already had three decades of work behind her. Most of it was stored in the crannies and recesses of her home studio. But *The Destruction of the Father* and *Confrontation* made clear that she was not receding into her own history. Far from it, the sixty-six-year-old artist was emerging with a vengeance.

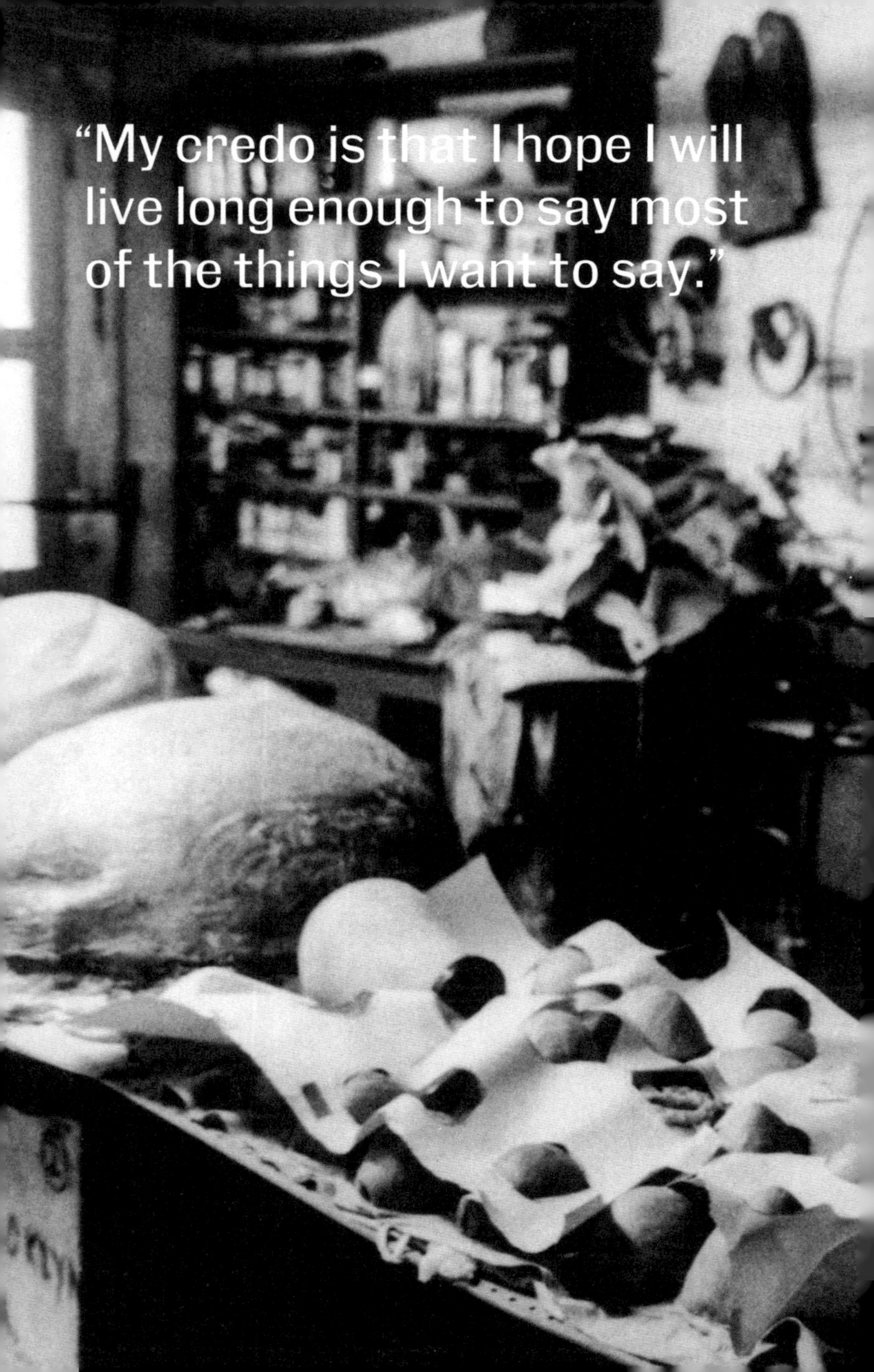

"My credo is that I hope I will live long enough to say most of the things I want to say."

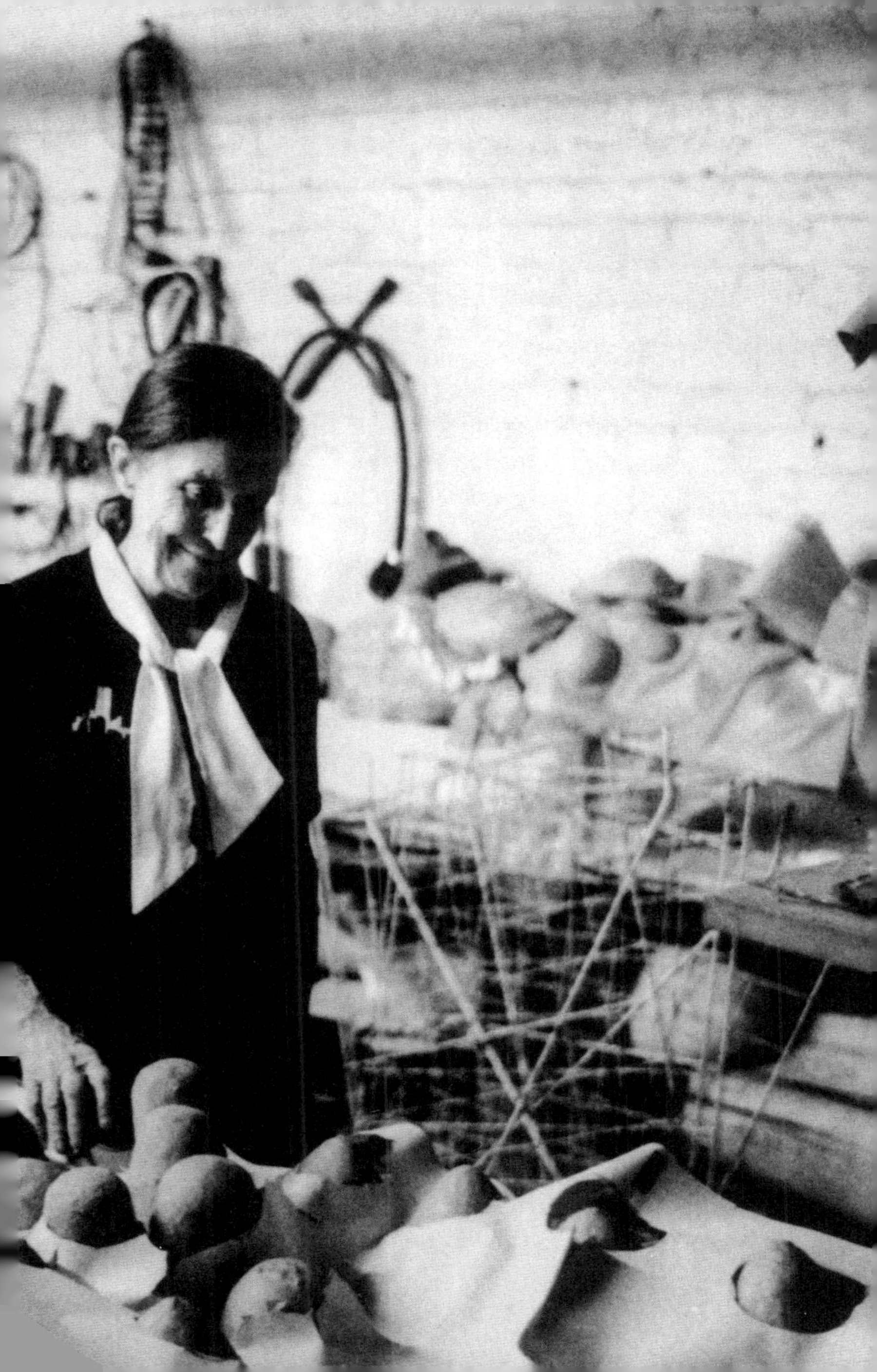

A Calmer Place
Bourgeois often leads us *inside,* to emotionally charged interiors. Just as important—because rarer—are her landscapes of peace and respite. The turbulence clears, and we find ourselves in a place of meditation and escape—a hinterland of shapely hills and soothing, repetitive distances. Instead of being aggressively cut or carved, these works are often painted or stitched. Red gives way to peaceful blue. Sharp forms yield to flows and curves. And the maternal body is always present in the landscape's "mounds and valleys and caves and holes."

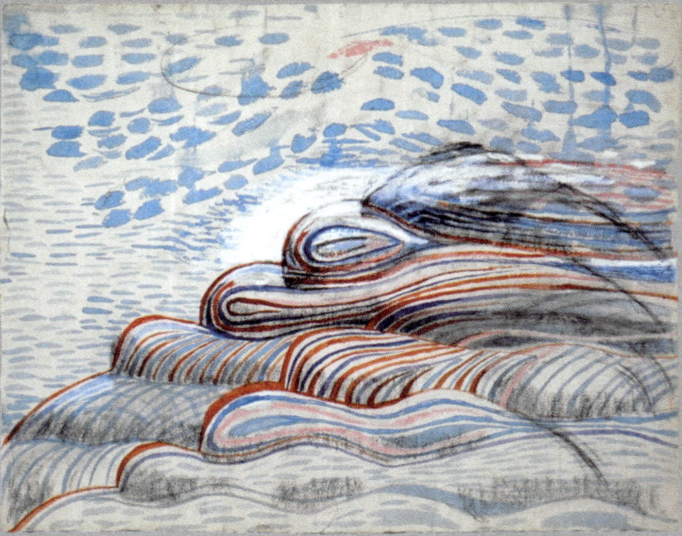

The Sweet Smell of Indigo, 1968. Watercolor, charcoal, and gouache on paper, 19¼ × 25 in. (48.9 × 63.5 cm)

The works are grounded in early memories of the hills and valleys around the village of Aubusson in central France—the landscape where Bourgeois stayed with her maternal grandparents when her father went to war.

But these works are also striking for the way they avoid specifics, as if to quell painful associations and keep difficult memories at bay. Remembered landscapes are reduced to abstract vistas filled with what Lucy Lippard called "hill-breast-clouds." The river that meanders through Aubusson is the Creuse, and in works such as *Vallée de la rivière sans berge* (The Valley of the Limitless River, 1968), it becomes a waterway of picture-book simplicity, its banks filled with treelike spheres that we sense could continue to infinity.

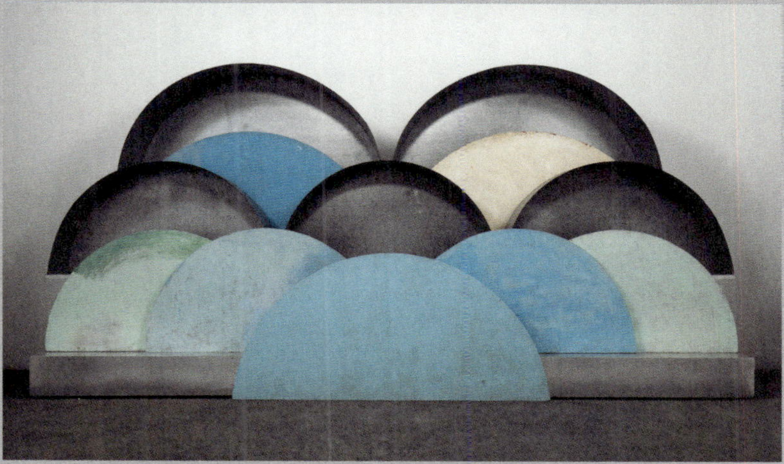

Clouds and Caverns, 1982–89. Metal and painted wood, 108 × 218 × 72 in. (274.3 × 553.7 × 182.9 cm)

These secretive, layered, hunkering shapes are made real in *Clouds and Caverns* (1982–89), a structure of huge aluminum "caverns" and painted wooden "clouds" that suggest a theatrical set for a play without conflict (the work, which Bourgeois used as a "perch"—her word for a secure place to observe from—in her Brooklyn studio, is large enough for someone to hide in). The neutral

Partial Recall, 1979. Painted wood, 108 × 90 × 66 in. (274.3 × 228.6 × 167.6 cm)

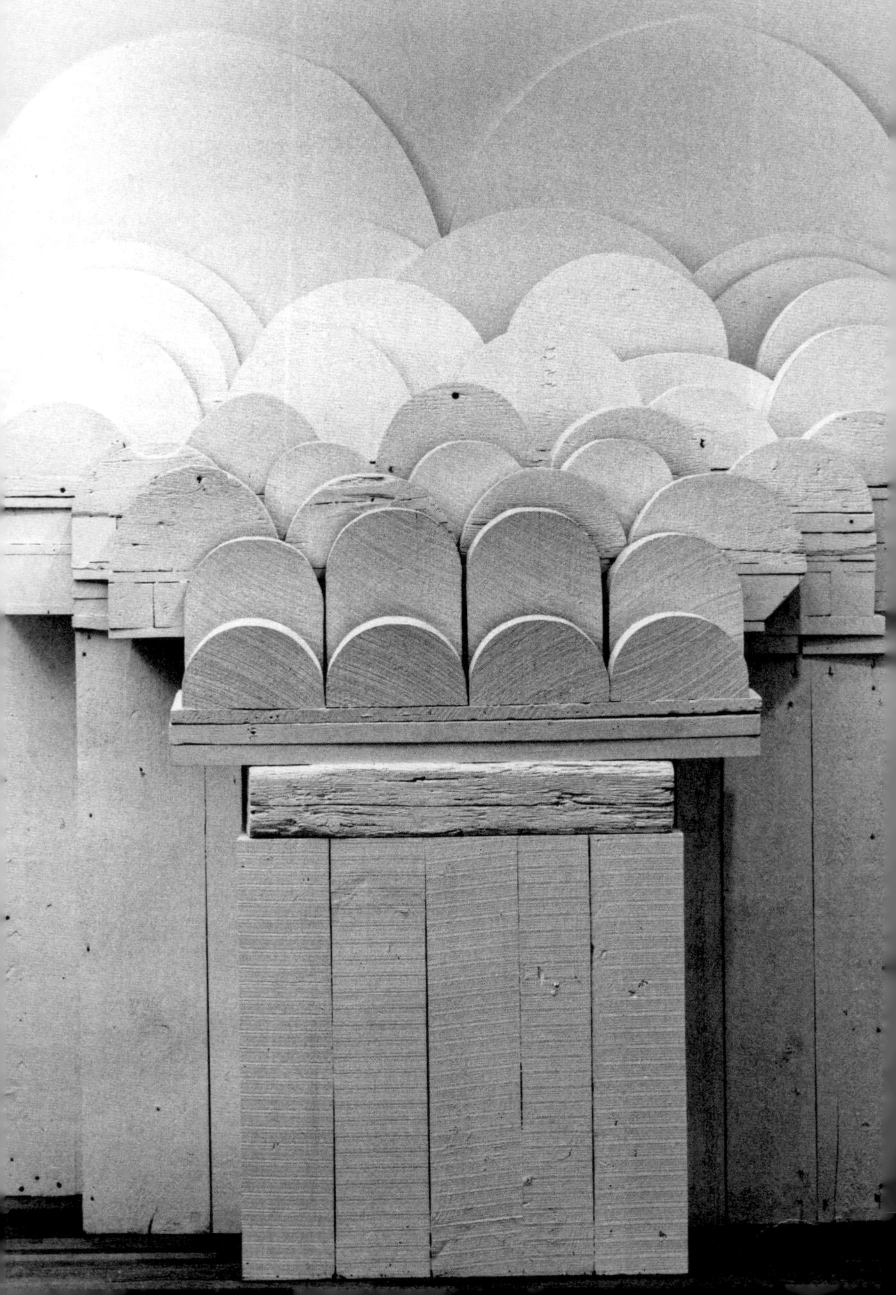

majesty of *Clouds and Caverns* is matched in *Partial Recall* (1979), a construction of white wooden forms–hills? people? tombstones?–that rise and enlarge as they recede. “After so much emotion,” Bourgeois wrote of these abstract altars, “they represent a search for, if not peace, actually forgiveness or forgetfulness.”

Of course, no form in Bourgeois's world has a fixed or final use. Her curves are less like words than syllables that she ceaselessly recombines to say what the moment demands. In a remarkable page from *The Insomnia Drawings* (1994–95; p. 59, bottom left), she effectively turns *Partial Recall* upside down, transforming the shadows between the scalloped forms into anxious volcanic peaks. The same shapes, in a page from her fabric book *Ode à la Bièvre*, become trees by a river again, as Bourgeois uses her own old garments to piece together a landscape of memory.

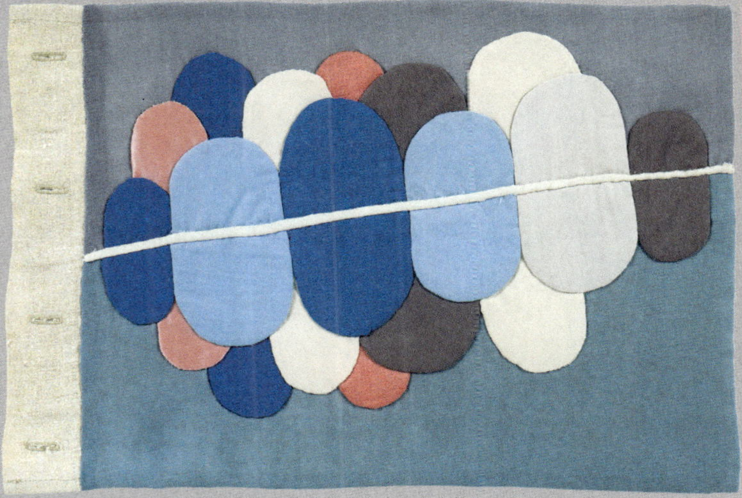

Ode à la Bièvre (detail), 2002. Fabric and lithograph book, 25 pages, each 11 × 15½ in. (27.9 × 39.4 cm)

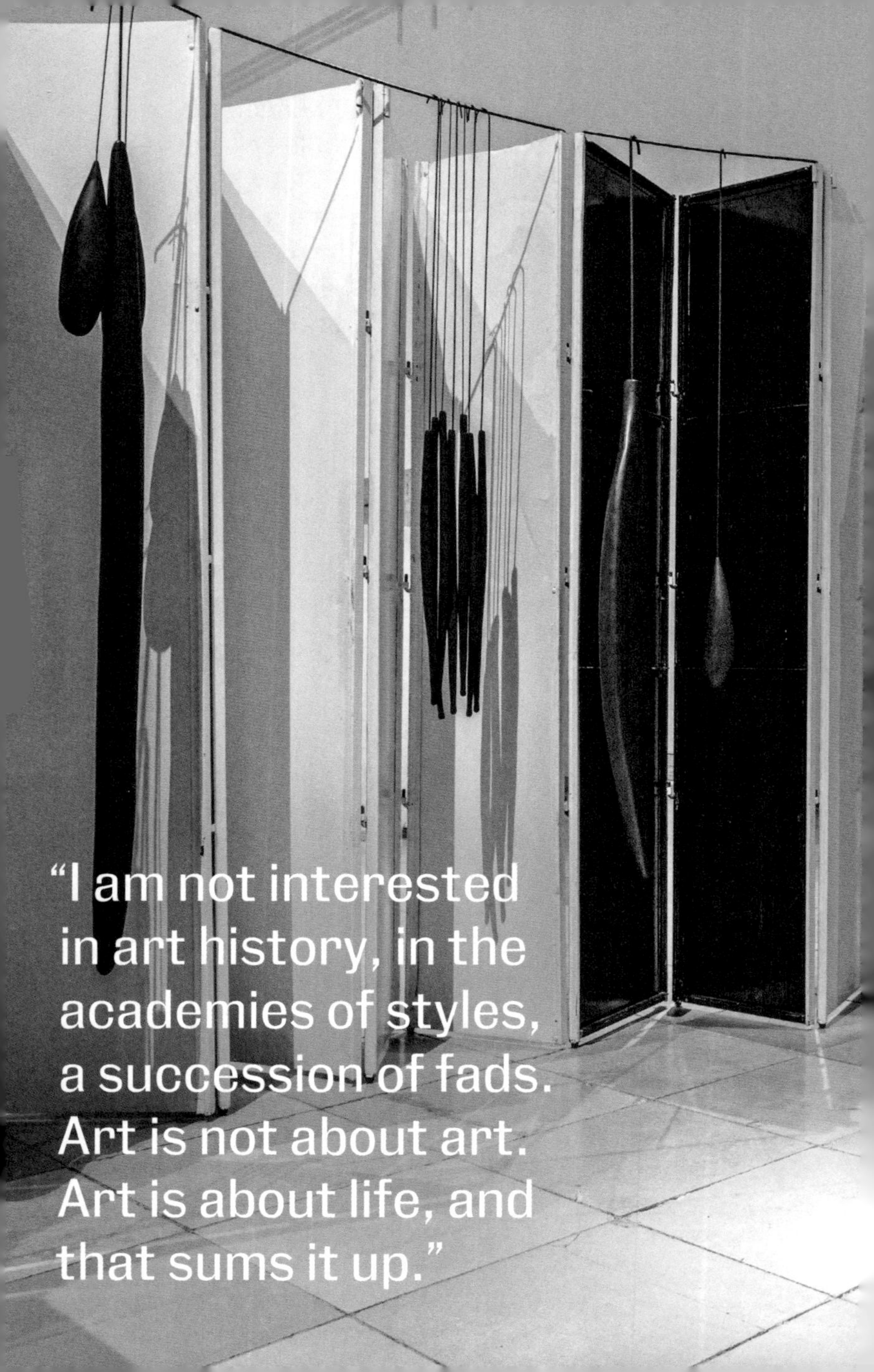

“I am not interested in art history, in the academies of styles, a succession of fads. Art is not about art. Art is about life, and that sums it up.”

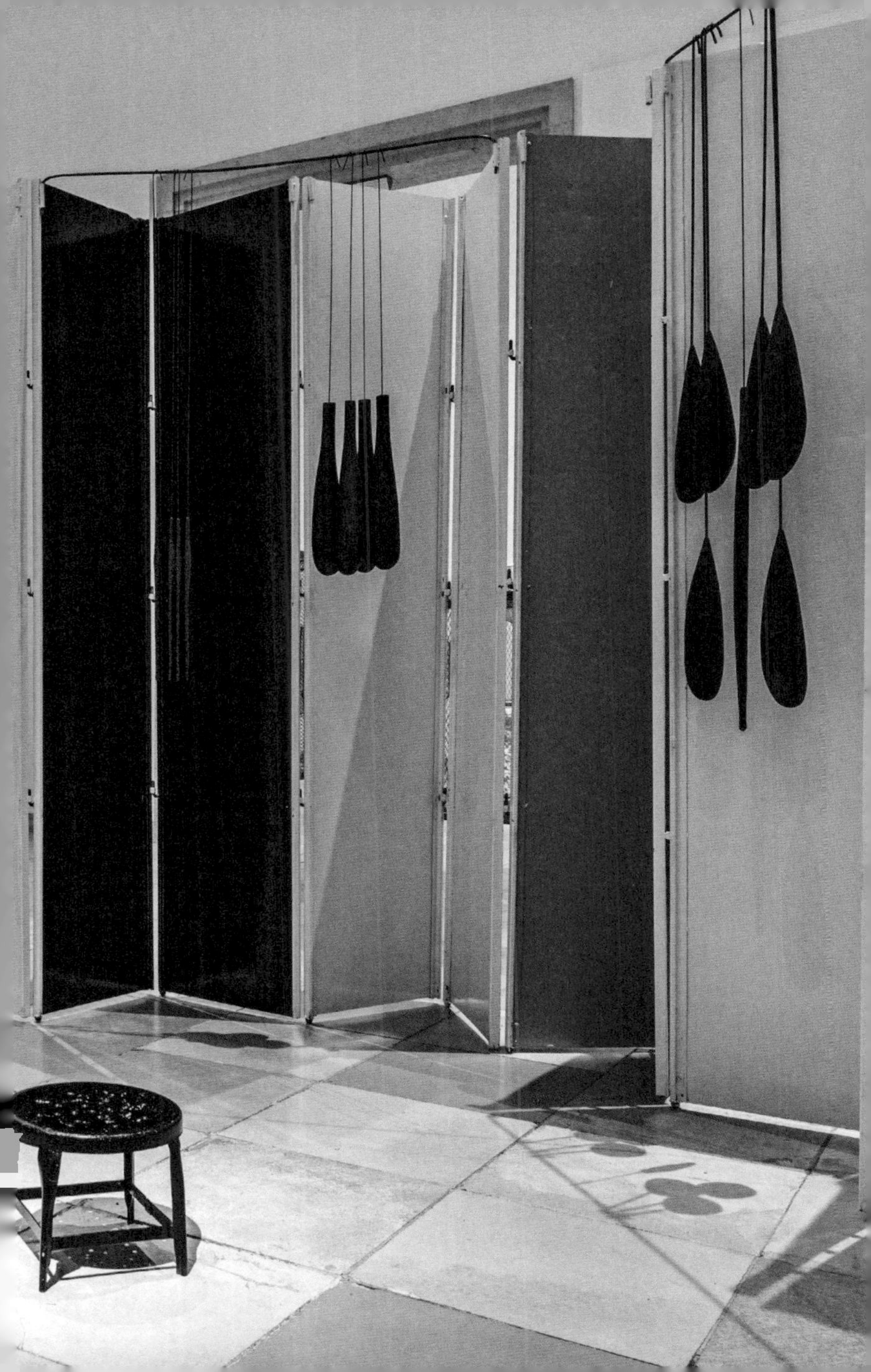

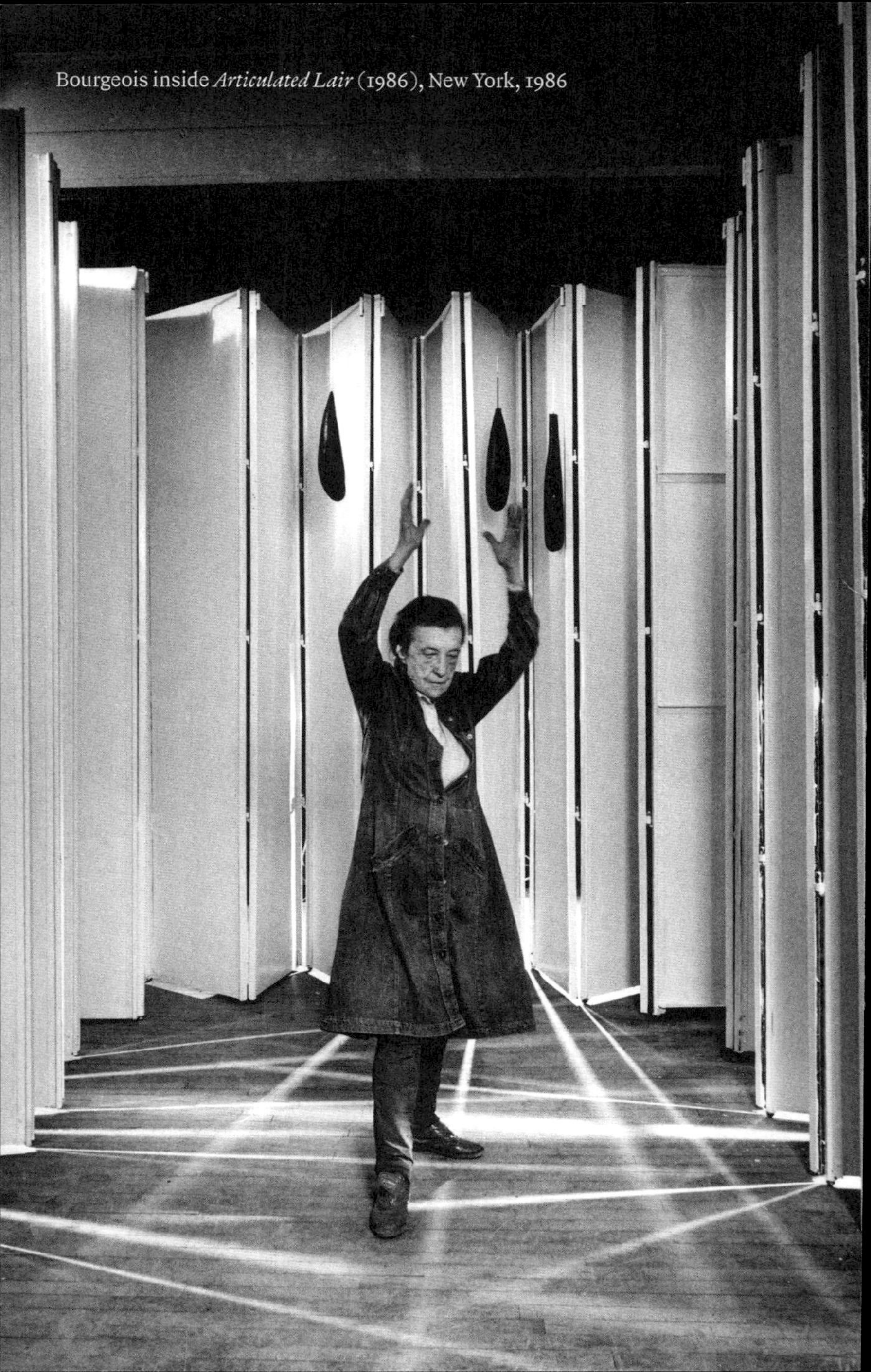

Bourgeois inside *Articulated Lair* (1986), New York, 1986

Her Own Architecture

The energies that were stirring in Bourgeois's installations of the 1970s found space to grow in 1980. After more than forty years of creating art in small rooms and her basement studio, Bourgeois moved her main sculptural practice into a vast and labyrinthine former sewing factory at 475 Dean Street in Brooklyn. This space became the engine room for one of contemporary art's extraordinary late flourishings.

The industrial warehouse, with its multiple entries and ranks of fluorescent lights, was unsettling at first for Bourgeois, who remarked at the time that a small turntable under a spotlight was all she required to make sculpture. The factory was soon serving its purpose, however, as a depot and sorting house for a lifetime of sculptures, which Bourgeois and her assistant, Jerry Gorovoy, had moved from the congested basement and storage spaces of her home in preparation for her retrospective at MoMA, curated by Deborah Wye. (Gorovoy was, like Wye and writer Robert Storr, part of a new generation fascinated by Bourgeois's achievement; over the next three decades, he became her essential supporter, confidant, model, and muse.) Simultaneously, the factory was starting to influence the production of new artwork, not only as a space in which to work at scale but as a source of materials left over from its former life.

As the daughter of tapestry restorers, Bourgeois loved all acts of rescue and repair. And as someone who feared abandonment, she identified passionately with castoffs and remnants. The most striking of her early acts of studio salvage is *Articulated Lair* (1986; pp. 100–101), in which she took long shelves from the factory and arranged them vertically to create a tall, pleated enclosure. A stool sits in this black, white, and blue space, as if waiting for a resident (or penitent), while pendulous black rubber forms, resembling tails and nests, seem to monitor from the peripheries. Bourgeois had been making small *Lairs* since the 1960s, but here she constructed an enclosure large enough to protect—or entrap—a person. This tension between shelter and constraint impels the work that comes next—the series of psychological structures known collectively as the *Cells*.

A cell is a place where a prisoner waits, or where a monk meditates. It also describes a basic biological unit: life at its most elemental. All three senses of the word are in play in the first six *Cells* from 1991, which created an immediate stir when they were exhibited at the Carnegie International in Pittsburgh late that year. Peeling doors and salvaged steel panels formed grimly enticing enclosures. Gaps and windows offered glimpses of objects arranged in psychological standoffs. Old surgical instruments, a carved marble ear, a collection of her empty perfume bottles: we sense that these objects have meaning for Bourgeois, without knowing their exact significance. Although they transmit loneliness, there is also a feeling of rescue and recognition—Bourgeois elevating objects that would otherwise have been discarded but in which she perceived "a little bit of soul."

The *Cells* multiply across the next nineteen years into a series sixty works strong, which range in feeling from sickroom fear to prayerful formality. Bourgeois's childhood is dead center in *Cell (Choisy)* (1990–93), where a raised guillotine threatens (or does it protect?) a pink marble replica of her early family home.

Precious Liquids (1992; p. 108) transforms a cedar water tower salvaged from the roof of the Brooklyn studio building into a psychosexual laboratory or distillery, its barnlike interior furnished with a drenched bed and towers of glassware for the metaphorical circulations of life's fluids. *Cell (Eyes and Mirrors)* (1989–93) and *Cell XV (For Turner)* (2000) have an air of ritual and alchemical experiment, with mirrors surveilling the stone eyes in the former and racked jars of blue liquid in the latter.

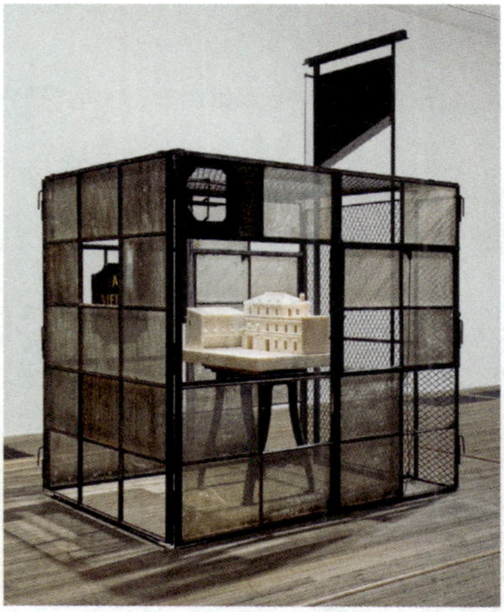

Cell (Choisy), 1990–93. Marble, metal, and glass, 120½ × 67 × 95 in. (306.1 × 170.2 × 241.3 cm)

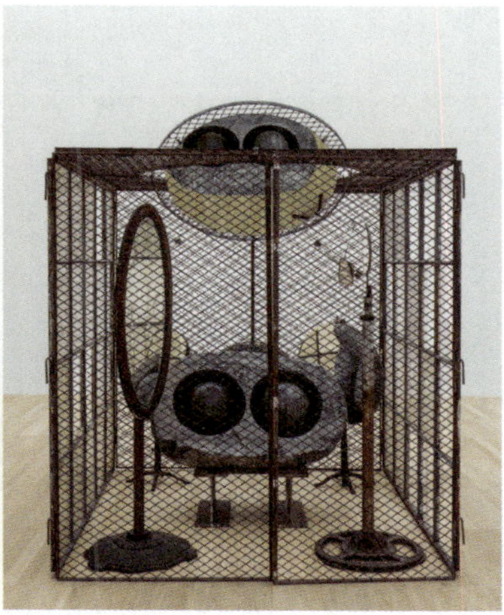

Cell (Eyes and Mirrors), 1989–93. Marble, mirrors, steel, and glass, 93 × 83 × 86 in. (236.2 × 210.8 × 218.4 cm)

If most of the *Cells* can be thought of as separate scenes, then *Passage Dangereux* (1997; pp. 106–7) is a work in several acts. Its linked steel chambers are crammed almost manically with found and memory-laden objects. Intriguing souvenirs of Bourgeois's past mingle with objects you're not sure you should be looking at. The story laid out room by room is one of dawning emotional and sexual awareness,

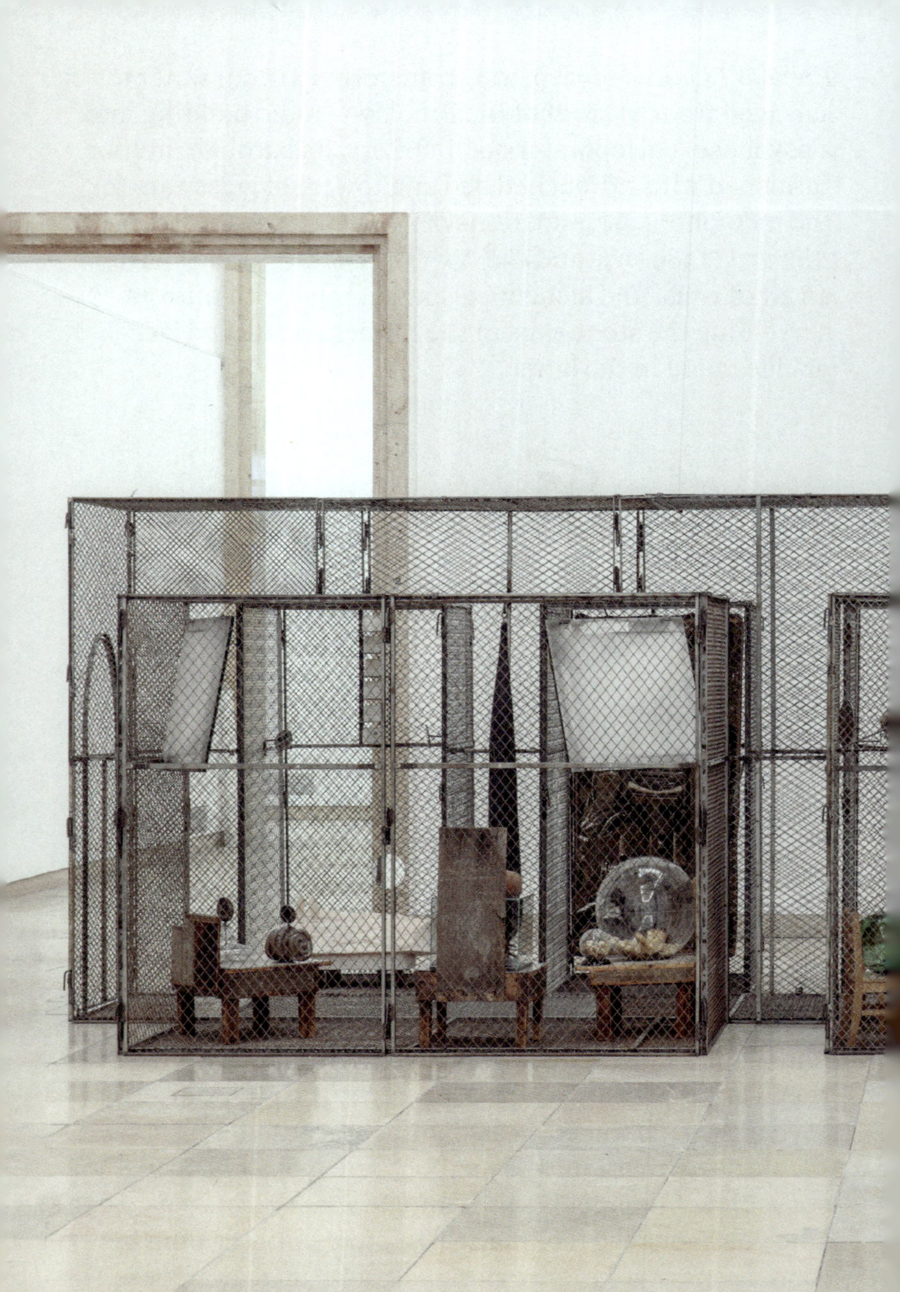

Passage Dangereux, 1997. Metal, wood, tapestry, rubber, marble, steel, glass, bronze, bones, flax, and mirrors, 104 × 140 × 345 in. (264.2 × 355.6 × 876.3 cm)

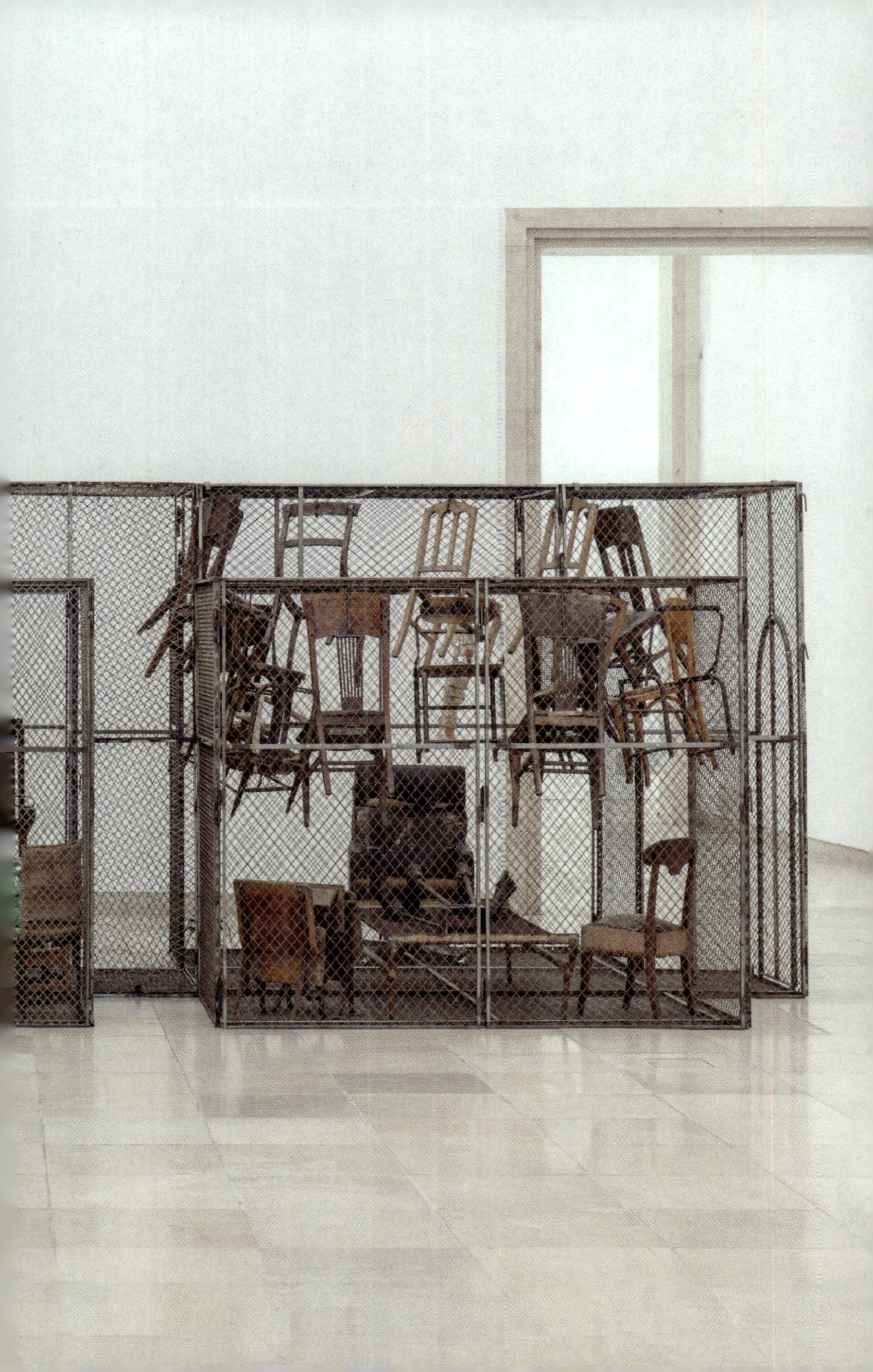

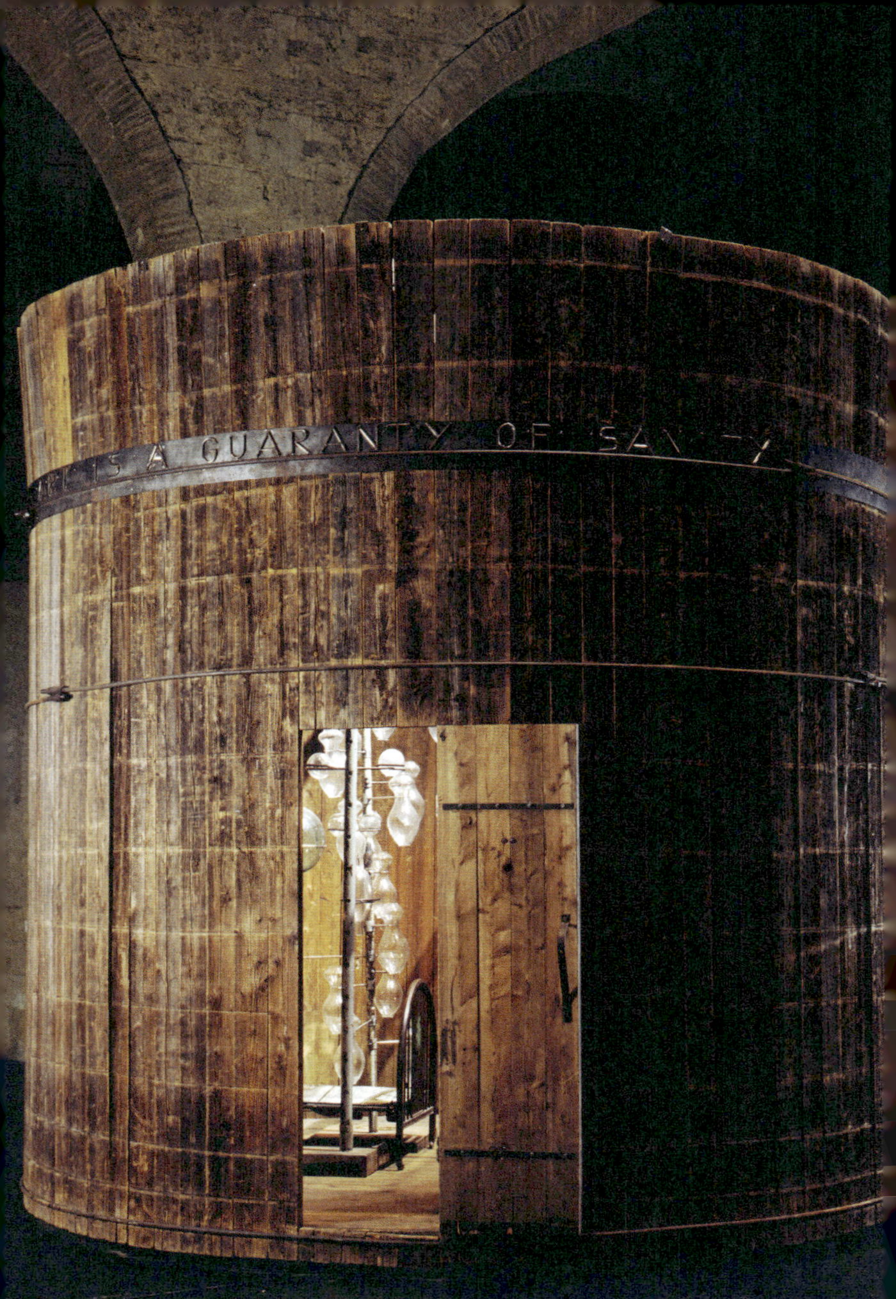

Precious Liquids, 1992. Wood, metal, glass, alabaster, rubber, fabric, embroidered fabric, water, and electric light, $167\frac{1}{2} \times 175\frac{1}{4} \times 175\frac{1}{4}$ in. ($425.5 \times 445.1 \times 445.1$ cm)

as experienced by a young girl who may be the artist herself. Here, for instance, are suspended chairs like those her father hung from the beams of an attic in her childhood home. Here are shirt cuffs inscribed with her father's name, and a bottle of Shalimar, her favorite perfume.

It is possible to track the symbolic significance of each object (diligent interpreters have done so). But what stays with a viewer, more than this-for-that meanings, is the gritty materiality of these elements, from the yellowing presence of bones in a bowl to the gut-wrenching coldness of copulating steel legs. We have stumbled, it seems, into some basement or backroom of the psyche, where Bourgeois is simultaneously storing up and ridding herself of her memories. As well as contemplating the memories and feelings that these objects evidently hold for the artist, our task as viewers is to reckon with the associations they may release in us. Forgotten scents, remembered fears—take the journey, if you're ready.

"I wanted to create my own architecture," Bourgeois said, "and not depend on the museum space." It is thrilling to think of all sixty-plus *Cells* as connected rooms in a twisting memory palace. Visitors to the studio when many *Cells* were in progress received glimpses of this larger order. Bourgeois herself acknowledged the effect in a note from this time: "The studio is the work of art I am just the intermittent visitor."

"I Am an Existential Maker"

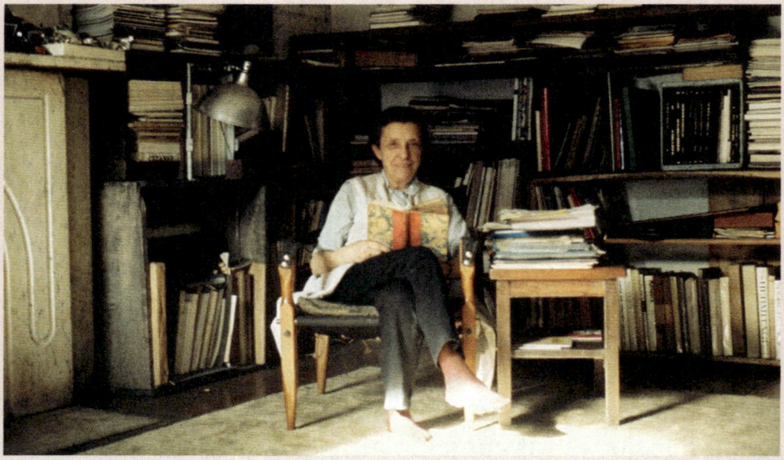

Bourgeois at home, New York, 1976

Bourgeois's sharp mind and contrarian spirit made her skeptical of groups and movements. Having battled through doubt to find her path in a monolithically male art world, she was unwilling to surrender her identity to any "ism" or authority. The Surrealists who arrived in New York during World War II inspired special irritation for this reason: "I objected to their lordly manner, to their success, to their pontificality." A lifelong feminist, Bourgeois participated in the women's art movement of the 1970s but bristled at being elevated as a role model or forebear. "I am not interested in being a mother," she explained. "I am still a girl trying to understand myself."

Bourgeois did feel a deep affinity, however, with one mid-century intellectual movement—Existentialism, which emerged in France during World War II. Formed in the writings of Jean-Paul Sartre, Simone de Beauvoir, and (Bourgeois's favorite) Albert Camus—who, despite the Existentialist thematics of his work, described his own philosophy as Absurdist—Existentialism was less an artistic style than an ethos for reckoning with modern uncertainty. Confronted with a war-shattered world where old gods and authorities had failed, the Existentialists asserted each person's responsibility to seek shared meaning and connection in the face of the absurd.

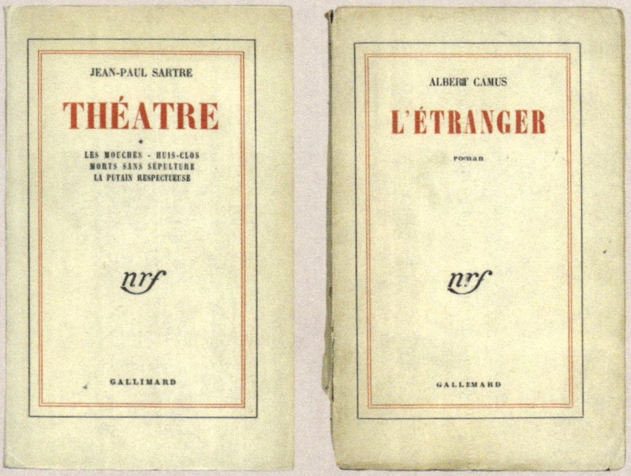

Bourgeois's copies of Jean-Paul Sartre's *Théâtre* (Paris: Gallimard, 1947) and Albert Camus's *L'Étranger* (Paris: Gallimard, 1942)

Jean-Paul Sartre (1905–1980)
Sartre emerged as Existentialism's foremost public philosopher soon after the end of World War II, when he delivered his 1945 lecture "Existentialism Is a Humanism" to huge crowds in Paris. His famous assertion that humans are "condemned to be free" points to Existentialism's appeal for Bourgeois. A philosophy that emphasized the daunting moral burden that comes with human agency was unsuited to gurus and acolytes.

In 1945, Bourgeois included Sartre alongside other anti-Nazi writers and artists in *Documents France 1940–1944: Art–Literature–Press of the French Underground*, an exhibition she organized at Norlyst Gallery in New York. Four decades later, as she embarked on her intensely theatrical installations of the 1980s, her thoughts circled back to Sartre's wartime play *No Exit* (1944). Her installation *Articulated Lair* (1986; pp. 100–101), she told friend and biographer Robert Storr, was like the set of Sartre's play—the angular room, laden with "booby traps," in which three damned souls realize they're trapped forever.

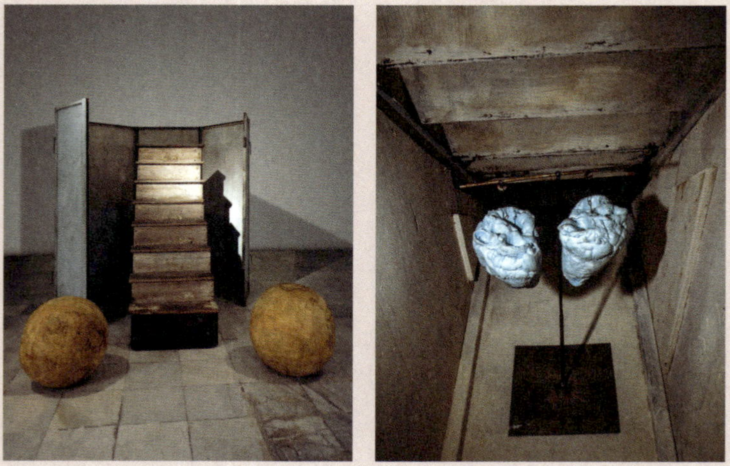

No Exit, 1989. Wood, painted metal, and rubber, 82½ × 84 × 96 in. (209.6 × 213.4 × 243.8 cm). Detail, right

Three years later, Bourgeois created an installation named *No Exit* (1989), which is less a homage to Sartre than a restaging of his question: Who would or could you live with forever? Two wooden spheres that recall Sisyphus and his burden (see Albert Camus, p. 114) flank wooden stairs that lead seemingly to nowhere. Within them is a secret: a small wooden door set into a closet at their rear opens to reveal two suspended hearts cast in blue rubber. The most famous line in Sartre's play declares that "Hell is other people." Bourgeois felt differently, as her two hearts affirm: "I say that Hell is the absence of others."

Simone de Beauvoir (1908–1986)
There are striking parallels between Bourgeois's and Beauvoir's early lives. Bourgeois said of her "I feel like a sister." Both were born into prosperous Parisian families; both adored learning and obtained their *baccalauréat*, a qualification that had only recently been opened to female students; and both felt pulled between the conflicting examples of an individualistic father and steadfast mother. For Beauvoir, this "imbalance, which made my life a kind of endless disputation," was the reason she became a thinker and writer. Bourgeois, similarly, regarded the tension between her father's emotionalism and her mother's rationality as a key to her life in art: "I am torn apart between the two."

Bourgeois read Beauvoir ("what she says is true," she remarked) and invoked the title of her 1945 play *The Useless Mouths* to describe her father's supercilious attitudes toward women. But her connection with Beauvoir lies less in specific references than in their shared trajectories as feminists and Existentialists—radical daughters who transformed their experience of contradiction into bracing thought and electrifying images. In the same postwar period during which Beauvoir was writing *The Second Sex* (1949), her mighty repudiation of "the eternal feminine," Bourgeois was creating the *Femme Maison* paintings and drawings. Clamped inside architectural structures, her "women houses" are quite literally "shut up in the home." For Beauvoir, this physical fact meant that "woman cannot herself establish her existence," and Bourgeois's thwarted, claustrophobic images speak to Beauvoir's description of its consequence: "Since woman is destined to be possessed, her body must present the inert and passive qualities of an object."

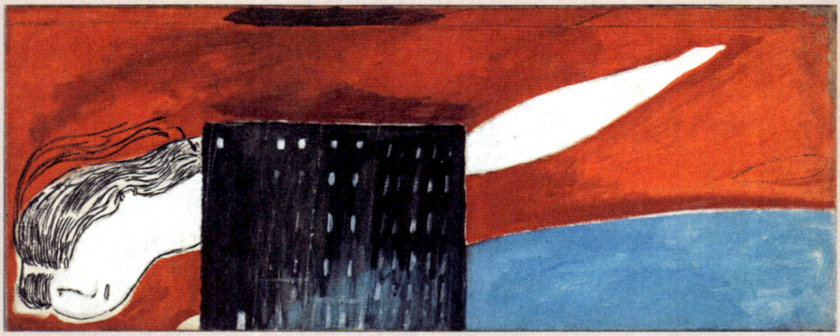

Fallen Woman (Femme Maison), 1946–47. Oil on linen, 14 × 36 in. (35.6 × 91.4 cm)

Albert Camus (1913–1960)

Algerian-born Camus, who by the 1940s was living in Paris and active in the Resistance, explored the challenge of persisting in a godless world in his 1942 essay on Sisyphus, the mythic figure who rolls his boulder up a mountain each day. In Camus's telling, Sisyphus finds a disillusioned happiness in his daily struggle: "The struggle itself towards the heights is enough to fill a man's heart."

Bourgeois described her emotional struggles in Sisyphean terms: "I am inhabited by a kind of boulder inside me that pushes me this way and that way, and it is made of existential anxiety." She saw artmaking, similarly, as a paradoxical climb—an act of absurd and necessary persistence that resumed each day in the studio.

A ferocious desire for resolution drove each new attempt, but each resolution was only temporary, so the next day involved another climb, a repetition that might lead to discovery. To be truthfully unconsoled—to know oneself—was preferable to false solace. A perverse strength and even transcendence came from one's refusals and repudiations.

In the same spirit of bleak hopefulness, Bourgeois often mentioned the dog from Camus's 1942 novel *The Stranger*—an abject creature so mistreated by its owner that it flees, leaving its former tormentor distraught. Camus's bitter little parable clearly held a difficult truth about love for Bourgeois, who offered it as an allegory of her father's relationship with her and of her own "tough love" for her art. Marked with a tick in another of her books by Camus is the line "Art is the distance that time gives to suffering."

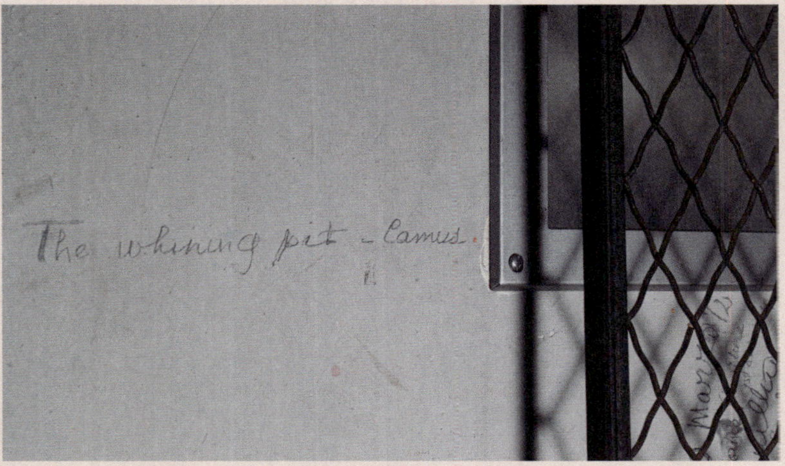

Reference to Camus written by Bourgeois on the wall of her home studio, New York. The phrase may relate to the character Salamano and his whining dog in *L'Étranger*.

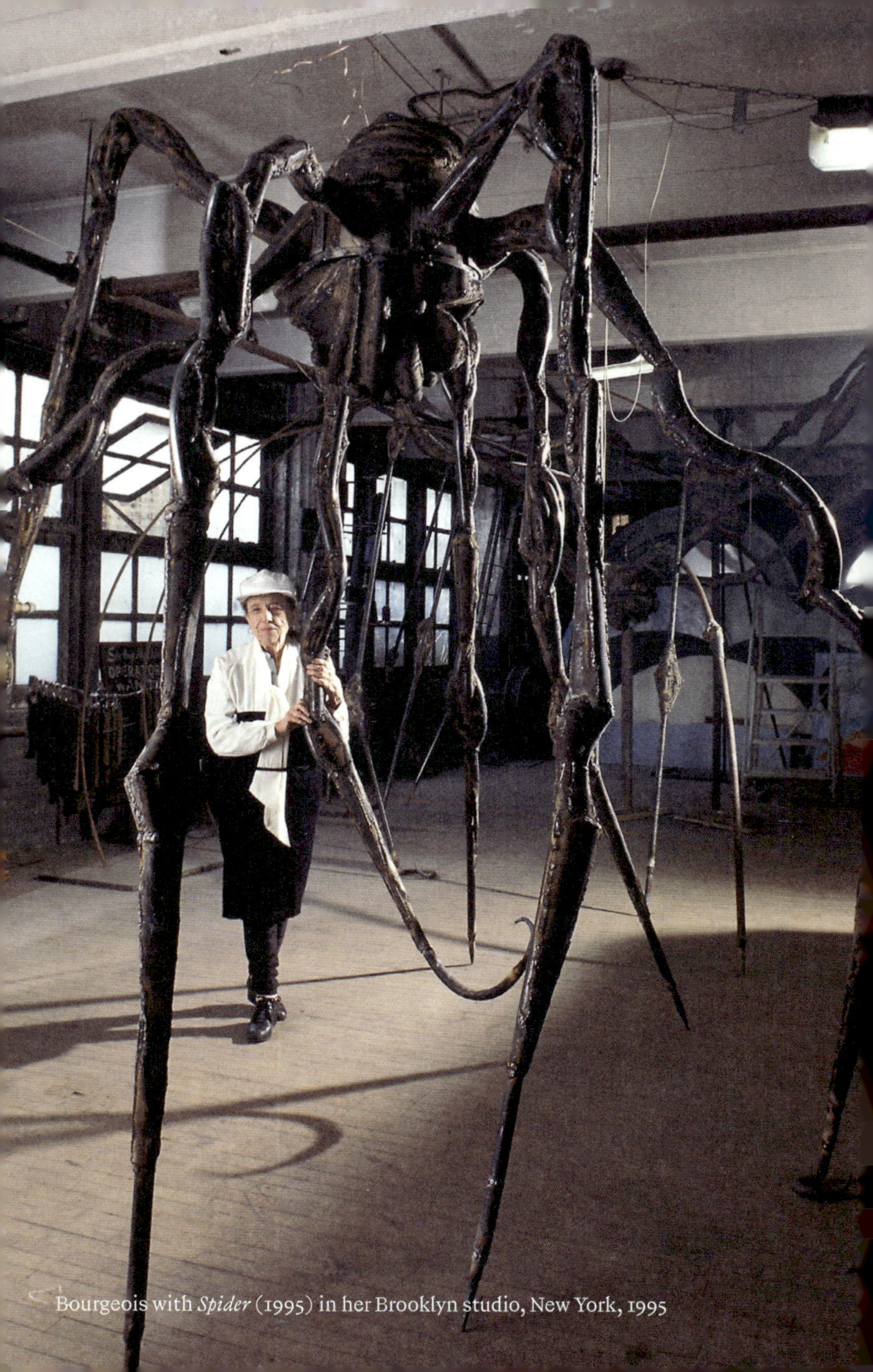

Bourgeois with *Spider* (1995) in her Brooklyn studio, New York, 1995

Spiders

In 1994, a new creature unfolded from the industrial clutter of Bourgeois's Brooklyn studio. It had been glimpsed long before, in a 1947 drawing of a Cyclops-eyed spider with a furry torso. But the drawing hardly readies a viewer for the first of Bourgeois's steel spiders—a nine-foot-high terror with a steel-mesh torso and legs like articulated spears.

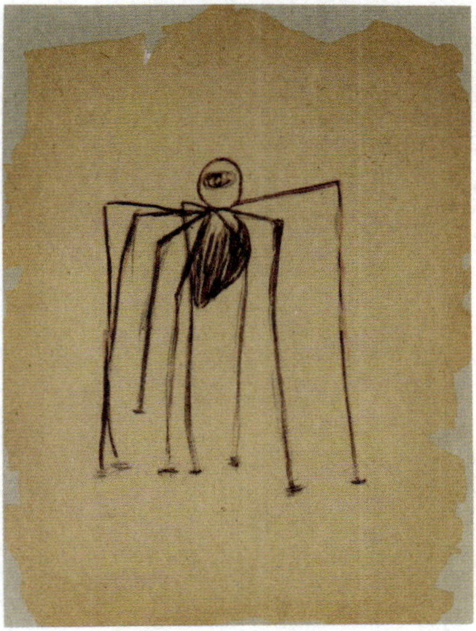

Spider, 1947. Ink and charcoal on paper, 11½ × 8¾ in. (29.2 × 22.2 cm)

This first spider was, like most of Bourgeois's works at this time, born from what was left behind; she made the early spiders from steel pipes, tubing, and other relics from the studio's previous life as a factory (one even has an old bowling ball for a head, with the two finger holes as close-set eyes; p. 118, bottom). Imaginatively speaking, the spiders are also made from pieces of Bourgeois's past; their bodies sometimes look like 1960s *Lairs*, and their legs recall her slim, pointed *Personages*.

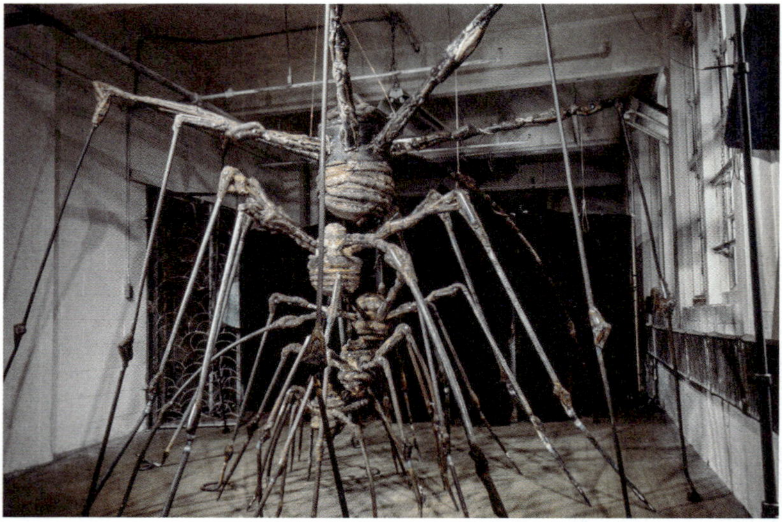

The Nest, 1994. Steel, 101 × 189 × 158 in. (256.5 × 480.1 × 401.3 cm)

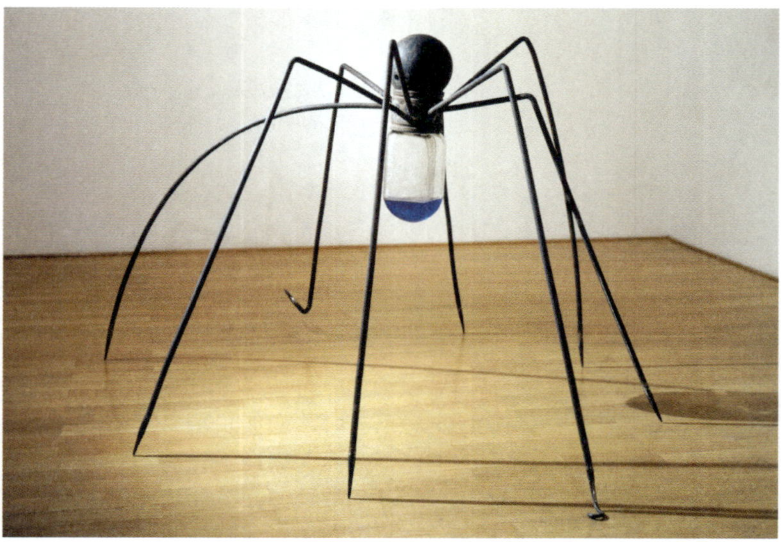

Spider, 1994. Steel, glass, water, and mixed media, 45¾ × 78 × 68 in. (116.2 × 198.1 × 172.7 cm)

Over the next decade, spiders vast and small scuttled from the Brooklyn studio and foundry out into the world. Along the way, they attracted many disquisitions on myths and cultural narratives of the spider, among them the tale of the weaver Arachne, who, after her suicide, became a spider. These tales were entwined, in turn, with the stories that Bourgeois told of the spider, in which the creature is cast as a manifestation of her mother, Joséphine: rational, reasonable, patient.

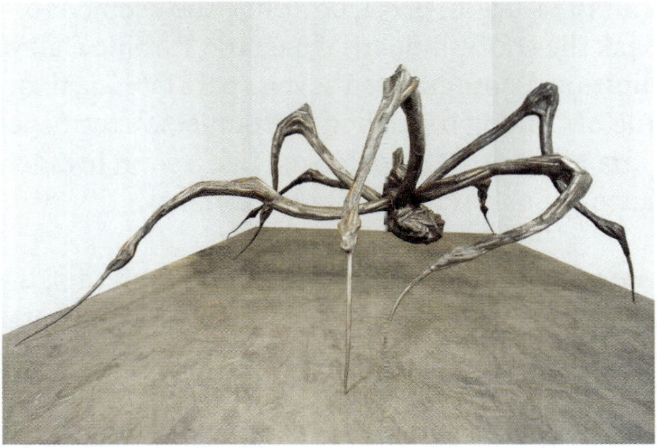

Crouching Spider, 2003. Bronze, silver nitrate patina, and stainless steel, 106½ × 329 × 247 in. (270.5 × 835.7 × 627.4 cm)

Meeting Bourgeois's spiders in person is much less reassuring. *The Nest* (1994) is a clustered family of five, whose legs form a horribly dense forest. *Crouching Spider* (2003) is a marvel of coiled menace that seems ready to spring up and stab you. And a much smaller *Spider* from 1994 has scabby welds and burn marks, as if it has come through an apocalypse. Far from seeming neat and restorative, these sculptures are marvelously creepy. All of them are upstaged and outdone by the thirty-foot-high *Maman* (1999; p. 121).

Maman, which means "Mommy," debuted in Tate Modern's Turbine Hall when the museum opened in 2000. Bourgeois, the first artist commissioned for this immense space, marked the moment with a sculpture of a mother. More than that, she gave her matriarch the aggressive strength usually associated with masculine monuments. *Maman* rose on legs of flexed steel plate whose welds suggested veins and tendons. Ten marble eggs were caged in her belly, like bombs waiting to be dropped. Stationed on a platform near the steel-plate towers *I Do*, *I Undo*, and *I Redo* (all 1999–2000; p. 152, bottom), she seemed to bring back the sooty, industrial past the Turbine Hall was rehabilitating. Photographed seven years later against a backdrop of London fog to herald Bourgeois's retrospective at the Tate Modern, *Maman* looked like a sci-fi invader about to advance upon the city and its inhabitants.

But *Maman*'s power is more fundamental than this; it comes from a psychological shift. Spiders inspire outsize fear among humans, but physically they are tiny. The spider's fantasy, as Robert Storr writes, is to become more powerful than those who would destroy it. Bourgeois, who reckoned with her own fears, has made her spider-mother gigantic, granting a small and threatened being all the force it ever dreamed of.

Maman's significance shifts as she travels. In 2024, she was installed above lush green rice paddies in Khao Yai Art Forest, Thailand. There, the heavy-metal intruder became a nature deity, a goddess who appeared to have grown from the landscape.

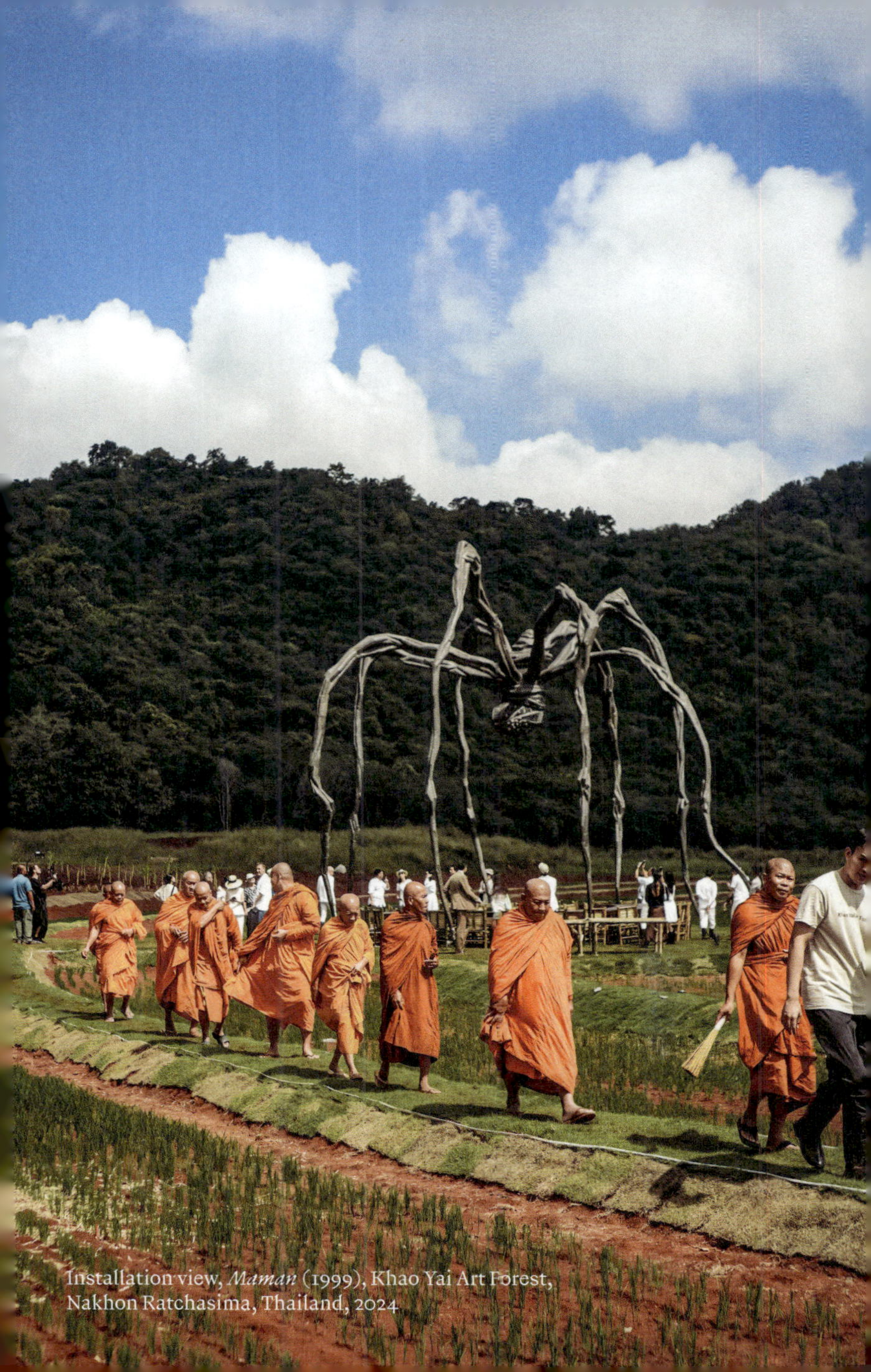

Installation view, *Maman* (1999), Khao Yai Art Forest, Nakhon Ratchasima, Thailand, 2024

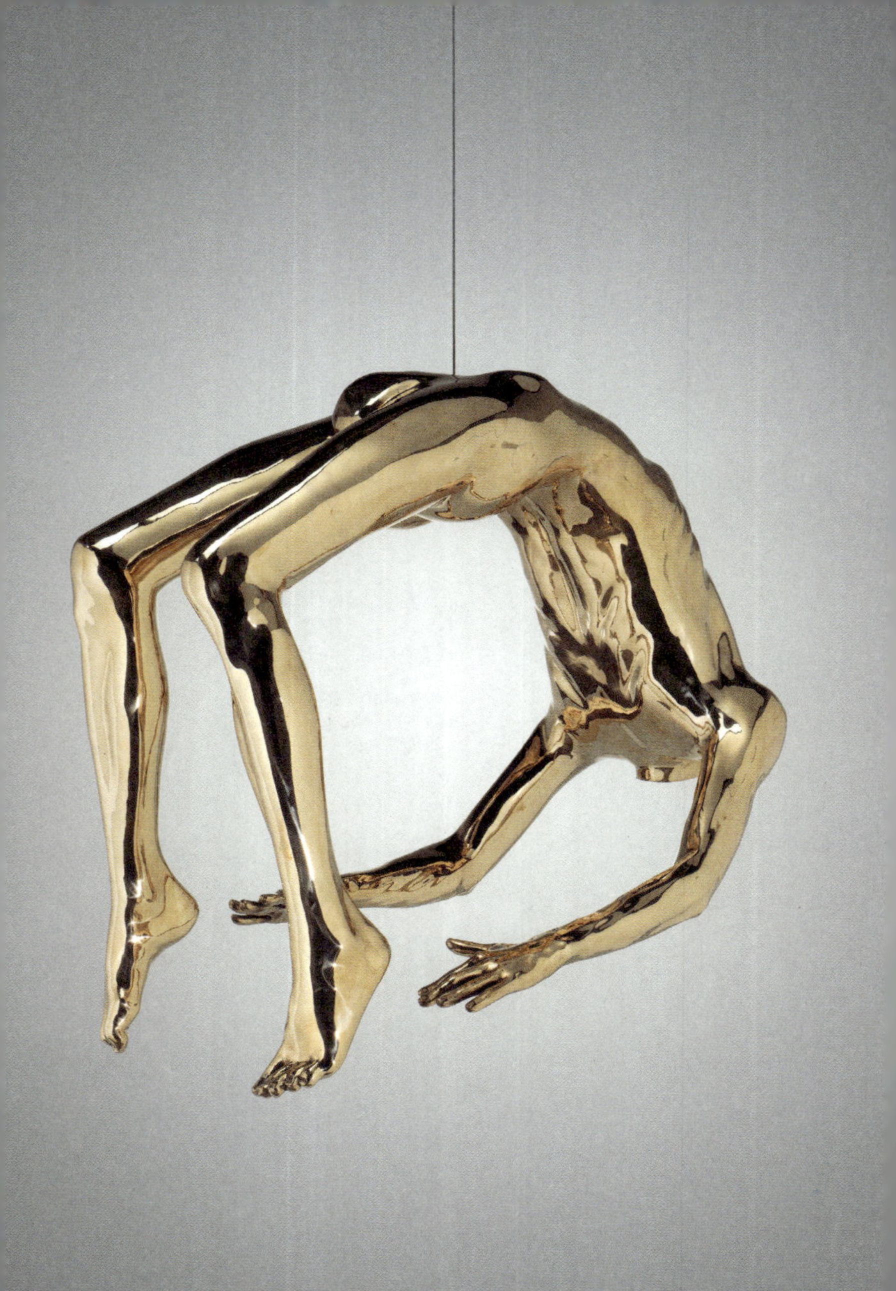

Arch of Hysteria, 1993. Bronze, polished patina, 33 × 40 × 23 in. (83.8 × 101.6 × 58.4 cm)

***Arch of Hysteria* (1993)**

Not the body as it normally appears, but the body altered by emotion. Raised up, supercharged, bent to the point of breaking. Bourgeois is a sculptor of the human figure in extremis, of physical states that communicate psychological ones. Here, she cranks up the tension between form and feeling to its limit. The long-limbed male body, suspended by a wire, arches backward to form a near-circle. Walking around the figure, we sense, in our spines, how painful it would be to do this (Jerry Gorovoy, who modeled for this sculpture, recalls the heat of the plaster as it set around his body). At the same time, we sense the nearness of release—the fingers nearly reach the heels. Bourgeois is responding in part to the idea of the female "hysteric," as embodied in French neurologist Jean-Martin Charcot's photographs of women arcing up from their beds. But *Arch of Hysteria* just as clearly draws power from a tradition of beautiful and harrowed male bodies, notable among them the broken yet radiant figure of Christ in the *Pietà of Villeneuve-lès-Avignon*—a fifteenth-century masterpiece that Bourgeois knew from her time as a guide at the Louvre. *Arch of Hysteria* is an ecstatic body for the late twentieth century, hovering between trauma and transcendence.

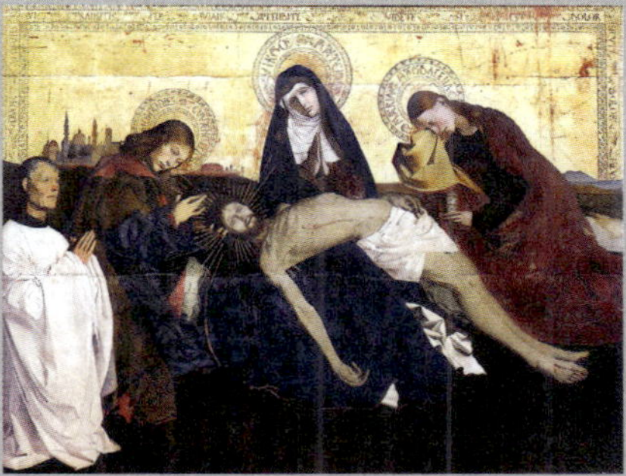

Enguerrand Quarton, *Pietà of Villeneuve-lès-Avignon*, mid-15th century. Oil and gold on wood, 64³⁄₁₆ × 86¼ in. (163 × 219 cm)

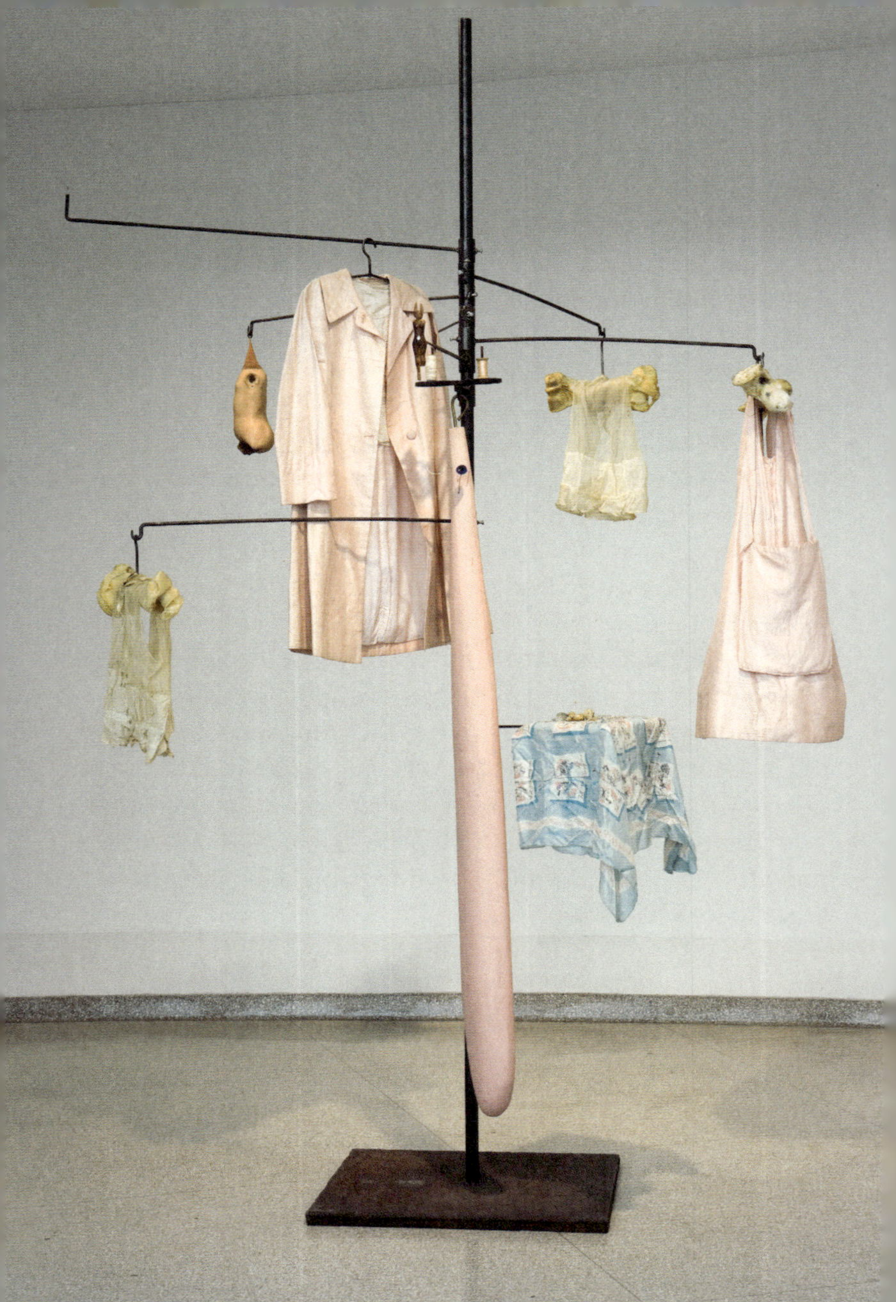

Pink Days and Blue Days, 1997. Steel, fabric, bone, wood, glass, rubber, and mixed media, 117 × 87 × 87 in. (297.2 × 221 × 221 cm)

Fabric Works: An "Unconscious Collection"

In contrast to the basement of Bourgeois's home, which was a place for work, the upper levels were spaces dedicated to memory. Among the things she saved there were clothes and textiles collected across a lifetime. As someone scared of abandonment, she took intense pleasure in holding on to these objects: "It's my past and as rotten as it was I want to take it and hold it tight in my arms."

In 1993, Bourgeois and Gorovoy began to unpack her closets and drawers, bringing out armfuls of garments which they arranged by color and hung from the exposed pipework in her basement. Bourgeois's family connections to tapestry restoration gave her a feeling for the past lives of textiles, and every object in this stockpile connected her physically to pivotal people and moments. Here were Robert's shirts and monogrammed handkerchiefs, her father's starched cuffs and her mother's blouses, clothing worn by her sons when small, and decades of her own garments—an "unconscious collection," as Bourgeois called it, that she now put to use in her art.

The first body of work she created was anything but nostalgic. In a series of "pole pieces" from the mid-1990s, which includes *Pink Days and Blue Days* (1997) and *Untitled* (1996), Bourgeois airs her fabric memories sparingly, selecting family groupings of garments and suspending them from stark steel coatracks and hangers of bone. With their movable arms of differing lengths, these structures resemble crude orreries, but instead of the movement of heavenly bodies, they plot personal distances and proximities. The empty garments move on their own lonely orbits, close but never touching, sometimes accompanied by desolate little figures and counterweights that have the air of talismans. Far from welcoming us into the warmth of an archive, the pole pieces feel scarecrowlike, cautionary.

By contrast, there is an alarming fullness to the second group of works in fabric. Often working with skilled seamstresses, as her mother had in the tapestry workshop, Bourgeois created a family of stitched and stuffed bodies whose softness only sharpens their sting. There are grappling couples (p. 131, bottom), knife women, arched bodies, and a host of upholstered heads. The patching and patterning of these figures often scrambles their sexual and emotional identities. Breasts stare, necks become phallic, and three heads spring from one body. A dark, hectic, and mischievous laughter plays through this body of work, as if Bourgeois is conquering a lifetime's fears by making dummies and mannequins of all of them. Details pierce, like the tiny steel shoes of the frayed odalisque in *High Heels* (1998; p. 131, top). "They say something unsayable," filmmaker Jane Campion observed.

Bourgeois had long been focused emotionally on her relationship with her father. In these late works, this focus shifted to her mother as a mainstay and repairer. Sculpting in fabric was a way to bind herself back to her "best friend," while simultaneously unpicking her own profoundly mixed feelings about motherhood. The mighty *Spider* (1997; p. 128) from the *Cells* is, on one hand, a tribute to Joséphine as weaver and mender, providing her with a place to rest on a throne lined with an old tapestry (Bourgeois recalled Joséphine being at her happiest when sitting and embroidering in the sun). At the same time, this *Cell*, with its tattered tapestry linings, is a moldering memory cage, whose occupant cannot cut the ties to her past, her family, or her responsibilities.

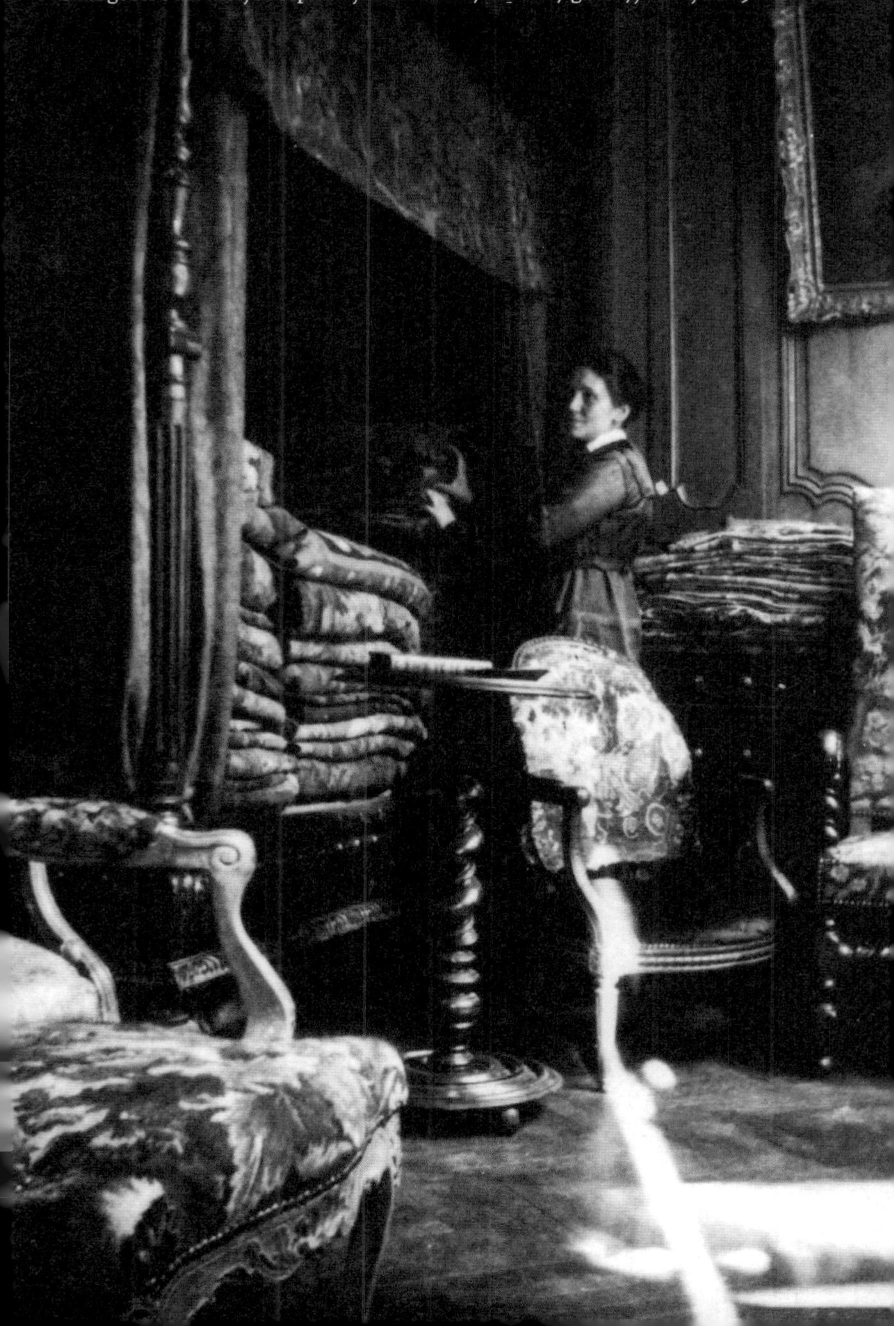

Bourgeois's mother, Joséphine, in the family tapestry gallery, Paris, ca. 1911

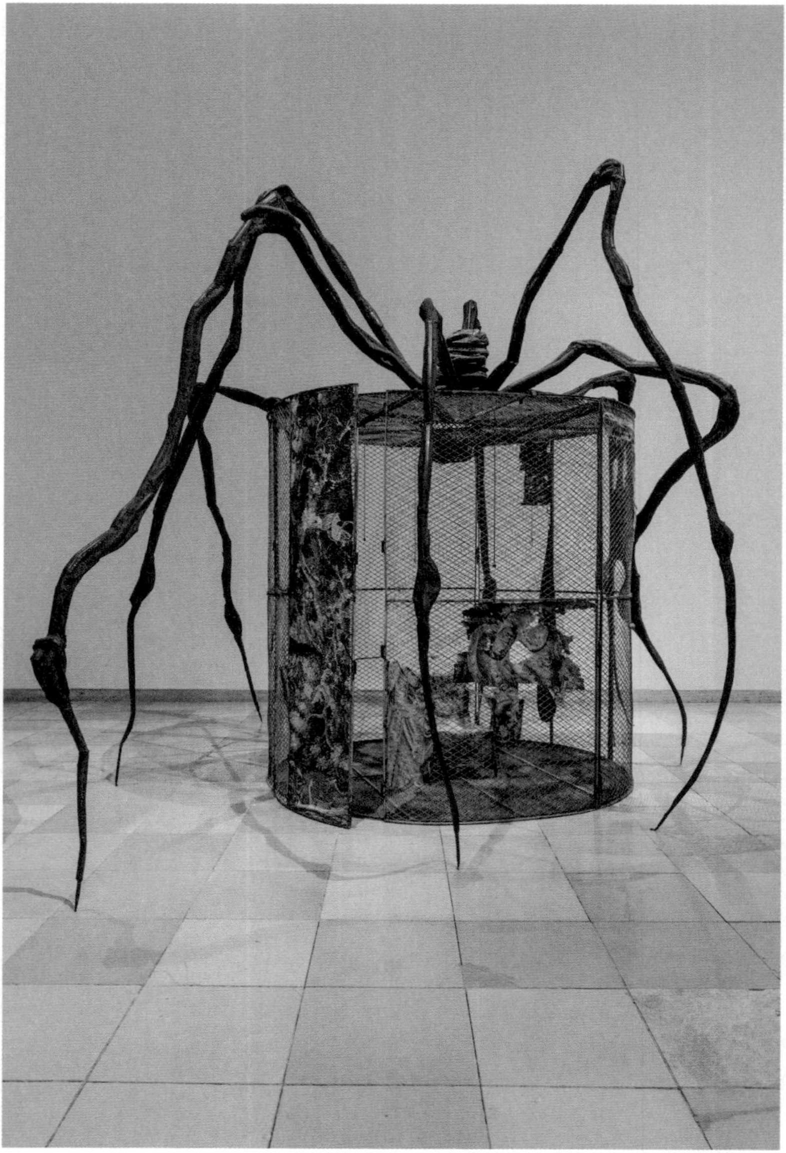

Spider, 1997. Steel, tapestry, wood, glass, fabric, rubber, silver, gold, and bone, 177 × 262 × 204 in. (449.6 × 665.5 × 518.2 cm)

Ambivalence about motherhood runs like a current through Bourgeois's late fabric sculptures, many of which are made more affecting by being small enough to cradle. *Do Not Abandon Me* (1999) is a rough-stitched portrayal of the separation that defines us all at the beginning. The newborn child, though separate from its mother, is still umbilically tethered, and the plea of the title seems to be spoken simultaneously by child and mother. *The Good Mother* (2003), meanwhile, selflessly feeds her threads of milk to a symbolic family of five. But this tiny votive figure is immobilized—tied forever to this place and this function. Her complement in Bourgeois's world of emotional polarities is the cruel-courageous figure of the "bad mother," who turns away from family (breast milk spilling on the ground) toward other forms of creation.

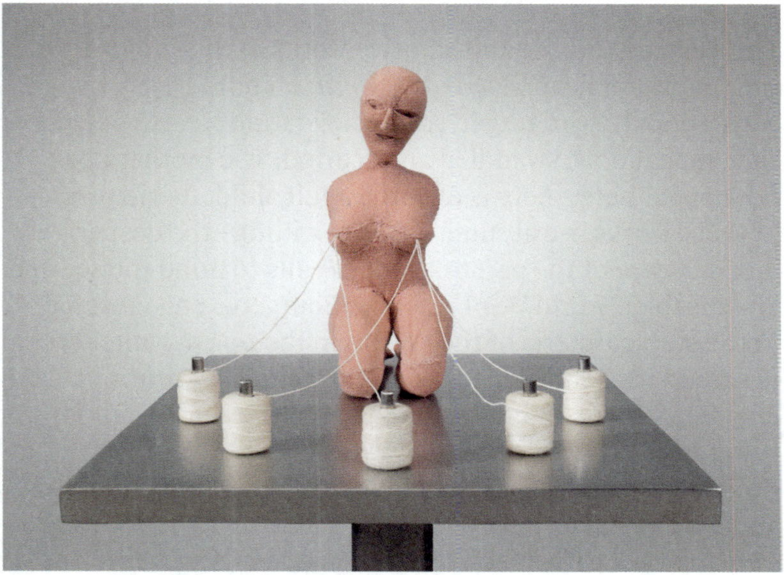

The Good Mother, 2003. Fabric, thread, and stainless steel, 43 × 18 × 15 in. (109.2 × 45.7 × 38.1 cm)

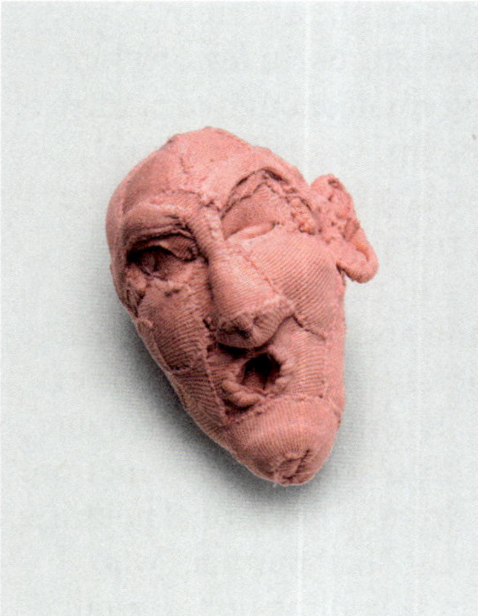

Pierre, 1998. Fabric, 8¾ × 5¾ × 5¾ in. (22.2 × 14.6 × 14.6 cm)

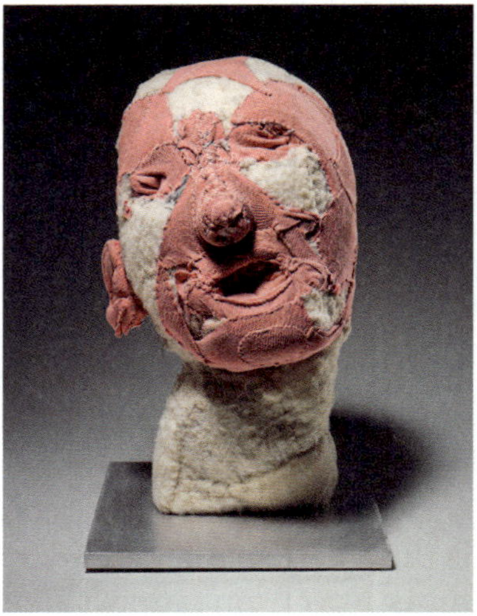

Untitled, 1998. Fabric and stainless steel, 20 × 12 × 13 in. (50.8 × 30.5 × 33 cm)

The most disturbing and emotive works in this group are the sculptural heads *Pierre* and *Untitled* (both 1998), in which prickly stitching in soft jersey fabric creates objects that appear both swaddled and scarred. The mother does not appear here; there is only the adult child. As viewers of these works, we assume—if we're willing—the desperately anxious gaze of the parent. *Untitled* calls to mind the scarred and disabled World War I veterans Bourgeois encountered in the staff cafeteria of the Louvre in the 1930s, while *Pierre* is named for her troubled brother, who was institutionalized and died in 1960. It is a relief to turn to the gentler fabric towers and collages of the following decade, in which Bourgeois—again echoing her mother's efforts as a repairer and pacifier—stacks soft blocks of fabric in nursery colors or rearranges patterned fabrics in mesmerizing webs. To the end, she held to her credo: "I do, I undo, I redo."

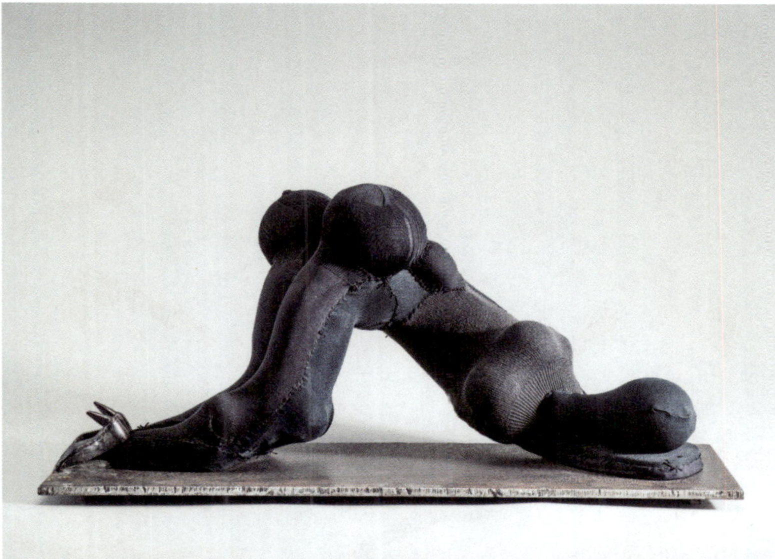

High Heels, 1998. Fabric and steel, 14 × 29½ × 8 in. (35.6 × 74.9 × 20.3 cm)

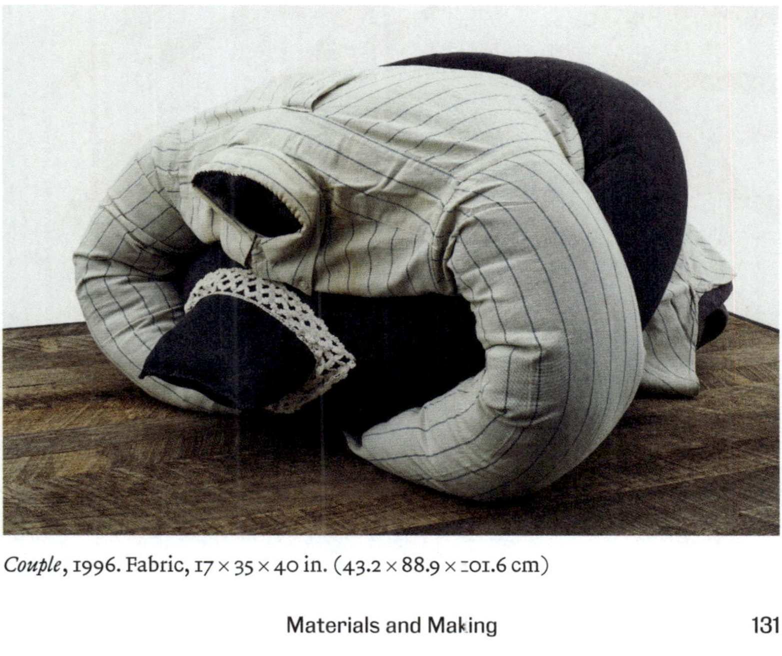

Couple, 1996. Fabric, 17 × 35 × 40 in. (43.2 × 88.9 × 101.6 cm)

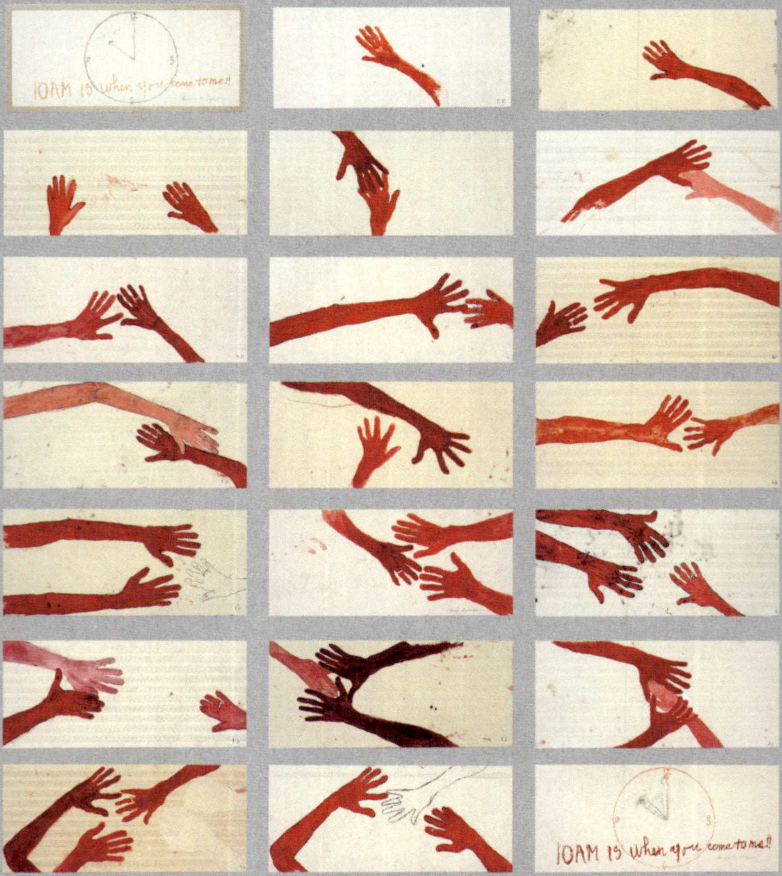

10 AM Is When You Come to Me, 2006. Etching and watercolor on paper, suite of 20, each $14\frac{7}{8} \times 35\frac{3}{4}$ in. (37.8×90.8 cm)

Studio Time
Bourgeois's fears and anxieties arrived unscheduled. There was no telling where or when. The studio and its routines, by contrast, were known and consolingly reliable. During the busy years in the Brooklyn studio, she would often wait on her Chelsea stoop at 10 a.m. for Gorovoy to collect her. After her preferred breakfast of marmalade straight from the jar, the day would begin with purpose.

The Dean Street studio was no hermit's retreat in this period of full-tilt sculptural production. As was the case when Bourgeois worked with craftsmen in Italian workshops and foundries, intense to-and-fro with expert makers was part of her daily round. "I give credit to people who are related to a certain tool, a certain craft," she said in 1993. Welders and foundry workers were among her trusted technical allies, and she spoke with fascinated respect of the stonemason who felt nothing for her art but was passionately interested in what he could achieve with his drill.

Nonetheless, the mornings were semisacred; 11 a.m. was her best time. The din and distraction of construction and welding were contained in the rear rooms of the warehouse. Gorovoy, while also overseeing production, was the protector of Bourgeois's quietude. Interruptions and unplanned "visits" could enrage her; she seldom listened to music or news while working. All this order was maintained, paradoxically, to promote a kind of inner wildness—the freedom to enter the state of deep material play that Bourgeois called "the spell."

The structure of the day mattered even more to Bourgeois in her last decade, when she worked in her parlor at home. Time—the ticking of the mortal clock—became a subject, and even a medium. The portfolios

Dawn (2006), *Hours of the Day* (2006), and *The Waiting Hours* (2009) mark the passing of time page by page, overlaying the cadence of studio days with thoughts of cosmic duration. And time becomes an urgent measure of love and need in *10 AM Is When You Come to Me* (2006; p. 132).

The title refers to the morning hour at which Gorovoy arrived to set the day's work in motion. Across a series of wide sheets of music paper (themselves designed for notating time), Bourgeois's small hands, with their wedding band, reach for and sometimes meet Gorovoy's. Emotional energy, in the form of thickening and thinning red paint, seems to pass between artist and assistant. On other pages, Bourgeois's arms flail alone amid finger trails of paint. The result is both a plea and a tribute to Bourgeois's great friend and supporter—an emotional score in which the consolations of love never quite outrun the fear of separation.

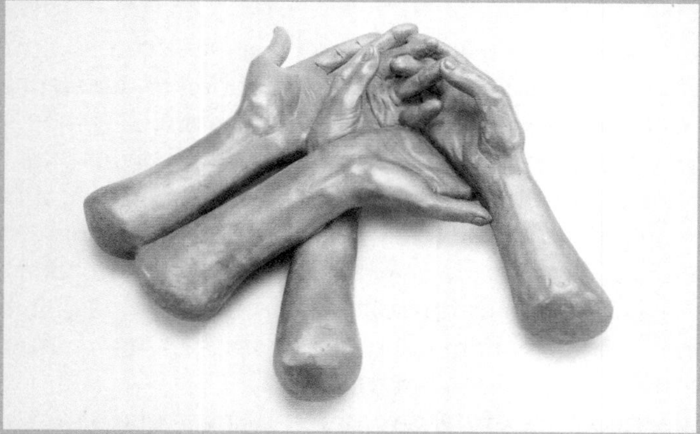

The Welcoming Hands, 1996. Bronze, 6 × 18 × 18 in. (15.2 × 45.7 × 45.7 cm). Opposite, Bourgeois with Gorovoy creating the cast for *The Welcoming Hands* in her Brooklyn studio, New York, 1995

“You are born alone. You die alone. The value of the space in between is trust and love.”

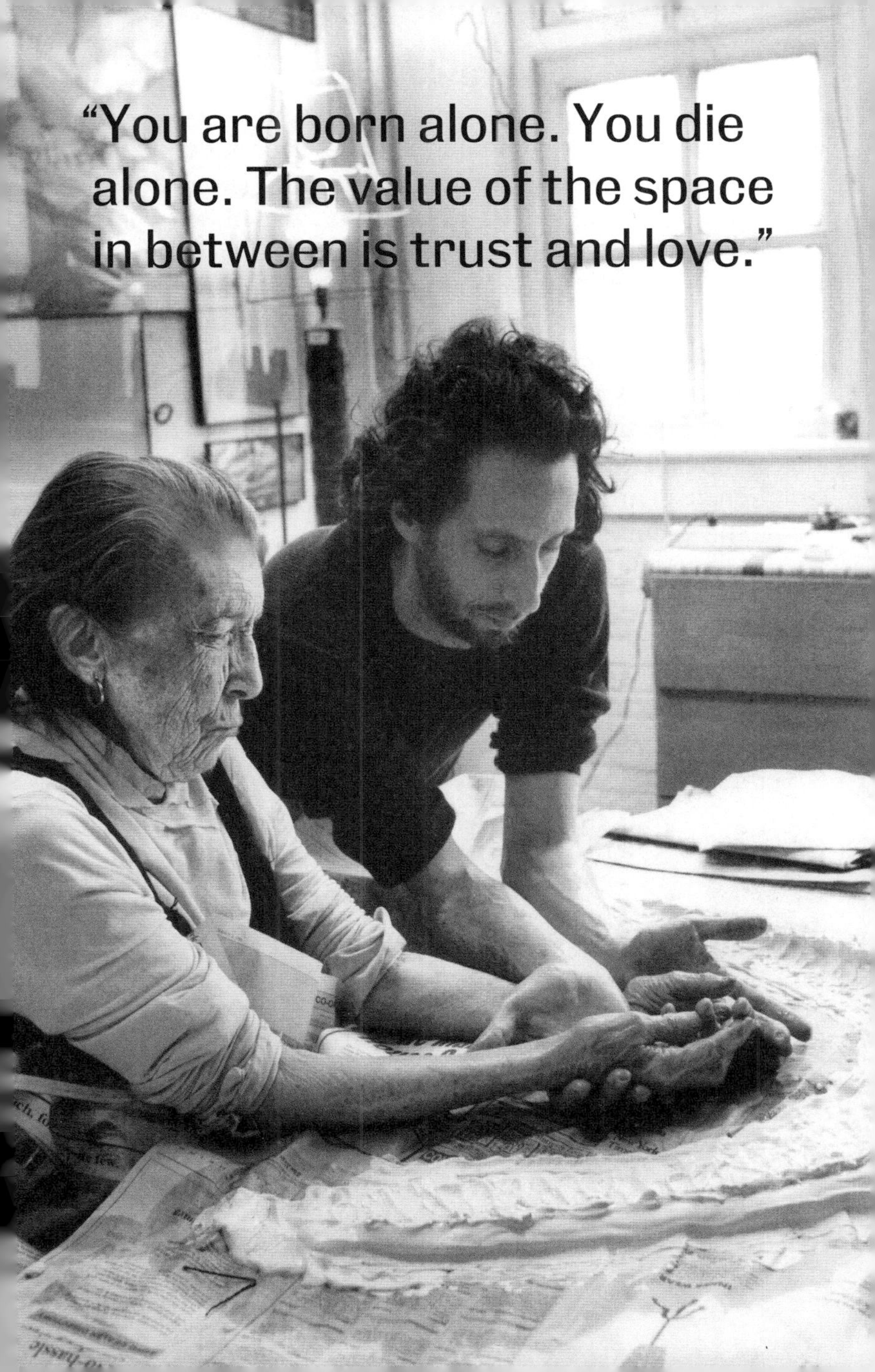

“Alive and Awake”

Some artists become monuments: admired, but only from a distance. Bourgeois is an artist of the opposite kind, still alive for artists today. The multifariousness of her work, its desire for truth, its vital unpredictability—all this has made it urgent and inspiring for subsequent generations.

Richard Serra (US, 1938–2024)
“I feel closeness to the expression of violence in her sculpture and to the acerbity of her writing, and I admire her demonic intelligence. At the same time, her visceral emotionalism unsettles me—the fragmentation of the body, the breasts, the vaginas, the penises, the organs of the body, the amputated legs, arms, hands; then the other trajectory, the need to conjoin opposites, to conjure up disparate elements, to force together male and female, to fuse human and animal.”

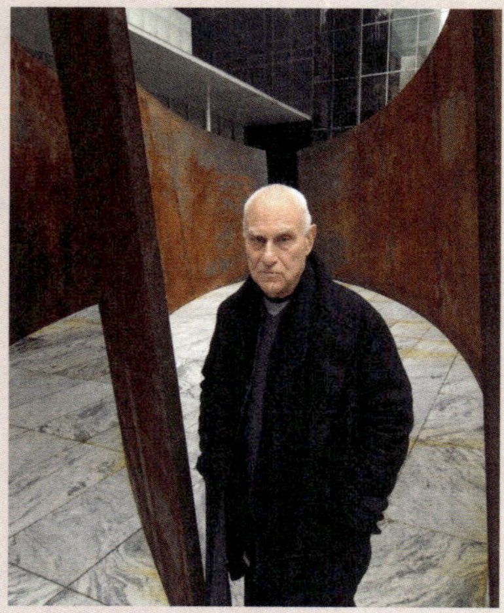

Richard Serra with his work at MoMA, New York, 2007

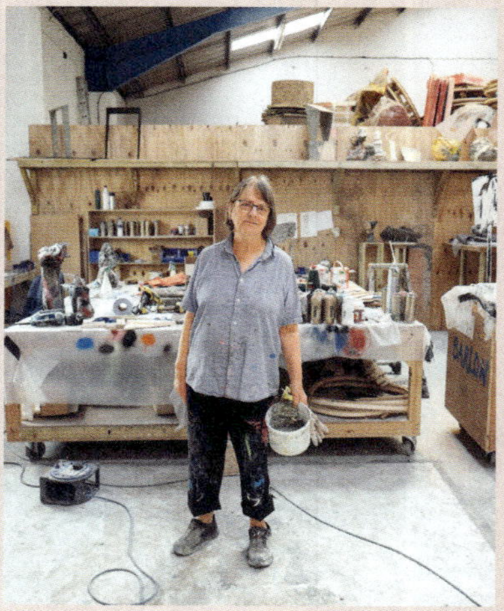

Phyllida Barlow in her studio, Bermondsey, London, 2018

Phyllida Barlow (UK, 1944–2023)
"To me, the great appeal of Louise is the fact that she was inventing with very little, a simple repertoire of shapes, but my God, what invention. In the early works, there's a real stumbling to find out how you make the clay do this, how you make the wax do this. The work *Avenza Revisited II* (1968), with the living presence of her fingers in the plaster. Or *Le Regard* (1963), with latex over fabric and this vicious cut in it. It speaks about a discovery. It's alive and awake."

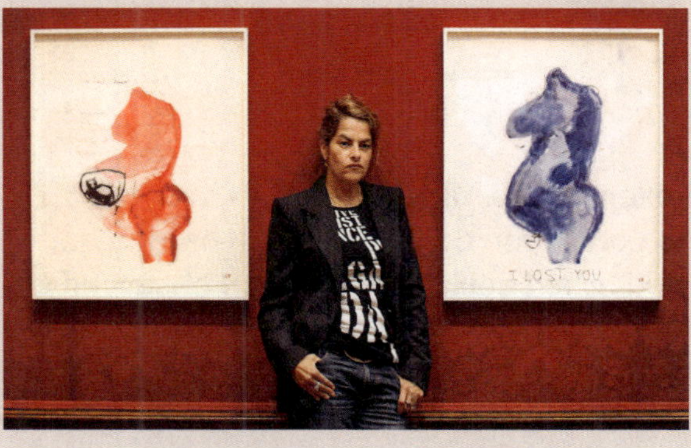

Tracey Emin in the exhibition of works she made in collaboration with Bourgeois, *Do Not Abandon Me*, Hauser & Wirth, London, 2011

Tracey Emin (UK, b. 1963)
"The one thing that I see I do have in common with Louise is the repetitive emotion in my work. Louise would make work about something, and then she'd make work about it again, then she might make another work about it again, later—always a recurring theme. And I have that in my work too—because it's real: I'm still angry. I'm still upset. I'm still furious. I'm still jealous. I'm still heartbroken. I'm still confused."

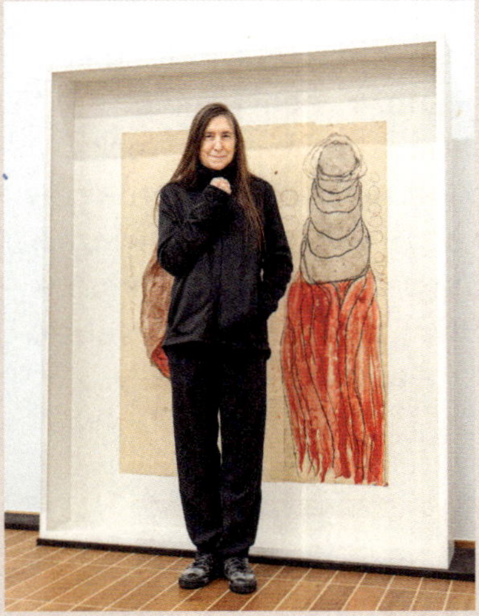

Jenny Holzer in the exhibition she curated of Bourgeois's work, *The Violence of Handwriting Across a Page*, Kunstmuseum Basel, 2022

Jenny Holzer (US, b. 1950)
"I sat with Louise for the first time in her house, surrounded by artwork in progress. I observed that Louise was a relentless worker. There is much evidence of her relentlessness, even when tormented or maybe especially when tormented. There was a bright red wax ear on the table, so we talked about the brutality but the necessity of red—about finding and ensuring the right color as if this were the most serious thing in the world. Regarding her legacy, I believe it's less what she anticipated and more that she identified and tirelessly represented essentials. The essentials endure."

Igshaan Adams (South Africa, b. 1982)
"Louise reminds me of my grandmother. She is that absolutely honest and direct person with whom you always know where you stand. In discovering her work early on, I felt the freedom to dig into my own history and not care who was impressed. There was so much chaos

inside me. My biggest moment was realizing that painful past experiences were my wealth—that I could have the conversations I wanted through making. I think often of her quotes about turning hate into love, and about the needle as a tool for restoration."

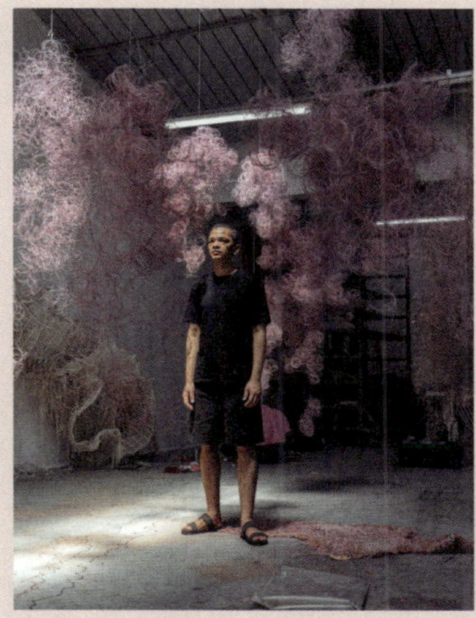

Igshaan Adams in his studio, Cape Town, 2023

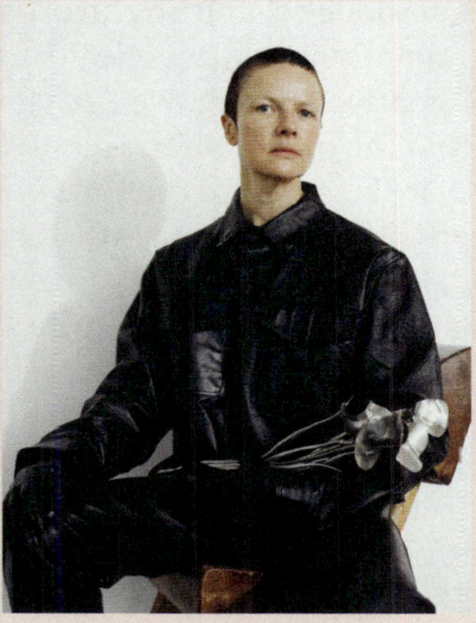

Isabelle Albuquerque in her studio, Los Angeles, 2025

Isabelle Albuquerque (US, b. 1981)
"By speaking to the maternal, Louise also speaks to the universal. Every human has a mother. This relationship, however fraught, also connects us to every other person. It took eighty years for Louise to discover how to make *Maman* (1999)—to create a form that protects, frightens, and connects us to life the way that our mothers do. I love that you can clutch *Maman's* legs, like a child, or lie under her as if she were a tree. All that steel and toughness, but the form is alive and flowing with energy. I dream of making sculpture that scares and seduces like that."

“What Has Kept Me Going”

Remarks prepared for art students at Rutgers University, New Jersey, ca. 1984

What has kept me going and still keeps me going is the knowledge that being an artist is a privilege. And the second thing—which is a consequence of the first—is that one must not ask too much. Well, what do I mean by that? Simply that the pursuit of happiness is fine—we all want to believe in it—but most of the time it is just that, a pursuit. Now the privilege of being an artist consists of three things. First, to have something of your own to say. And then—and this is a fight to the finish—to be able to communicate that to people. At best a school can help you with the second part, but it is obviously up to you what you are going to say, what spark you have, what subject. Now what does this all have to do with making a living? I do not know. When you start to define being an artist in those terms—as a profession like any other profession—you place yourself on a downward spiral. You begin to think: “How am I going to survive?” “I hate my job.” “I am a prisoner of the people who depend on me, of people’s expectations for my success.” “I know that there is loads of money out there but the system is so crooked none of it is going to come my way.” “I know there are hundreds of galleries in New York and I have a right to be in one but I’m not—or I’m not in the one I want to be in.” The important thing about all these statements is that they are all true—or could be true. But the mistake is to confuse art with a “right” at all. One has no birthright to be an artist. One is lucky to be one and that is all. So why have I mentioned these pessimistic things? Well, in fact, it is to say—as I have said—that things really are not so bad all the same. You are privileged to be what you are, and you have your whole life—fifty years—to figure out how it will be. But if this seems too general, all I can say is that after fifty years as an artist it is *my* privilege to say it just the same. That is all.

I cannot speak of style in general terms. I can only speak of mine, and my style is dictated entirely by the life I lead. That is to say by what I do—and I have a very hard time doing it. It is dictated by how much I am able—this is the dangerous thing—how much I am able to deprive myself. In other words style deals with limitations, and I am afraid we have to talk of discipline. You are made, you are forged by what you can resist and by your failures. My style, the way I work comes from all the failures, all the temptations I have resisted, all the fun I didn't have, all the regrets. Style is made like a statue that you hack away at—and it's made by all the things you have given up. All the things that you intensely desire to which you say, "No."

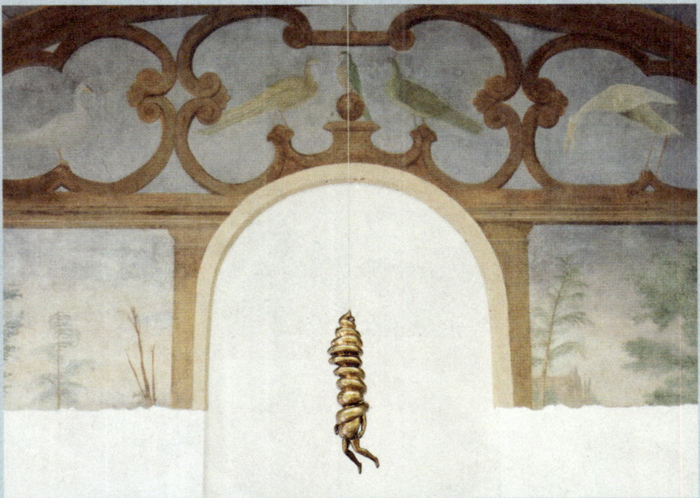

Installation view, *Spiral Woman* (1984), in *Louise Bourgeois: Unconscious Memories*, Galleria Borghese, Rome, 2024

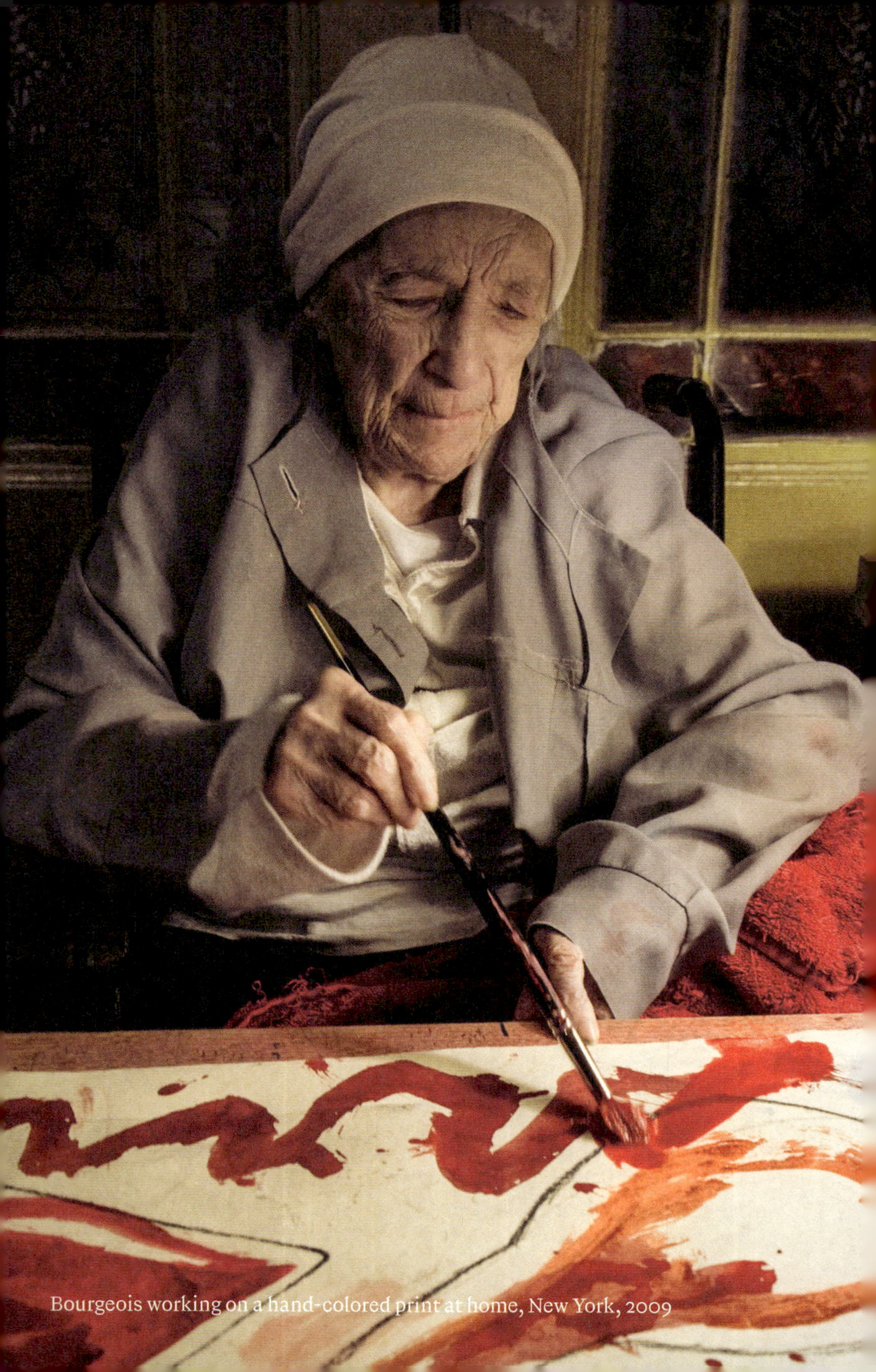

Bourgeois working on a hand-colored print at home, New York, 2009

To Infinity

There are many loops, echoes, and returns in Bourgeois's long creative life. As a young artist and mother in the 1940s, she sometimes worked on prints at the kitchen table. Sixty years later, her last great run of work emerged from a similar setting.

Bourgeois seldom ventured away from her Chelsea home after her Brooklyn studio was demolished in 2005, but she was joined in her parlor throughout these years by friends, carers, and collaborators. Her famed Sunday salons brought young artists into her world at a time when she was increasingly tethered to home. These were also years in which print publishers, including Felix Harlan and Benjamin Shiff, brought their resources to Bourgeois, effectively turning her modest parlor into an improvised and wildly inventive print studio. Like Matisse with his radical late cutouts, Bourgeois was drawn to paper for its intimacy and immediacy, working on etching plates and printed sheets that filled and sometimes overspilled her worktable. Shiff, an empathetic collaborator, lived nearby and ferried sheets and materials back and forth for Bourgeois to "undo and redo." The resulting works form a ragged and moving song of mortality.

In the 1940s, Bourgeois relished the demanding incisiveness of engraving, noting that strong biceps were needed to drive the burin through metal. The works of her last years are defined instead by soaking and releasing—the artist who had grown up beside rivers ending with an aesthetic of flow. Wielding a brush loaded with red-pink gouache on sheet after sheet of drenched paper, she created endless visual diaries of gestation, birth, feeding, and flowering—amniotic

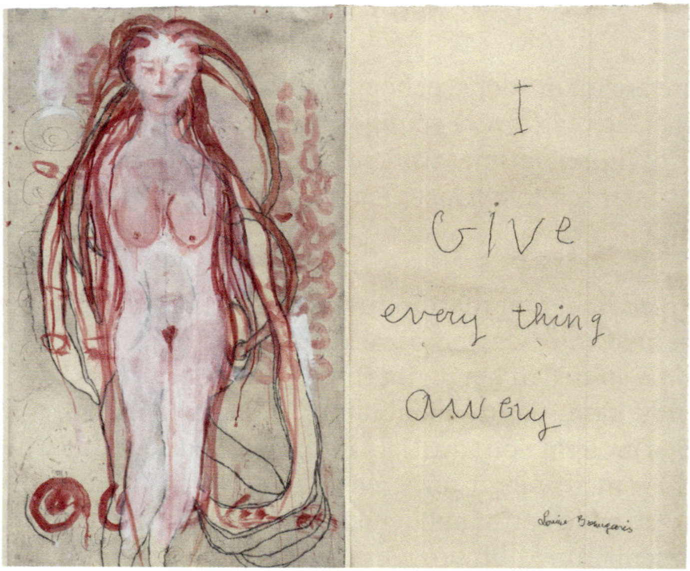

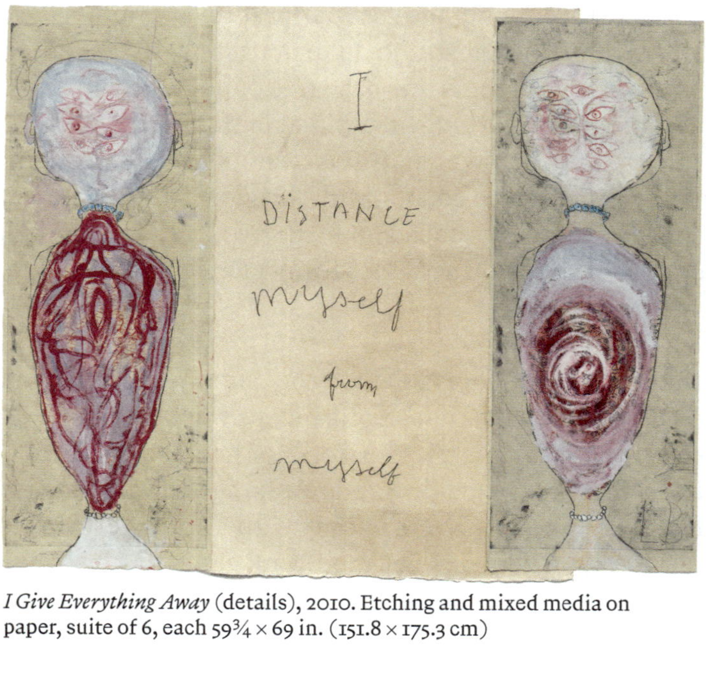

I Give Everything Away (details), 2010. Etching and mixed media on paper, suite of 6, each 59¾ × 69 in. (151.8 × 175.3 cm)

images in which, Bourgeois said, she identified with the baby rather than the mother. Meanwhile, the large six-part work *I Give Everything Away* (2010) is a pulsing testament and swan song, opening with an apparition of Bourgeois's younger, long-haired self, moving through scenes of growth and bursting, and ending with the shakily handwritten "I am packing my bags." The most open and affecting of these late works is the series *À l'Infini* (To Infinity, 2008–9; pp. 146–47), in which Bourgeois extrapolated a world both womblike and cosmic from a loose network of etched forms.

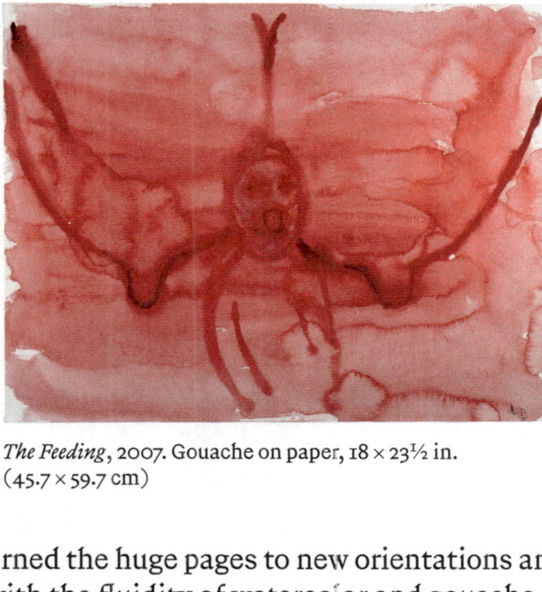

The Feeding, 2007. Gouache on paper, 18 × 23½ in. (45.7 × 59.7 cm)

As she turned the huge pages to new orientations and worked with the fluidity of watercolor and gouache, Bourgeois found and released images from across her lifetime, among them spirals, spheres, knots, spiders, entwined lovers, a pregnant woman, and a kicking baby. Even as the artist approached her ninety-eighth year, she was still defiantly making—connecting beginning and end while opening herself, as ever, to the unknown.

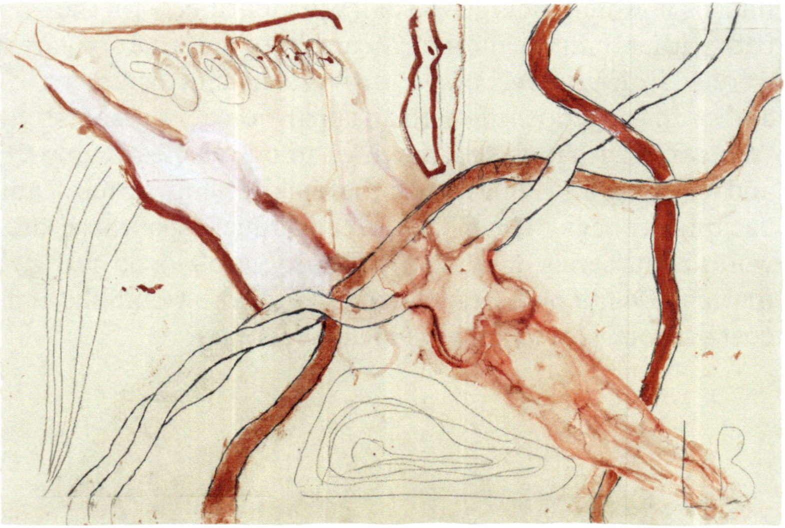

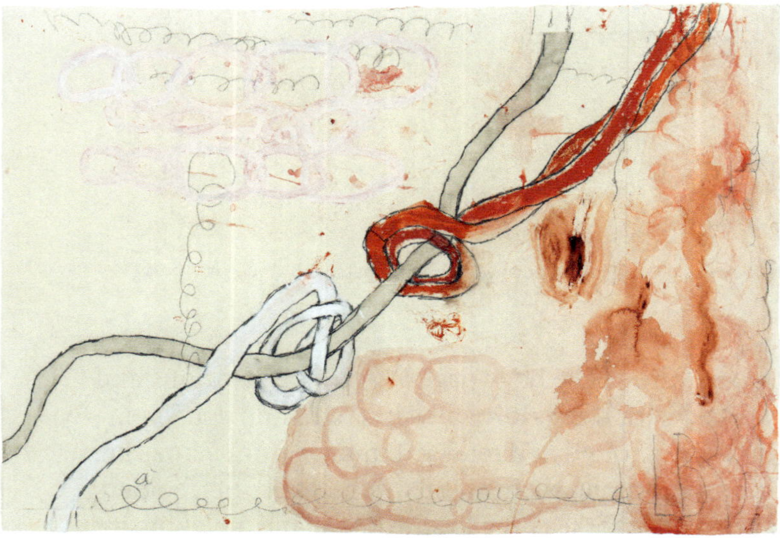

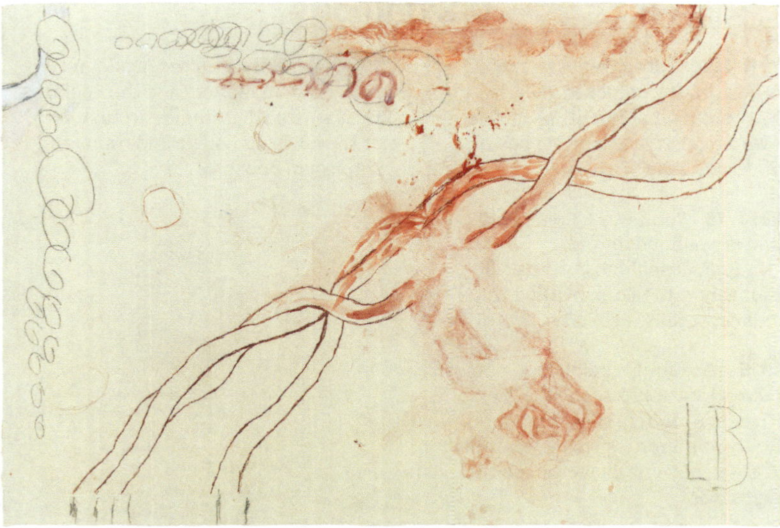

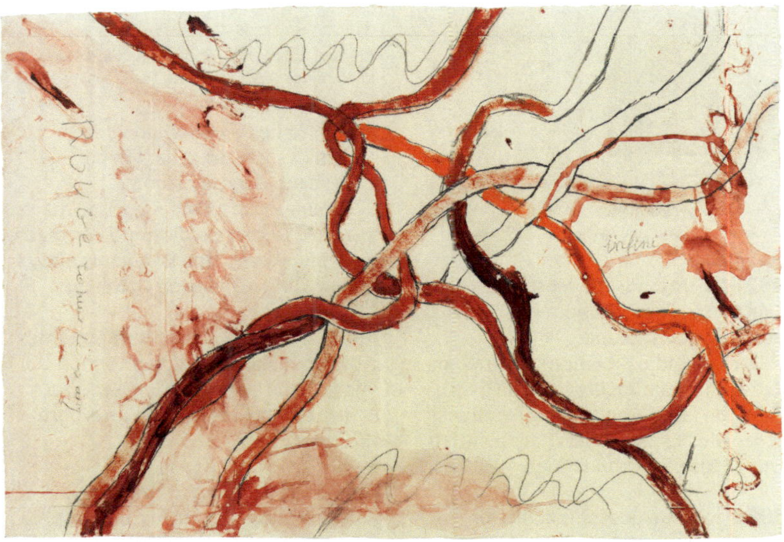

À l'Infini (details), 2008–9. Etching and mixed media on paper, suite of 16, each 40 × 60 in. (101.6 × 152.4 cm)

Chronology

1911 Louise Joséphine Bourgeois is born on December 25 in Paris. Her parents, Louis and Joséphine, own a tapestry restoration business and sales gallery.

1914–18 World War I. Louis fights and is wounded in 1916.

In 1918, Joséphine becomes ill, probably with Spanish influenza, and never fully recovers.

1919 The family establishes a tapestry restoration atelier along the Bièvre River in Antony, a suburb of Paris. Bourgeois later assists in the workshop, drawing missing elements for damaged tapestries.

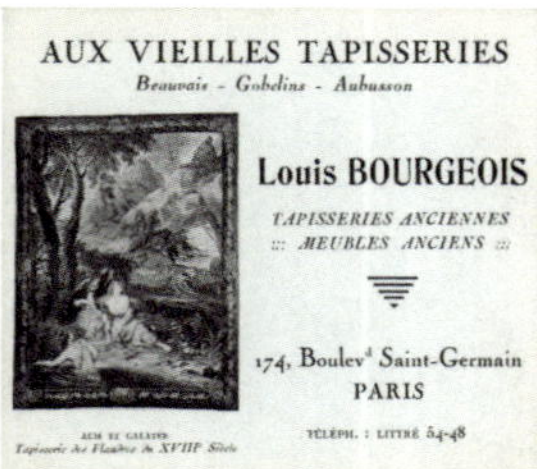
AUX VIEILLES TAPISSERIES
Beauvais - Gobelins - Aubusson

Louis BOURGEOIS

TAPISSERIES ANCIENNES
MEUBLES ANCIENS

174, Boulev[d] Saint-Germain
PARIS

TÉLÉPH. : LITTRÉ 54-48

Louis Bourgeois's business card for Aux Vieilles Tapisseries, Paris, ca. 1920–30

1921–27 Attends the prestigious Lycée Fénelon in Paris. Withdraws in 1927 to care for Joséphine.

In 1922, Sadie Richmond is hired to teach the children English and lives with the family, on and off, for almost a decade. She and Louis have an affair, one of his many infidelities.

1932 Mother, Joséphine, dies on September 14. Bourgeois attempts suicide in the Bièvre and is saved by her father.

Briefly studies geometry and calculus at the Sorbonne.

1933–37 Enrolls in the Académie de la Grande Chaumière and the École des Beaux-Arts. Also studies art history at the École du Louvre and trains as a museum docent.

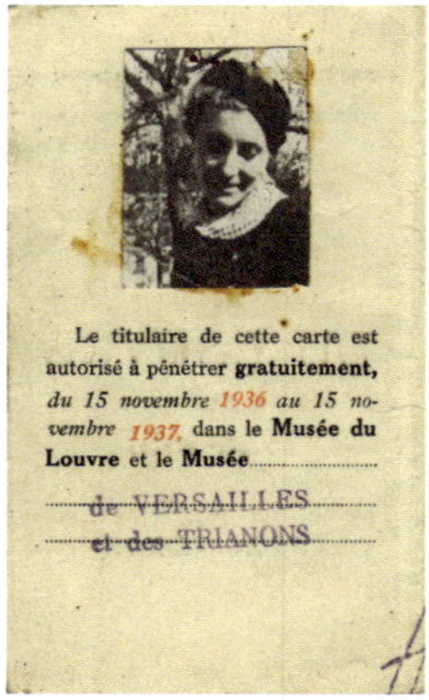
Le titulaire de cette carte est autorisé à pénétrer **gratuitement,** *du 15 novembre 1936 au 15 novembre 1937,* dans le **Musée du Louvre** et le **Musée** de VERSAILLES et des TRIANONS

Museum pass for Musée du Louvre and Musée de Versailles et des Trianons, Paris, 1936–37

1938 Studies with Fernand Léger.

Opens a small art gallery in her father's tapestry salesroom.

On August 24, meets American art historian Robert Goldwater. They marry on September 12, and Bourgeois moves to New York, arriving on October 12.

1940 The Bourgeois-Goldwater family grows to include an adopted son, Michel, who arrives in New York from France on May 21. Jean-Louis is born shortly after, on July 4.

1941 The family moves to the Stuyvesant Apartments at 142 East Eighteenth Street, New York, and purchases a country home in Easton, Connecticut.

A third son, Alain, is born on November 12.

1945 *Paintings by Louise Bourgeois*, her first solo exhibition, opens on June 4 at Bertha Schaefer Gallery, New York.

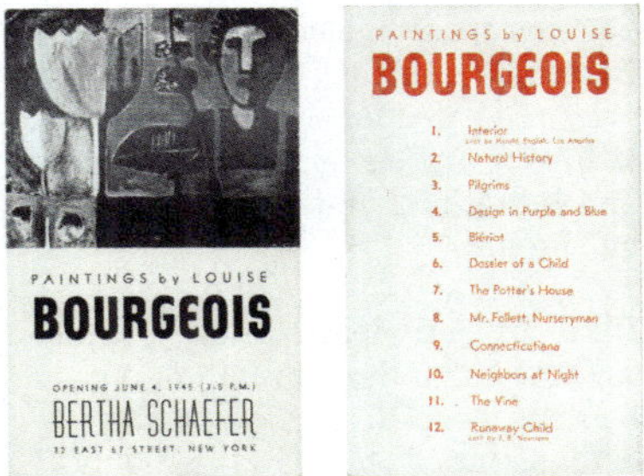

Announcement for *Paintings by Louise Bourgeois*, Bertha Schaefer Gallery, New York, 1945

1946 Begins creating her first mature sculptures, the *Personages* (p. 48), on her apartment building's roof.

1947 Self-publishes *He Disappeared into Complete Silence* (p. 49). Works on the engraving plates at Atelier 17, Stanley William Hayter's renowned printmaking studio.

Second solo exhibition, *Louise Bourgeois: Paintings*, at Norlyst Gallery, New York, includes the *Femme Maison* paintings (pp. 44–45).

1949 First solo exhibition of sculpture, *Louise Bourgeois: Late Work 1947–1949, 17 Standing Figures in Wood* at Peridot Gallery, New York.

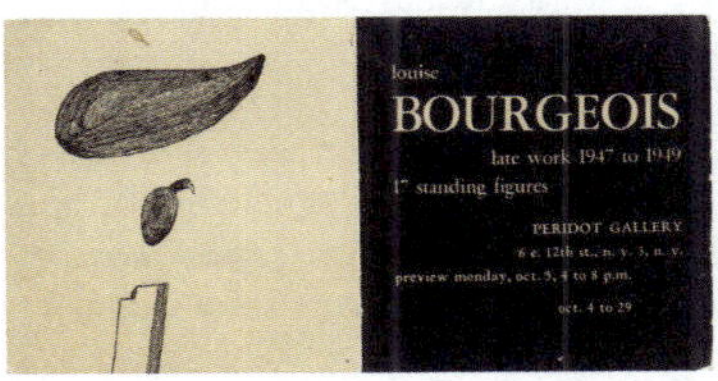

Announcement for *Louise Bourgeois: Late Work 1947–1949, 17 Standing Figures in Wood*, Peridot Gallery, New York, 1949

1950 Peridot Gallery presents *Louise Bourgeois: Sculptures*.

Participates in "Artists' Sessions at Studio 35," a symposium on contemporary American art moderated by Alfred H. Barr, Jr., Richard Lippold, and Robert Motherwell.

Departs for a year-long stay in France with family, during which Goldwater conducts research for a Fulbright scholarship. Maintains a studio in Paris until 1955.

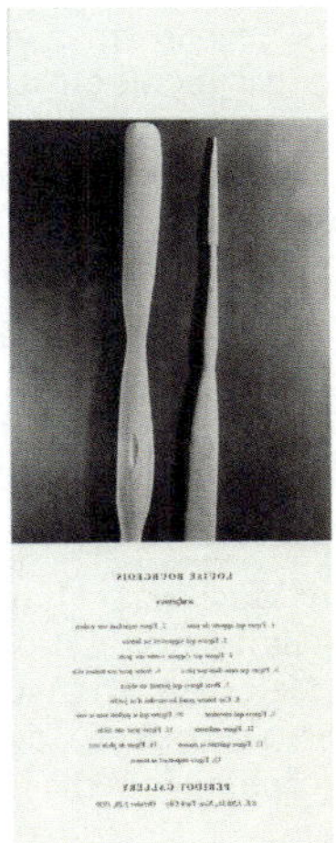

Announcement for *Louise Bourgeois: Sculptures*, Peridot Gallery, New York, 1950

1951 The Museum of Modern Art (MoMA) acquires *Sleeping Figure* (1950), a *Personage*.

Father, Louis, dies in Paris on April 9.

Bourgeois enters a deep depression and begins psychoanalysis in New York, which she undergoes regularly until the mid-60s and then on and off until the mid-80s.

1952 Begins writing extensively as part of the analytic process. This effort essentially replaces her artistic practice for much of the following decade.

1953 *Louise Bourgeois: Drawings for Sculpture and Sculpture* opens at Peridot Gallery.

1956 Establishes a bookstore, Erasmus Books and Prints, which closes in 1960.
Whitney Museum of American Art, New York, acquires *One and Others* (1955).

1957 Becomes an American citizen.

1958 Moves to an apartment at 435 West Twenty-Second Street after the Stuyvesant Apartments are demolished.

1961 Experiments with new materials such as plastic, latex, and rubber in a series of biomorphic sculptures loosely referred to as *Lairs*.

1962 Moves to 347 West Twentieth Street, where she lives for the rest of her life.

1963 Begins teaching sculpture, and then printmaking, first at Brooklyn College, and later at Pratt Institute, the School of Visual Arts, and Cooper Union. Continues teaching into the late 1970s.

1964 Stable Gallery, New York, presents several *Lairs* in her first solo exhibition of new work since 1953.

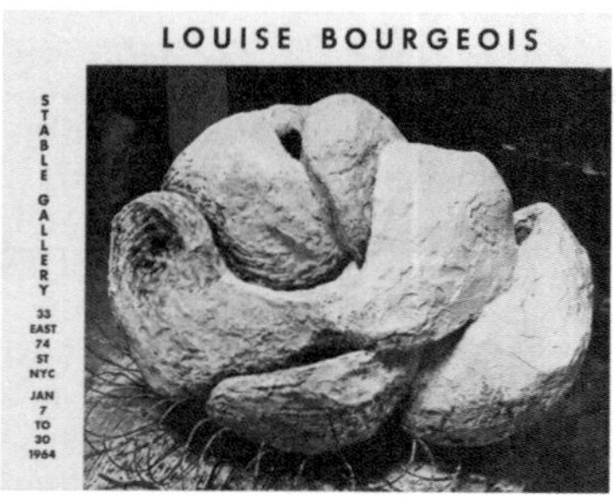

Poster for *Louise Bourgeois: Recent Sculpture*, Stable Gallery, New York, 1964

1966 Included in *Eccentric Abstraction*, a seminal group exhibition curated by Lucy Lippard at Fischbach Gallery, New York. Her works are shown with those by younger artists including Eva Hesse and Bruce Nauman.

1967–70 Travels frequently to Carrara and Pietrasanta, Italy, to work in marble and bronze.

1970–73 Participates in the Feminist Art Movement through exhibitions, benefits, panel discussions, and demonstrations but never explicitly identifies as a Feminist artist.

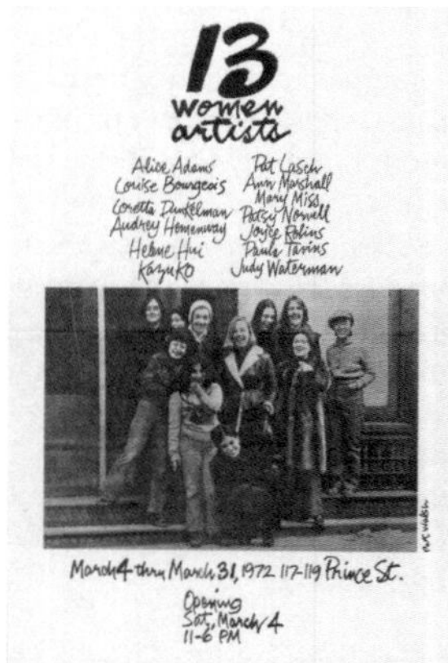

Announcement for *13 Women Artists*, 117–119 Prince Street, New York, 1972

1973 Goldwater dies at home on March 26.

1974 Debuts *The Destruction of the Father* (1974; p. 89) in her first solo exhibition in ten years, *Louise Bourgeois: Sculpture 1970–1974*, at 112 Greene Street Gallery, New York.

1978 Stages the performance *A Banquet / A Fashion Show of Body Parts* inside the installation

Confrontation (1978; p. 91) on the closing day of her solo show at Hamilton Gallery of Contemporary Art, New York.

1980 Meets Jerry Gorovoy when he includes her in a group exhibition at Max Hutchinson Gallery, New York. Gorovoy becomes Bourgeois's principal assistant and close confidant. (After her death, he becomes president of her foundation, The Easton Foundation.)

Acquires a large studio in an old garment factory at 475 Dean Street in Brooklyn.

1982 *Louise Bourgeois: Retrospective*, curated by Deborah Wye, opens at MoMA and travels across the United States.

Robert Mapplethorpe photographs Bourgeois with *Fillette* (1968; p. 24) for the catalogue, her first monographic publication.

Produces *Partial Recall*, a slideshow with voiceover narrative recounting her childhood, in conjunction with the exhibition. *Artforum* publishes the related photo essay, "Child Abuse."

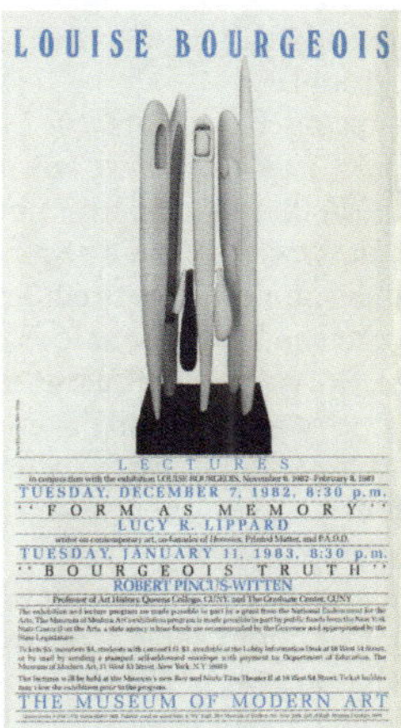

Poster for *Louise Bourgeois: Retrospective*, Museum of Modern Art, New York, 1982–83

1985 First solo exhibition in Europe, *Louise Bourgeois: Rétrospective, 1947–1984*, opens at Galerie Maeght-Lelong, Paris.

1989 First museum retrospective in Europe opens at the Frankfurter Kunstverein, Germany, and travels through 1991.

1990 Son Michel dies on April 27.

1991 Debuts six *Cells* at the *Carnegie International* in Pittsburgh. This series of architectural environments ultimately encompasses sixty works.

1992 Shows *Precious Liquids* (1992; p. 108), a *Cell*, at *Documenta IX* in Kassel, Germany.

Presents the installation and related performance *She Lost It* at The Fabric Workshop, Philadelphia.

1993 Represents the United States at the Venice Biennale.

Meets collector Ursula Hauser, who goes on to assemble one of the largest private collections of Bourgeois's work after seeing *Legs* (1989) in Venice and later acquiring the sculpture.

1994 The Brooklyn Museum presents *Louise Bourgeois: The Locus of Memory*, which includes her first large-scale *Spider* (1994). The show travels until 1996.

MoMA opens *The Prints of Louise Bourgeois*, curated by Wye. It is accompanied by the first volume of Bourgeois's print catalogue raisonné.

Begins *The Insomnia Drawings* (1994–95; p. 59).

1995–96 *Louise Bourgeois: Pensées-plumes*, a drawing retrospective curated by Marie-Laure Bernadac, is held at the Musée National d'Art Moderne, Centre Pompidou, Paris.

Begins incorporating clothing and fabric from throughout her life into her work. Her first fabric sculptures are installed in the bell tower of St. Pancras Church, London, for a 1996 exhibition.

1997 Awarded the National Medal of Arts by US President Bill Clinton.

1999 Kunsthalle Bielefeld, Germany, presents *Louise Bourgeois*, curated by Thomas Kellein.

Participates in the Venice Biennale and is awarded the Golden Lion for Lifetime Achievement.

Museo Nacional Centro de Arte Reina Sofía, Madrid, presents *Louise Bourgeois: Memory and Architecture*.

2000 Commissioned to create the inaugural installation for Tate Modern's Turbine Hall in London. Debuts the monumental spider *Maman* (1999) and three architectural towers: *I Do*, *I Undo*, and *I Redo* (all 1999–2000).

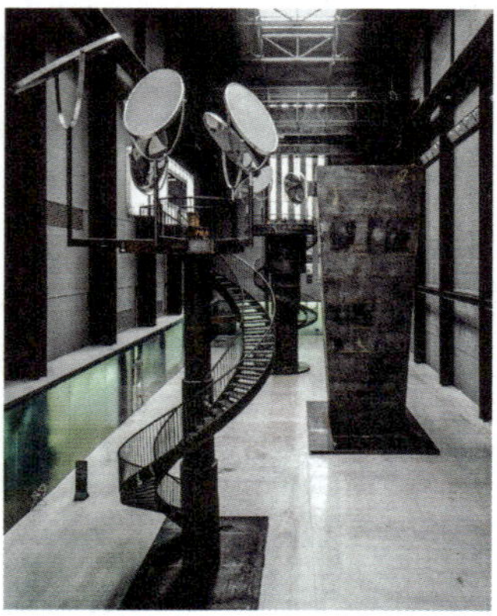

Installation view, *Louise Bourgeois: I Do, I Undo, I Redo*, Tate Modern, London, 2000

2001 *Louise Bourgeois at the Hermitage* is the first show of a living artist at the State Hermitage Museum, Saint Petersburg, Russia.

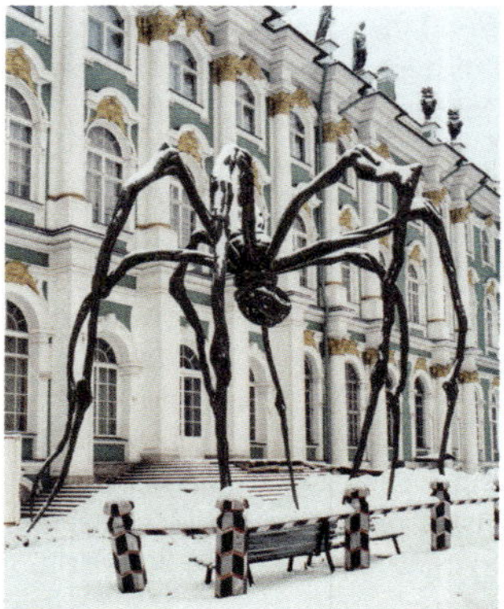

Installation view, *Maman* (1999), State Hermitage Museum, Saint Petersburg, Russia, 2001–2

2005 Forced to vacate her Brooklyn studio when the building is demolished for redevelopment.

2007 *Louise Bourgeois: Retrospective*, curated by Frances Morris, Marie-Laure Bernadac, and Jonas Storsve, opens at Tate Modern. It travels to the Centre Pompidou, Paris; Guggenheim Museum, New York; Museum of Contemporary Art, Los Angeles; and Hirshhorn Museum and Sculpture Garden, Washington, DC.

Commissioned to create *The Damned, the Possessed, and the Beloved* (2007–10), her last *Cell*. Installed posthumously in 2011, the work sits inside a glass pavilion designed by architect Peter Zumthor at the Steilneset Memorial in Vardø, Norway, a monument to the ninety-one people—mostly women—tried and executed there for witchcraft in the 1600s.

2008 Awarded a Commander of the Legion of Honor by French President Nicolas Sarkozy at her home on September 21.

2010 Dies on May 31 in New York.

Additional Resources

Bourgeois's work has generated scholarship as varied and probing as her practice itself, offering readings that span the biographical, psychoanalytic, feminist, formalist, and more. These publications represent the most essential of what has been written, providing readers ways into a career that unfolded across seven decades and myriad mediums—including sculpture, installation, drawing, painting, printmaking, and writing. Taken together, these resources offer a picture of an artist whose life and work were inseparable, whose emotional range was vast, and whose influence continues to deepen with time.

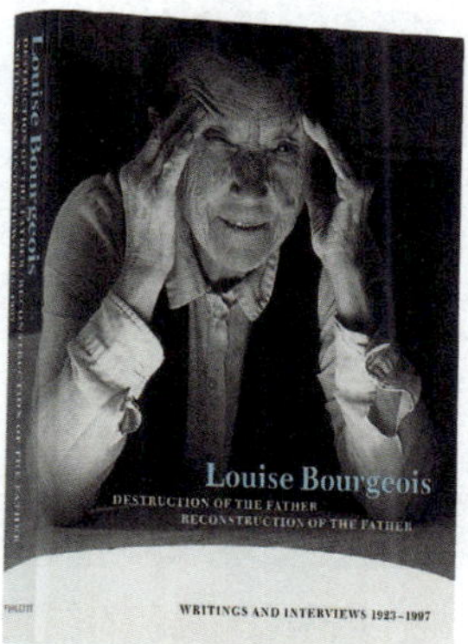

Destruction of the Father / Reconstruction of the Father: Writings and Interviews, 1923–1997 (Violette Editions, 1998), edited by Marie-Laure Bernadac and Hans Ulrich Obrist, brings together diaries, correspondence, artist statements, and interviews spanning seven decades, offering direct and often startling insight into the personal motivations and obsessive themes that animated Bourgeois's practice. The book has been translated into French, German, Spanish, Italian, and Portuguese.

Louise Bourgeois (Tate, 2007), edited by Frances Morris to accompany the traveling retrospective that began at Tate Modern, takes an unconventional approach to the exhibition catalogue. Organized by topic from A to Z, it assembles short essays by critics and art historians—including Julia Kristeva, Linda Nochlin, and others—on individual works, recurring motifs, and key contexts of the artist's practice. It remains one of the most accessible introductions to Bourgeois's work available.

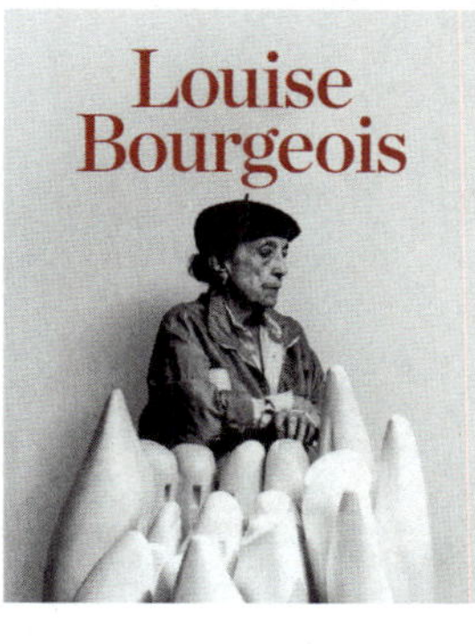

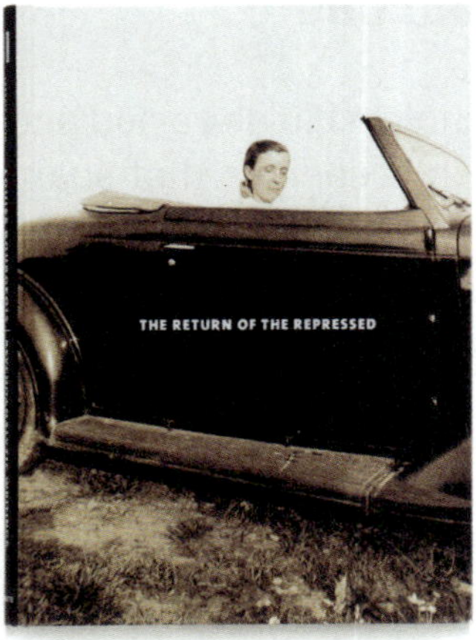

The Return of the Repressed (Violette Editions, 2012), a two-volume publication edited by Philip Larratt-Smith, draws on Bourgeois's previously unpublished psychoanalytic writings, which are presented alongside essays by scholars including Juliet Mitchell and Mignon Nixon, offering a sustained examination of the psychological dimensions of her art.

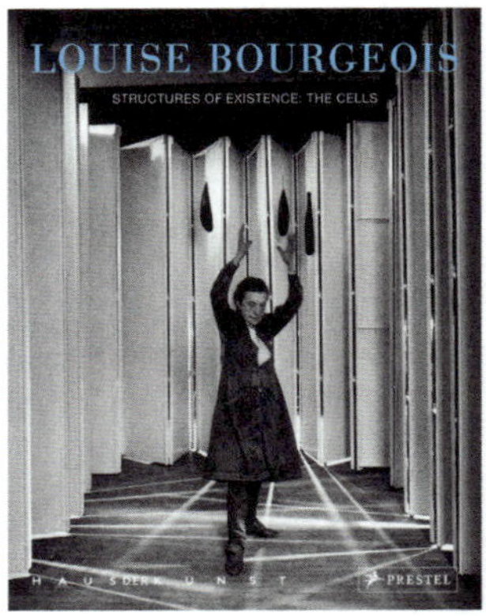

Structures of Existence: The Cells (Prestel / Haus der Kunst, 2015), edited by Julienne Lorz, is the definitive study of the eponymous installations Bourgeois developed across the final two decades of her life. The book—featuring contributions by Lynne Cooke, Jerry Gorovoy, Griselda Pollock, Nancy Spector, and others—examines the *Cells* as environments suspended between memory and fantasy, exposure and concealment, and moves interpretation of the inexhaustibly interpretable series decisively beyond biography.

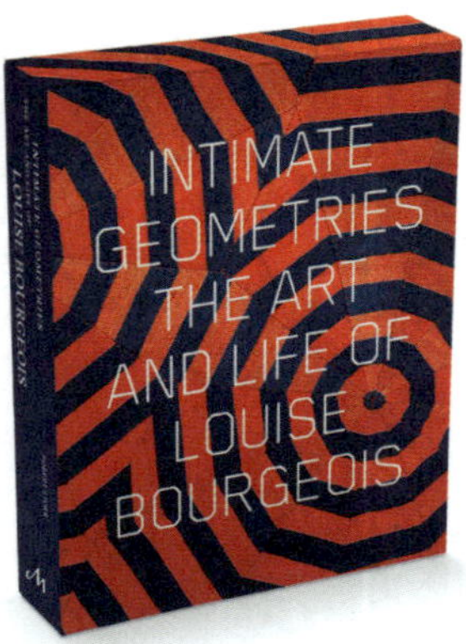

Intimate Geometries: The Art and Life of Louise Bourgeois (Monacelli Press, 2016) is curator and writer Robert Storr's monograph on Bourgeois, developed over more than three decades. Writing from close personal knowledge of the artist and drawing on extensive research, Storr traces the entire arc of her career. The veritable tome is notable above all for its close attention to the chains of association that propel the formal and material development of the work.

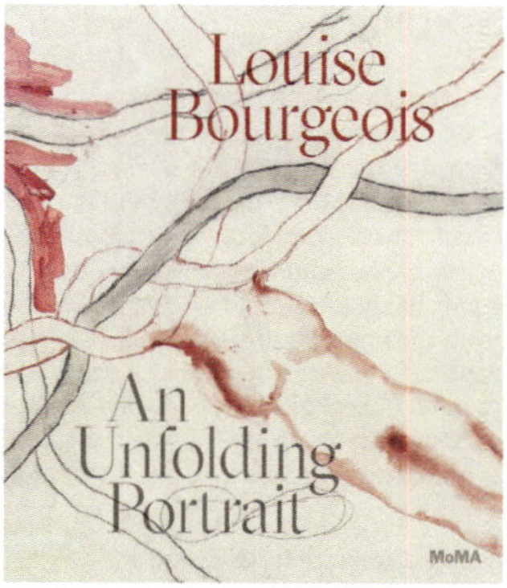

Louise Bourgeois: An Unfolding Portrait (Museum of Modern Art, 2017), by Deborah Wye, is a generously illustrated study of Bourgeois's prints and books—a body of some 1,400 artworks that runs through her entire career. Grounded in Wye's four decades of scholarly engagement with Bourgeois, and accompanied by interviews with the printers and publishers who collaborated with the artist, the book sheds light on her creative process as it traces the evolving states and variants that led to her final compositions.

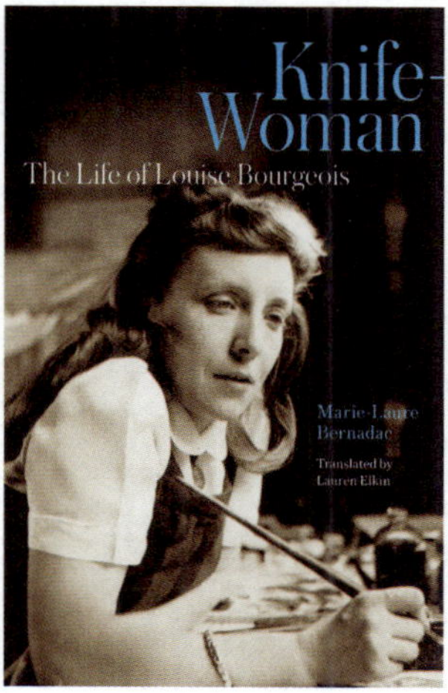

Knife-Woman: The Life of Louise Bourgeois (Yale University Press, 2025), by Marie-Laure Bernadac, is a focused biography of Bourgeois by a longtime curator and friend of the artist. Mining Bourgeois's diaries, correspondence, and psychoanalytic writings, Bernadac holds life story and criticism in balance, illuminating the choices that shaped the work without reducing them to their sources.

Scan this QR code to access additional material, including archival footage of Bourgeois at work as well as the online catalogue raisonné of Bourgeois's prints and books created by the Museum of Modern Art, New York.

Sources

Most quotations from the artist are from Louise Bourgeois, *Destruction of the Father / Reconstruction of the Father: Writings and Interviews, 1923–1997*, ed. Marie-Lauré Bernadac and Hans Ulrich Obrist (London: Violette Editions, 1998), which includes additional source information and is henceforth cited as *Destruction*. Quotations from the Louise Bourgeois Archive / The Easton Foundation, New York, are identified by object number (LB or AV) or the initials TEF. In extracts of Bourgeois's writings, punctuation and line breaks have been retained as closely as possible.

p. 4: "What is important . . ." is from "Statements from Conversations with Robert Storr" (1980s–90s), in *Destruction*, p. 217.

p. 13: "If there is magic . . ." is from Christiane Meyer-Thoss, *Louise Bourgeois: Designing for Free Fall* (Zurich: Ammann, 1992), p. 121.

p. 23: "Thought feathers" is from "Interview with Marie-Laure Bernadac" (1995), in *Destruction*, p. 293; "my work in the studio . . ." is from Bourgeois's audio-visual recording, ca. 1974 (AV-00987_02); "the spell" is from Donald Kuspit, *Bourgeois: An Interview with Louise Bourgeois* (New York: Vintage Books, Elizabeth Avedon Editions, 1988), p. 31.

p. 25: "Dirty" is from Hal Foster in Hal Foster, Rosalind Krauss, Yve-Alain Bois, and Benjamin H. D. Buchloh, *Art Since 1900: Modernism, Antimodernism, Postmodernism* (London: Thames & Hudson, 2004), p. 506; "comic" is from Elaine Showalter, "Lumps, Bumps, Bulbs, Bubbles, Bulges, Slits, Turds, Coils, Craters, Wrinkles and Holes," in *Tate Etc.*, no. 11, Autumn 2007: p. 58.

p. 27: "It is not conscious motivation . . ." is from *Album* (1994), in *Destruction*, p. 285.

p. 29: "Oysters and champagne" is from "Interview with Douglas Maxwell" (1993), in *Destruction*, p. 246.

p. 33: "Art is a privilege . . ." is from Kuspit, *Interview with Louise Bourgeois*, p. 67; "total, friendly silence" is from "Conversations with Robert Storr," p. 217; "passion for the third dimension" and "Louise, you are not a painter . . ." are from "Interview with Douglas Maxwell," p. 243.

p. 34: "I had found a diamond" is from "On *The Sail*" (1988–89), in *Destruction*, p. 170; "the runaway girl" is from Bourgeois's December 2, 1996, diary entry (TEF). See also "Select Diary Notes 1991–1997," in *Destruction*, p. 365. The phrase serves as the title of a painting (ca. 1938; p. 41) and also relates to a gouache work titled *Home for Runaway Girls* (1994).

p. 36: "Emotional geometries" ("geometry" in the original) is from "Interview with Michael Auping" (October 25, 1996), in *Destruction*, p. 352; "chaos could be licked" is from oral history interview with Louise Bourgeois by Colette Roberts, April 14, 1968, Archives of American Art, Smithsonian Institution, part 3, p. 57.

p. 37: "The Euclidean is comforting . . ." is from "The Puritan" (1990), in *Destruction*, p. 55.

p. 38: "Set out with something . . ." is from Bourgeois's loose sheet of writing, 1944 (LB-1149). See also "Select Diary Notes 1939–1944," in *Destruction*, p. 41.

p. 42: "The hustle and bustle . . ." is from Bourgeois's letter to Louis Bourgeois, October 28, 1938 (LB-1006); "between the bed and the window" is from Bourgeois's letter to Louis Bourgeois, December 27, 1938 (LB-1009); "I do not need much . . ." is from Bourgeois's October 26–27, 1949, diary entry (TEF).

p. 46: "Suddenly I had this huge sky space . . ." is from an October 31, 1982, article in the *New York Times* by Michael Brenson, cited in Robert Storr, *Intimate Geometries: The Art and Life of Louise Bourgeois* (New York: The Monacelli Press, 2016), p. 126.

p. 50: "This very small, intense woman . . ." is quoted in Storr, *Intimate Geometries*, p. 129; "the reason was a psychological one . . ." is from "Interview with Susi Bloch" (1976), in *Destruction*, p. 105.

p. 54: "You can not arrest the present . . ." is from *Album*, p. 285.

p. 56: "Thought feathers" is from "Interview with Marie-Laure Bernadac," p. 293.

p. 60: "An artist's words . . ." is from "An Artist's Words" (1954), in *Destruction*, p. 66; "I dreamt about you . . ." is from Bourgeois's letter to Robert Goldwater, September 24, 1938 (LB-1715); "I want to be the owner . . ." is from "Conversations with Robert Storr," p. 219; "The sound of a pebble . . ." is from Bourgeois's loose sheet of writing, ca. April–May 1959 (LB-0877); "ashamed like a fox . . ." is from Bourgeois's March 12, 1975, diary entry (TEF).

p. 61: "I am a collection . . ." is from Bourgeois's loose sheet of writing, ca. 1957 (LB-0251); "I don't want to understand . . ." is from Bourgeois's loose sheet of writing, February 8, 1952 (LB-0452); "she looked like a peacock feather . . ." is from Gary Indiana, "A Coney Island of the Viscera," *Ursula*, October 9, 2019, https://www.hauserwirth.com/ursula/25821-gary-indiana-psychoanalytic-writings-louise-bourgeois/.

p. 62: "Season in hell" is from Philip Larratt-Smith, "The Case of LB," in Philip Larratt-Smith and Juliet Mitchell, *Louise Bourgeois: Freud's Daughter* (New York: Jewish Museum; New Haven, CT, and London: Yale University Press, 2021), p. 106; "she talks with a hatchet . . ." is from Bourgeois's loose sheet of writing, September 29, 1955 (LB-0126); "Never let me be free . . ." is from Bourgeois's loose sheet of writing, ca. 2008 (LB-0516).

pp. 65–68: The writings in this section are from Bourgeois's diaries from the dates indicated (TEF) except for May 3, 1963, which is from Bourgeois's loose sheet of writing (LB-0370).

p. 71: "Unconscious landscapes" is from "Two Conversations with Deborah Wye" (October 14, 1981), in *Destruction*, p. 126.

p. 73: "It is really in this statuary . . ." is from oral history interview with Bourgeois, 1968, part 3, p. 56.

p. 75: "Volcanic unconscious" is from Bourgeois's September 11, 1980, diary entry (TEF). See also "Select Diary Notes 1980–1987," in *Destruction*, p. 130.

p. 76: "I take it over with my fantasy . . ." is from Kuspit, *Interview with Louise Bourgeois*, p. 59; "If I want, a thing becomes . . ." is from Bourgeois's loose sheet of writing, December 20, 1967 (LB-0664).

p. 78: "Well you certainly cannot be hysterical" is from Nigel Finch, dir., *Louise Bourgeois: No Trespassing* (London: Arena Films, BBC, 1994).

p. 81: The studio inventory is recorded in Bourgeois's loose sheet of writing, ca. 1963 (LB-2001); "fight to the finish" is from "Meanings, Materials, and Milieu—Reflections of Recent Work by Louise Bourgeois: From an Interview with Robert Storr," in *Destruction*, p. 142; "hack away" is from Meyer-Thoss, *Designing for Free Fall*, p. 195.

p. 82: Bourgeois's exchange with Finch is from Finch, *No Trespassing*.

p. 85: "The tools . . ." is from Bourgeois's loose sheet of writing, ca. 1958 (LB-0303). "To animate a cube . . ." is from Bourgeois's loose sheet of writing, ca. 1962 (LB-0787).

p. 87: "I organize a sculpture . . ." is from Meyer-Thoss, *Designing for Free Fall*, p. 189.

p. 89: "The challenge of my being alone . . ." and "I am an artist with the whole house . . ." are from Bourgeois's June 6, 1974, diary entry (TEF).

p. 90: "a very murderous piece" is from "Statements 1979," in *Destruction*, p. 116; "Attempts to bring . . ." is from Lucy Lippard, "Louise Bourgeois: From the Inside Out," *Artforum* 13, no. 7, March 1975: p. 27.

p. 91: "This was an old woman . . ." is from "The Heart of Something: An Interview with Chris Kraus," in *Louise Bourgeois: Has the Day Invaded the Night or Has the Night Invaded the Day?* (Sydney: Art Gallery of New South Wales, 2023), p. 45.

p. 93: "Creature" is from Meyer-Thoss, *Designing for Free Fall*, p. 182.

p. 94: "My credo . . ." is from oral history interview with Bourgeois, 1968, part 3, p. 58.

p. 96: "Mounds and valleys . . ." is from "Two Conversations with Deborah Wye," p. 126.

p. 97: "Hill-breast-clouds" is from Lippard, "From the Inside Out," p. 28; Storr described Bourgeois's use of *Clouds and Caverns* as a "perch" in *Intimate Geometries*, p. 511.

p. 99: "After so much emotion . . ." is from "Symbolic Architecture" (July 11, 1981), in *Destruction* p. 136.

p. 100: "I am not interested in art history . . ." is from Kuspit, *Interview with Louise Bourgeois*, p. 81.

p. 103: Comment about only needing a turntable is from Bourgeois's audio-visual recording, ca. 1985 (AV-01254_01).

p. 104: "A little bit of soul" is from footage recorded by Jacqueline Kaess-Farquet in 1991 in Bourgeois's Brooklyn studio.

p. 109: "I wanted to create my own architecture . . ." is cited in Julienne Lorz, ed., *Louise Bourgeois: Structures of Existence; The Cells* (Munich, London, New York: Prestel, 2015), p. 28; "The studio is the work of art . . ." is from Bourgeois's March 23, 1994, diary entry (TEF).

p. 110: "I am an existential maker" is from Pandora Tabatabai Asbaghi and Jerry Gorovoy, *Louise Bourgeois: Blue Days and Pink Days* (Milan: Fondazione Prada, 1997), p. 254; "I objected . . ." is from Bourgeois's filmed interview with Kate Horsfield and Lyn Blumenthal, Video Data Bank, School of the Art Institute of Chicago, 1975; "I am not interested in being a mother . . ." is from "Feminism," in Frances Morris, ed., *Louise Bourgeois* (London: Tate Publishing, 2007), p. 130.

p. 111: "Condemned to be free" is from Jean-Paul Sartre, *Existentialism and Humanism*, trans. Philip Mairet (London: Methuen, 1948), p. 34. Originally delivered as a lecture, "Existentialism Is a Humanism," in Paris on October 29, 1945.

p. 112: "Booby traps" (hyphenated in the original) is from Jean-Paul Sartre, "No Exit" (1944), trans. Stuart Gilbert, in *No Exit and Three Other Plays* (New York: Vintage International, 1989), p. 30. Bourgeois's remarks about the similarity between *Articulated Lair* (1986) and the set of Sartre's play are from "Meanings, Materials, and Milieu," p. 143.

p. 113: "I say that Hell . . ." is from "Meanings, Materials, and Milieu," p. 143; "I feel like a sister" and "what she says is true" are from Bourgeois's interview with Ann Gibson, audio-visual recording, May 1982 (AV-01380_02); "imbalance . . ." is from Simone de Beauvoir, *Memoirs of a Dutiful Daughter*, trans. James Kirkup (London: Penguin Books, 1963), p. 41; "I am torn apart . . ." is from Marion Cajori and Amei Wallach, dirs., *The Spider, the Mistress, and the Tangerine* (New York: Art Kaleidoscope Foundation and Zeitgeist Films, 2008); comment about her father and Simone de Beauvoir's *The Useless Mouths* is from Bourgeois in Kuspit, *Interview with Louise Bourgeois*, p. 20.

p. 114: "Shut up in the home, woman cannot herself . . ." and "since woman is destined . . ." are from Simone de Beauvoir, *The Second Sex*, trans. and ed. H. M. Parshley (London: Jonathan Cape, 1953, repr. 1956), pp. 504 and 175; "The struggle itself . . ." is from Albert Camus, *The Myth of Sisyphus*, trans. Justin O'Brien (London: Penguin, 2013), p. 89; "I am inhabited by a kind of boulder . . ." is from Bourgeois's audio-visual recording, March 1976 (AV-00856_01).

p. 115: "Tough love" is from "Interview with Douglas Maxwell," p. 239.

p. 125: "It's my past . . ." is from Bourgeois's loose sheet of writing, ca. 1963 (LB-0202); "unconscious collection" is from Bourgeois's loose sheet of writing, ca. 1995 (LB-2172).

p. 126: "They say something unsayable" is from Jane Campion, "To the Depths: About Me and Louise," in *Has the Day Invaded the Night?*, p. 59; "best friend" is from "Ode à ma mère" (1995), in *Destruction*, p. 321.

p. 130: Variations on the phrase "I do, I undo, I redo" appear in Bourgeois's loose sheet writings from January 29, 1958 (LB-0272), ca. 1960s (LB-1097), ca. 1962 (LB-0976), and ca. 1963 (LB-0827).

p. 133: "I give credit to people . . ." is from Deborah Wye, *Louise Bourgeois: An Unfolding Portrait* (New York: Museum of Modern Art, 2017), p. 29; Bourgeois spoke about the stonemason in "On *The Sail*," p. 171.

p. 135: "You are born alone . . ." is from Bourgeois's August 8, 1987, diary entry (TEF); see also "Select Diary Notes 1980–1987," p. 132.

pp. 136–39: Richard Serra, speech at memorial in honor of Louise Bourgeois, Museum of Modern Art, New York, September 28, 2010; Phyllida Barlow, edited from *Fruitmarket Segments*, podcast, "Future Bourgeois: Phyllida Barlow, Elisabeth Lebovici, and Mignon Nixon in conversation," July 2, 2025, https://fruitmarket.podbean.com/e/future-bourgeois-phyllida-barlow-elisabeth-lebovici-and-mignon-nixon-in-conversation; Tracey Emin, from "Tracey Emin on the iconic Louise Bourgeois," in *London Evening Standard*, February 1, 2022, https://www.standard.co.uk/culture/exhibitions/tracey-emin-louise-bourgeois-hayward-gallery-b979690.html; Jenny Holzer, edited from "The Intolerable is a Climate We Share," interview with Sebastian Frenzel, in *Ursula*, April 29, 2022, https://www.hauserwirth.com/ursula/37275-the-intolerable-is-a-climate-we-share-jenny-holzer-on-louise-bourgeois/; Igshaan Adams, edited from an interview with the author, March 12, 2026; Isabelle Albuquerque, edited from an email to the author, February 4, 2026.

Additional Captions

Cover: Bourgeois with *The Quartered One* (1964–65) in her home studio, New York, 1964

pp. 4–5: Bourgeois with *The Quartered One* (1964–65) in her home studio, New York, 1965

pp. 6–7: Bourgeois drawing at home, New York, 1970

pp. 8–9: Bourgeois's Brooklyn studio, New York, 1982

pp. 10–11: Bourgeois's Brooklyn studio, New York, 1985

pp. 12–13: Bourgeois's spider sculptures in progress in her Brooklyn studio, New York, 1995

pp. 14–15: Bourgeois's Brooklyn studio, New York, 2000

pp. 16–17: Bourgeois in her home, New York, 2000

pp. 18–19: *Arch of Hysteria*, 2004. Fabric, 5 × 20¼ × 9 in. (12.7 × 51.4 × 22.9 cm)

pp. 26–27: Bourgeois with *Eyes* (1995) in her Brooklyn studio, New York, 1995

pp. 38–39: Bourgeois in her home studio, New York, ca. 1946

pp. 54–55: Bourgeois in her exhibition at Xavier Fourcade Gallery, New York, 1979

pp. 78–79: Bourgeois in her home studio, New York, 1974

pp. 86–87: Bourgeois working on *The Destruction of the Father* (1974), New York, 1974

pp. 94–95: Bourgeois with elements of *Confrontation* (1978) in her home studio, New York, 1982

pp. 100–101: *Articulated Lair*, 1986. Painted steel, rubber, and metal, 111 × 258 × 193 in. (281.9 × 655.3 × 490.2 cm)

p. 160: Bourgeois's Brooklyn studio, New York, 1982

Credits

8–9: Allan Finkelman. 12–13, 16–17, 26–27, 116, 135: © Jean-François Jaussaud. 14–15, 18–20, 22, 30–31, 36–37, 41, 45, 49, 52 (top left), 57 (top right, bottom), 58 (top left, top right), 59, 60 (right), 61, 72 (top left, bottom left), 74, 81, 83 (top), 97, 99, 114, 117, 119, 122, 129–30, 131 (top), 132, 134, 145–47: Christopher Burke. 24: © Robert Mapplethorpe Foundation, used by permission. 25: Gianfranco Gorgoni © Maya Gorgoni. 32, 63, 83 (bottom), 102, 112 (right), 118: Peter Bellamy (102, © Peter Bellamy). 33: Brassaï. 43, 51, 52 (top right, bottom right), 89, 144: Ron Amstutz. 46, 54–56, 96: Eeva Inkeri. 50: Aaron Siskind. 52 (bottom left): Sarah Muehlbauer. 57 (top left): Beth Phillips. 58 (bottom): Zindman Fremont. 70: Studio Fotografico, I. Bessi, Carrara. 72 (right): Adam Rzepka. 73: Philippe Migeat, dist. RMN. 76: Felicity Jenkins. 77: Peter Passuntino. 78–79, 86–87, 110: Mark Setteducati. 80: © Claudio Edinger. 88, 92, 98, 160: Peter Moore (88 [detail from original photograph] and 92, © Northwestern University; Peter Moore Photography Archive, Charles Deering McCormick Library of Special Collections, Northwestern University Libraries). 91, 124: David Heald. 94–95: © Inge Morath. 100–101, 106–7, 128: Maximilian Geuter. 105, 152 (bottom): Marcus Leith. 108: Frédéric Delpech. 111: courtesy Editions Gallimard. 112 (left): Raphael Lobato. 115: David Walker. 121: Krittawat Atthsis and Puttisin Choojesroom. 123: Mbzt / Wikimedia Commons (CC BY-SA 4.0). 131 (bottom): Jon Etter. 136 (left): David Corio / Redferns / Getty Images; artwork © 2026 Estate of Richard Serra / ARS, New York. 136 (right): Cat Garcia. 137: Dan Kitwood / Getty Images. 138: Xandra M. Linsin. 139 (left): © Mario Todeschini. 139 (right): Olivia Malone. 141: Agostino Osio. 142: Alex Van Gelder. 152 (top): Andrea Stappert. 153 (top), 154 (top): courtesy Violette Editions. 153 (bottom): courtesy Tate Publishing. 154 (bottom): courtesy Monacelli Press, a Phaidon Company. 155 (top): courtesy The Museum of Modern Art, New York. 155 (bottom): courtesy Yale University Press.

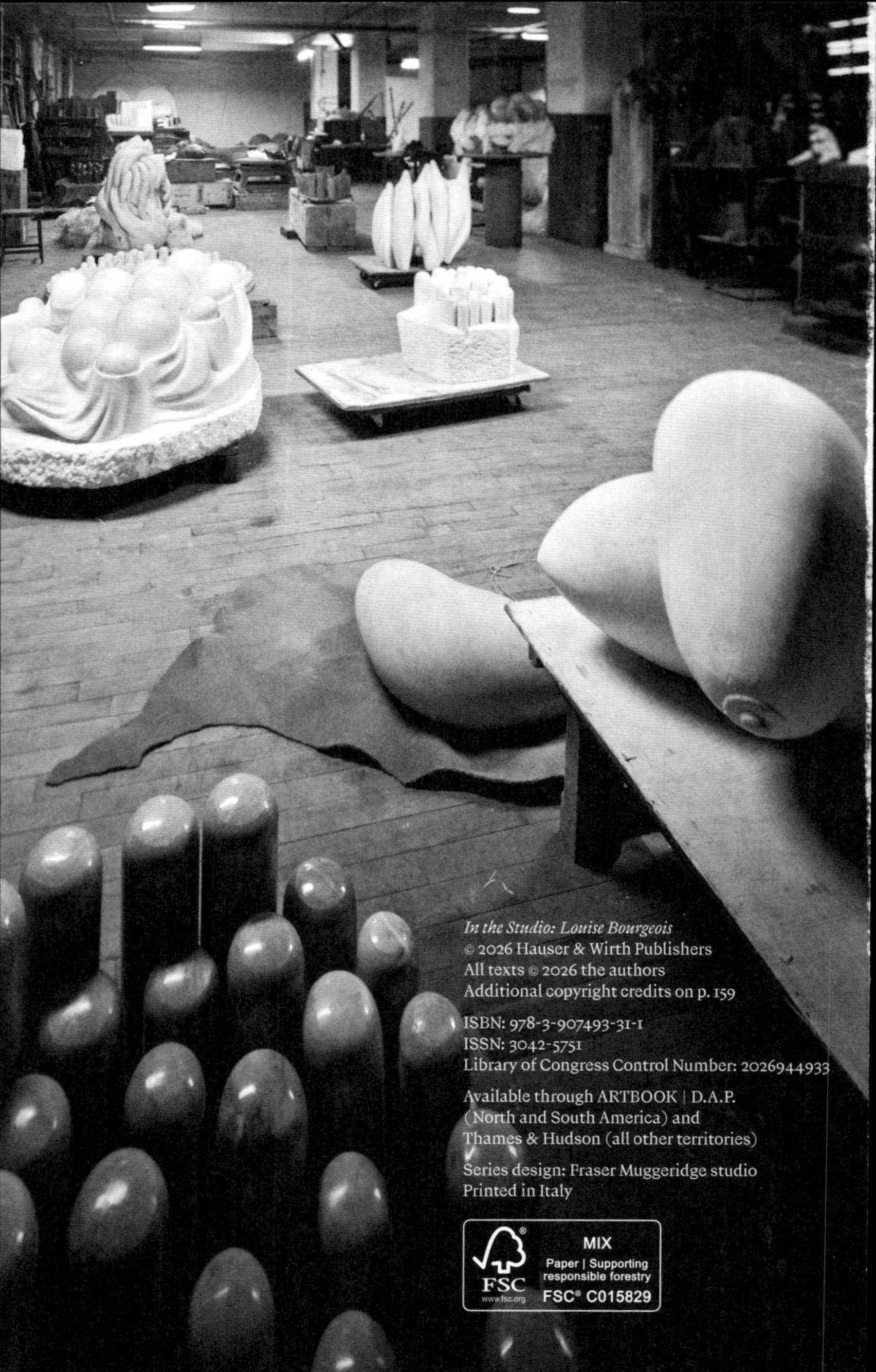

In the Studio: Louise Bourgeois

ISBN: 978-3-907493-31-1
ISSN: 3042-5751
Library of Congress Control Number: 2026944933

Available through ARTBOOK | D.A.P.
(North and South America) and
Thames & Hudson (all other territories)

Series design: Fraser Muggeridge studio
Printed in Italy

MIX
Paper | Supporting responsible forestry
FSC www.fsc.org
FSC® C015829